Focus on Grammar

TEACHER'S MANUAL

A
HIGH-INTERMEDIATE
Course for
Reference
and Practice

Margaret Bonner

Longman

Focus on Grammar: A High-Intermediate Course for Reference and Practice, Teacher's Manual

Longman, 10 Bank Street, White Plains, NY 10606

Editorial Director: Joanne Dresner
Development Editor: Marjorie Fuchs
Production Editor: Carol Harwood
Text Design Adaptation: Circa 86, Inc.
Cover Design: A Good Thing, Inc.

ISBN: 0-201-65690-6

4 5 6 7 8 9 10-CRS-99 98 97

Contents

Introduction

Focus on Grammar: A High-Intermediate Course for Reference and Practice helps high-intermediate students of English understand and practice basic English grammar. However, teaching the rules is not the ultimate goal of the course. Rather, the aim is for students to use the language confidently and appropriately. This Teacher's Manual provides suggestions for teaching the high-intermediate level Student's Book. The first part contains general teaching suggestions that apply to every unit. The next part gives practical teaching suggestions, along with culture and background notes to accompany specific exercises in the book. The Teacher's Manual also provides ready-to-use diagnostic and final tests for each part in the Student's Book. In addition, there are answer keys for the diagnostic and final tests as well as a tapescript for all the listening activities from the Student's Book.

Focus on Grammar recognizes different styles of language learning and provides a variety of activities to accommodate these different styles. Some learners prefer an analytical, or rule-learning approach. Others, especially younger learners, respond best to exposure to the language in meaningful contexts. Indeed, the same students may adopt different styles as they learn. Furthermore, some students respond better to visual, and some to auditory instruction.

As teachers, we want to help the rule-learners in our classes become more able to take risks and plunge into communicative activities. We also want to encourage the risk-takers to focus on accuracy. It stands to reason that a varied approach, such as that offered by *Focus on Grammar*, will accommodate more students, more of the time.

General Suggestions

INTRODUCTION

Each unit in *Focus on Grammar: A High-Intermediate Course for Reference and Practice* is introduced by a text that presents the grammar in a realistic context. Each text is recorded on cassette so that students can practice listening to the structures as well. A variety of formats is offered, including magazine and newspaper articles, advertisements, book and movie reviews, and interviews. The unit's target structure is always highlighted in boldface type for easy identification.

The unit-by-unit teaching suggestions provide a great deal of assistance in presenting the texts and guiding students' reading and discussion of the material. This includes:

- cultural and background information
- discussion topics to activate students' own knowledge about the subject
- focus questions to guide their reading
- comprehension questions to elicit the main idea and details of the text
- inference and opinion questions to encourage students to extend their thinking about what they have just read
- simple definitions of potentially unfamiliar vocabulary
- suggestions for relating the grammar structure to the text

Following is a procedure for using these aids to present the Introduction. Since classes and teaching styles differ widely, however, we urge teachers to adapt this procedure as needed. For example, teachers may prefer to have students listen to some of the texts before reading. Some teachers will prefer to discuss the meaning of words after students have seen the words in context, while others may want to talk about vocabulary before students read. We emphasize that what follows is a suggested procedure that teachers can use flexibly according to the needs of their classes.

1. Preview the reading. Before students read the text, introduce the context—for example, magazine article, review, or advertisement. If possible, bring in other examples for students to examine to give them an idea of the type of language and content that they can expect in this context.

2. Present cultural and background information as necessary, and activate students' own knowledge of the topic. See the unit-by-unit Teaching Suggestions with Culture, Background, and Vocabulary Notes for

specific ideas on initiating discussions that will elicit students' knowledge and thoughts of the subject before they read the introductory text.

3. Provide focus questions to give students a purpose for reading.

4. Have students read the text. Go over unknown vocabulary as necessary. As much as possible have students try to guess the meaning from context. It is also important for students to realize that they do not need to know every word in order to understand the text. A list of potentially unknown words, along with simple definitions, is provided for your convenience. Use the list to help students as needed, rather than teaching the whole list.

5. Have students answer the focus questions.

6. Have students listen to the text. You may ask them to listen only, or to listen and read along in their books.

7. Ask the main idea and detail questions, and let students find the answers in the text. You may want to write the questions on the chalkboard and have students work in pairs to answer them.

8. Ask the inference and opinion questions and discuss possible answers with the class.

9. Elicit examples of the grammar structure from the text and write them on the chalkboard. Using the suggestions in the Grammar in context section, point out how the grammar structure conveys the meaning of the text.

GRAMMAR CHARTS

After the opening text, grammar is presented in grammar charts. At this point in the lesson, students have been introduced to the structures in context, and they are now ready to look at the form in isolation. Do not rush through this part of the lesson. It is important to give students time to take in the patterns.

1. Write the paradigms on the chalkboard and circle or underline important features such as forms of *be* in the passive.

2. Alternatively, supply a number of examples, and ask students to induce the rule. Then write the paradigm on the chalkboard.

3. Give additional examples, and encourage students to supply their own if they are ready.

4. Use magazine pictures or other simple cues for a drill so that students become accustomed to producing the form. See the unit-by-unit notes in this Teacher's Manual for suggestions on classroom drills.

GRAMMAR NOTES

The grammar notes pull together and make explicit the information about meaning, use, and form that the students have encountered in the introductory reading and grammar charts. The notes also offer information about degrees of formality that will help students use the forms appropriately as well as correctly.

The language presented in *Focus on Grammar: A High-Intermediate Course for Reference and Practice* is the English of daily life in the United States and Canada. Contractions, short answers, *who* to refer to an object, *will* with *I* and *you,* are practiced, although more formal usage is mentioned in the grammar notes.

Common grammatical terms are used throughout the book because they make grammar explanations clearer and because students often have learned them in their own language. Students need only understand the terms as they are used, not produce them.

1. Ask students to read each note. Write the examples on the chalkboard and highlight important features.

2. Give additional examples and ask students to supply their own. You may wish to have them work in pairs or groups to write examples.

3. At each note, check students' comprehension by asking them to complete a sentence stem or fill in the blank in a sentence. When they are ready, move on to the next step.

FOCUSED PRACTICE EXERCISES

In these exercises, students practice using the forms that have been presented in the preceding sections. Since there are objective answers to the questions in this section, you may assign these exercises as homework, or students may do them alone for self-study in class. In class, most exercises may be done in pairs. Pair work gives students the opportunity to work through answers together and discuss the application of the grammar rules. All the exercises are contextualized, so they convey cultural information as well as grammar practice. Have your students practice the conversations after they have completed the exercises.

Here is a procedure for the focused practice exercises. You may wish to spend more or less time setting up the exercises, depending on how proficient your class is.

1. Have students skim the exercise quickly. Elicit or explain the setting of the conversation or the text.
2. Explain the vocabulary and supply cultural and background information as necessary.
3. Go over the instructions, and have students complete one item in addition to the example.
4. Assign the exercise to be done in class or as homework. If students are working in class, circulate as they work to give help as needed.
5. When students complete the exercise, elicit the answers. Write them on the chalkboard or ask a student to do so.
6. When eliciting answers, have students read the entire sentence in which the answer appears, not just a single-word answer.
7. Give additional practice by having pairs of students act out the conversation for the class.

COMMUNICATION PRACTICE EXERCISES

The purpose of communication practice is to give students the opportunity to use the target structure in real information-gathering activities. In these exercises, students use the grammar in truly productive ways, and they have the opportunity really to "own" the structures. Students at the high-intermediate level are eager to communicate, and they enjoy this type of practice, which makes them more independent of the teacher. However, you must remain engaged with the class during communication practice. Circulate and work with each group, showing interest and enthusiasm in the discussion and eliciting further comments from students. Make sure students are engaged with one another. Ask about other group members' opinions. *(Edgar, what was Jiwen's opinion?)* The goal is fluency, so correct errors sparingly. Avoid making corrections that interrupt the flow of information. Instead, make them after a student has completed his or her statement or presentation.

Here are some suggested procedures for teaching the exercises in this section:

Practice listening: Each communication practice exercise begins with a listening.

1. Point out the situation of the listening.
2. Before playing the cassette or reading the tapescript, ask students to read over the items in the exercise or examine the pictures so they understand what they will be listening for.
3. Elicit questions, explain any unknown vocabulary, and give necessary cultural information.
4. Ask students to listen the first time with their pencils down.
5. Play the cassette or read from the tapescript included in this Teacher's Manual. If you are reading, read with a lot of expression and at a natural pace. Change positions so that you are indicating who the speaker is. You also can draw stick figures and label them with the characters' names. Point to the appropriate character as you change roles.
6. Tell students to listen again and do the task. Play the cassette again or read the tapescript.
7. Let students listen as many times as they have to in order to do the task.
8. Elicit the answers and write them on the chalkboard. Answer questions.
9. You may play the cassette or read the tapescript a final time for students to review using the corrected answers.

Pair and group activities: Most communication practice exercises are done in pairs or groups.

1. Go over the activity with students so they understand what is required.
2. Have students work in pairs or groups to perform the activity.
3. Circulate among the students to help them with the activity.
4. Have pairs or groups report to the whole class when they have finished an activity.

RECURRING EXERCISE TYPES

Quotable quotes: A number of lessons in *Focus on Grammar: A High-Intermediate Course for Reference and Practice* end with a discussion entitled *Quotable Quotes*. These are proverbs and quotations from famous people relating to the topic of the unit. The quotes provide a thought-provoking basis for discussion, which students can extend by bringing in examples from their own experiences and observations.

You may choose to assign different quotes to different groups or choose only some for discussion, and assign others for a writing exercise.

1. Have students work in groups.
2. Ask the groups to read the first quotation and then ask several students for their ideas about the meaning of the quotation.
3. Once the discussion is underway, turn it over to the groups to continue among themselves.
4. Go from group to group and participate. Encourage students to use their own experiences to illustrate their ideas.
5. Ask students to supply similar proverbs or sayings from their own cultures.

Information-gap exercises: In information-gap exercises, each student has different information necessary to complete a task.

Student A works with information in the unit. Student B is directed to turn to the back of the Student's Book.

The first time students do an information-gap exercise, take ample time to set up the activity and model it for the students. After the first time, they will be familiar with the activity and should have no trouble carrying it out.

1. Have students work in pairs. Assign one student to be Student A and the other to be Student B.
2. Make sure each partner is working on the correct page.
3. Explain what the task is.
4. Model the first one or two questions with a student in the class.
5. Circulate and help students who are having trouble.

Optional activities: The Teacher's Manual provides additional activities that you may do in class. There are also optional writing activities that may be assigned as homework. When correcting students' writing, concentrate on the structures presented in the unit, and do not correct all the errors in the writing.

Review or SelfTests: The units in *Focus on Grammar: A High-Intermediate Course for Reference and Practice* are grouped into ten parts. Each part is followed by a Review or SelfTest unit, which students may use to check their knowledge of the grammar found in that part. Students can then review any weak areas, thereby monitoring their own learning.

Teaching Suggestions with Culture, Background, and Vocabulary Notes

UNIT 1: Review and Integration: Present, Past, and Present Perfect

This first unit provides a review of verb tenses and aspects to which high-intermediate students have already been introduced. In addition, the unit provides activities suitable for the first few class periods, when students are introducing themselves and getting to know one another.

Each of the three numbered sections of Unit 1 contrasts two structures.

Section One: Simple Present Tense and Present Progressive

Section Two: Past Progressive and Simple Past Tense

Section Three: Present Perfect and Simple Past Tense

Each section consists of a reading, grammar charts and notes, focused practice, and communication practice, which includes a listening task.

All the structures that have been reviewed in Unit 1 are combined under Integration. It includes focused practice, a listening, and communication practice.

Some teachers will want to use the entire first unit, and give their students a thorough review of these verb structures. Others may wish to use only the first section with all classes, in order to give students a chance to get to know one another. After that, the diagnostic test can be used to pinpoint specific problems, and the teacher can choose which sections to use with which students.

SECTION ONE: SIMPLE PRESENT TENSE AND PRESENT PROGRESSIVE

INTRODUCTION

CULTURE NOTE: Baby-naming books are used by prospective parents to help them choose a name for their baby. As this review indicates, naming practices have changed in the past few years. Today, many people look for names that reflect their cultural origins. Others look for unique or meaningful names. In addition, naming practices vary greatly among different ethnic groups and nationalities, making this an excellent topic for cross-cultural comparisons.

Establish the context: The context is a book review. Ask students to look at the picture, the title, and the inset and guess what the book is about. Have a cross-cultural discussion about names. What are the most popular names in the students' country? Who chooses a baby's name? When is the decision made?

Focus questions:

> *According to the writer of this review, why do people sometimes put off choosing a name?* (It's a big decision. They don't want to make a mistake.)
>
> *What's the title of Sue Browder's book?* (*The New Age Baby Name Book*)
>
> *According to Browder, what does a distinctive name do for a child?* (It helps the child develop self-esteem.)
>
> *Is this book only for parents-to-be?* (No, it's not. It makes fascinating reading—even if you aren't becoming a parent.)

Comprehension questions:

Main idea:	*Are most Americans making up new names these days?* (No, they're not, but a lot of Americans are taking names from different sources.)
Details:	*What is happening to male and female names?* (The distinction between them is becoming blurred.)

Why are names like Kachina and Lateef becoming more common? (Parents are choosing names that reflect their ethnic backgrounds.)

What information about names does Browder's book supply? (their place of origin, meaning, and pronunciation)

Inference: *Why would teachers give better grades to students named David and Karen than to students named Elmer and Gertrude?* (These names are considered unattractive; teachers see students with these names as less attractive and less competent.)

Opinion: *Do people's names influence how others think of them?*

Vocabulary (optional): Explain as necessary: *solace* (comfort), *flawed* (with serious faults), *distinctive* (clearly marking a person as different from others), *self-esteem* (a good opinion of oneself; considered a positive trait), *trend* (the general direction of a social change), *blur* (to become less clear and distinct), *roots* (origins).

Grammar in context: Remind students that one use of the present progressive is to talk about events in the extended present (things that are happening these days, but not necessarily at the moment of speaking), for example:

We're studying English this semester. (We may not be studying at the moment.)

Have students find examples in the text of this use of the present progressive, for example:

You're still putting off choosing a name.

Carrie is becoming more popular than Caroline.

Explain that the simple present tense is often used in book reviews or in other writing to give a summary of the material. Elicit examples from the text, for example:

Browder explores the psychological effects of names.

Elicit examples of the simple present tense used to express things that are generally true, for example:

Most Americans still choose names that already exist.

GRAMMAR CHARTS

1. Review the simple present tense by having students interview a partner about his or her daily routine. Review question forms by brainstorming interview questions and putting them on the chalkboard for students to use in their interviews.

   What's your name?

   Where are you from?

   Do you come to class every day?

   What language do you speak at home?

   After the interview, ask students to introduce their partners to the class and give two or three facts about the partner in the introduction.

2. Practice forming negatives by making untrue statements and having students correct them.

   Teacher: *His name is Luis.*

   Student: *His name isn't Luis. It's Gregor.*

   Teacher: *She lives in an apartment.*

   Student: *She doesn't live in an apartment. She lives in a dormitory.*

3. Elicit the present progressive for all pronouns and put the paradigm on the chalkboard. Ask students to think about a recent change in their lives and write example sentences in the present progressive. Have them exchange the information with several students and then ask students to report about themselves and their classmates.

> *This semester I'm going to school full time.*
>
> *Nita isn't studying nursing this semester.*

GRAMMAR NOTES

Have students think of both positive and annoying traits of people they know and write examples for Grammar Note 4, for example:

> *My aunt is always doing something nice for us.*
>
> *My co-worker is always making long personal phone calls.*

EXERCISES

Exercise 1, page 4. CULTURE NOTE: Explain that a baby shower is a party for parents who are expecting a child. Friends bring gifts of things the parents will need for the child, such as blankets, clothing, and baby furniture.

After students do the exercise, have a brief discussion about whether they would prefer giving a child an original name or a traditional name, and why. Elicit the kinds of names people give their pets in cultures that your students know about. What are typical names for pet dogs, cats, or birds?

Exercise 2, page 4. Ask students' opinions about Conversation 1. Do they believe that names can influence people's lives? Do they know anyone whose name reflects what he or she does for a living?

Exercise 3, page 6. Ask students to look at the pictures and guess what the people's names are, before they do the listening. Ask them why they guessed as they did.

SECTION TWO: PAST PROGRESSIVE AND SIMPLE PAST TENSE

INTRODUCTION

CULTURE NOTE: Cultures have different systems for assigning names to children. In the United States, for example, it is the custom in some families for the oldest son to be named after the father. The term *Junior*, or the Roman numeral II or III after the name indicates what generation that person belongs to. In China it is considered disrespectful to give a child the same name as an older relative, living or dead. However, names that indicate what generation someone belongs to are sometimes assigned, often based on lines in a poem. Naming systems in different cultures have been studied by scholars and are the subject of many articles and even entire journals.

Establish the context: Ask students what rules people follow when they give names in their cultures. Is it permissible to name a child after a relative? Does it have to be a particular relative? Do people name children after religious figures and after qualities?

Tell students that the article discusses several naming practices that are used in different cultures.

Focus questions:

> *Why did Louisa Horvath name her daughter Doris?* (She was following tradition. Her great-aunt Dorothy died just before Louisa's daughter was born.)
>
> *Did Walter plan to follow his family's tradition with his own children?* (No, he didn't. He knew he was going to break the tradition.)
>
> *How did Ayadele get her name?* (From the weather. The sun was shining brightly when she was born.)

Why did Jahi's parents give him a name that meant "dignity"? (They wanted him to get an education.)

Comprehension questions:

Main idea: *Which of the following naming practices is NOT mentioned in the article?*

    a. naming after a relative

    b. naming after an incident that occurred around the time of birth

    c. naming after a religious figure

    d. naming after a quality that the parents want the child to have

      (Answer: c)

Details: *According to Jewish custom, can a child be named after a living relative?* (no)

    What did Native Americans believe about names? (Everyone should have a unique name.)

    Which naming system did Turtle's classmates follow when they gave her a nickname? (incident naming)

    How many naming systems are there? (many)

Inference: *Why might a Native American mother name her child* Helkimu? (Possible answer: Because she was gathering seeds when her labor started.)

Opinion: *If someone is named for a quality as Jahi was, can that name actually influence a person's life?*

Vocabulary (optional): Explain as necessary: *adhere to* (to follow), *deceased* (dead), *frowned upon* (disapproved of), *registers* (public records), *withheld* (refused to give), *at first glance* (the first time a person thinks about something), *derivation* (the source; the origin), *embody* (to represent; to become an example of).

Grammar in context: Have students provide examples from the text of the uses of the following structures:

• the past progressive to indicate an action that was in progress at a particular time in the past, for example:

      The Horvaths were adhering to an old Jewish custom. . . .

      The sun was shining brightly. . . .

• the simple past tense to express an action that was completed at a specific time in the past, for example:

      In the fourth grade one of the boys sneaked a baby turtle into my lunchbox.

      My parents named me Jahi.

• an action interrupted by another action, for example:

      It crawled out while I was eating lunch.

• two actions in progress at the same time, for example:

      While she was thinking about a name for her child, she was gathering beads for jewelry.

GRAMMAR CHARTS

1. Review simple past tense questions and statements. Put verbs on the chalkboard and have students form questions to ask one another about the previous day:

get up, eat breakfast, watch TV, go to work

What time did you get up yesterday?

Did you eat breakfast?

Elicit answers and write statements on the chalkboard, along with time expressions:

I got up at 6:00.

I ate breakfast at 6:30.

2. Elicit the entire paradigm for the past progressive and put it on the chalkboard. Ask students to say what they and their family members were doing at a particular time. Ask them to talk about something that was in progress and went on before and after that time, for example:

At 7:00 this morning, I was driving to work.

I was feeding my son. He was watching cartoons.

My parents were sleeping, but I was making my breakfast.

Using ideas from their sentences, illustrate the combinations of time clauses and go over their meaning:

I was driving to work when I got a flat tire. (The simple past tense is used with the past progressive to talk about an action that interrupts another action.)

I was feeding my son while he was watching cartoons. (The past progressive with *while* is used in both clauses to talk about two actions going on at the same time.)

When my parents got up, I made them breakfast. (The use of the simple past tense in both clauses means that first the parents got up, then he or she made them breakfast.)

I was going to stay home, but I decided to go to work. (*Was/were going to* expresses an intention. It usually means that the action didn't occur.)

GRAMMAR NOTES

1. Point out that in Grammar Notes 1 and 4, the broken line in the timeline indicates that the action may or may not continue after the specific point that is mentioned.

    They were living on Tenth Street in 1990. (The sentence doesn't indicate whether they moved in 1990 or continued to live there. More context is needed for this information.)

    When he came home, I was reading. (The sentence doesn't say whether the speaker stopped reading or continued reading after he came home. The context would supply the information.)

2. Have students think about plans they had made that did not work out, and ask them to produce more examples for Grammar Note 5.

    I was going to study French, but my family moved to Spain.

    We were going to name our first child after my mother, but the baby turned out to be a boy.

EXERCISES

Exercise 5, page 11. When students complete the exercise, have a brief discussion about how they or other family members got their names.

Exercise 6, page 12. Vocabulary (optional): Explain as necessary: *meteorologist* (a scientist who studies weather and climate).

After students complete the exercise, ask them to think of a very important moment in their lives, for example, when they met their spouses, girlfriends or boyfriends. Ask them what they were doing at the moment and what they did right after that.

I was working in the library when she came to check out a book.

When I saw her, I told my co-worker to go take a coffee break.

Exercise 7, page 14. Before the students listen, have them look at the three series of pictures and notice the differences among them. Have students tell a story for each set.

SECTION THREE: PRESENT PERFECT AND SIMPLE PAST TENSE

INTRODUCTION

CULTURE NOTE: In recent years more and more women in the United States and Canada have kept their last names after marriage. They do this to preserve their personal and professional identity, to maintain a credit rating in their own name, and, perhaps because of the increased divorce rates, to avoid several name changes during a lifetime. This trend also indicates the desires of families to affirm the equality of both parents and avoid having the family subsumed under the identity of the husband. Families are using a number of naming methods for their children. These include using both the mother's and the father's last names in a new, hyphenated last name (for example: Powers-Kroger), using the mother's last name for one child and the father's for another, and even having the children select their own last names at some time in their lives.

Establish the context: The context is a letter to a newspaper advice columnist and the columnist's reply. Ask students about this situation in their own cultures. Do women adopt their husbands' last names after marriage? Are there other times in a person's life when he or she changes names?

Focus questions:

Does Donna still perform with the Rockland Symphony Orchestra? (Yes, she does.)

Did the writer of the letter ever consider keeping her own last name? (No, she didn't.)

Does the couple know their son's opinion about his wife's decision to keep her own name? (No, they don't.)

Have families become weaker since more women started to keep their own names? (No, they haven't. A last name is not what keeps a family together.)

Comprehension questions:

Main idea: *Choose the sentence that best states John's opinion:*

a. Women should keep their last names in order to maintain their personal identity.

b. Social customs are changing quickly, and couples must make their own decisions about last names.

(Answer: b)

Details: *At the time of the letter, has the young couple gotten married yet?* (No, they haven't.)

Why does Donna want to keep her name? (She wants to keep her professional and personal identity.)

Have the parents been showing how they feel? (No, they haven't.)

Inference: *Why didn't the writer of the letter use her daughter-in-law's real name?* (Possible answer: She didn't want people to be able to identify her family.)

Opinion: *Is it ever appropriate to change your name?*

Vocabulary (optional): Explain as necessary: *maiden name* (birth name; a woman's last name at birth), *so-and-so* (an expression used instead of someone's real name), *committed* (firmly decided or promised to do something), *none of your business* (not your concern), *hyphenated surnames* (see the Culture Note).

Grammar in context: Give examples from the text of actions or situations that have been ongoing since some time in the past, and are still continuing. Point out that the progressive emphasizes that the action is ongoing and not finished.

> *My son and his girlfriend have been making wedding plans.*
>
> *She's been Donna so-and-so since she was born.*
>
> *Couples have been finding their own solutions.*

Give examples from the text of actions that were completed in the past.

> *I felt so proud when I became "Mrs. Smith."*
>
> *You and your husband showed a lot of self-control when you decided not to voice your opinion.*

GRAMMAR CHARTS

1. Review irregular past participles. Refer students to Appendix 1 in the Student's Book. Give students verbs and other cues and have them make sentences, for example:

   > *I/eat/sushi/never* (I've never eaten sushi.)
   >
   > *he/see/that movie/before* (He's seen that movie before.)
   >
   > *they/sell/all the tickets* (They've sold all the tickets.)

2. Review the irregular simple past tense. Refer students to Appendix 1 in the Student's Book. Have students tell you what they did last night.

3. Give students cues to practice the present perfect progressive and ask them to make sentences:

   > *he/talk on the telephone/twenty minutes*
   >
   > *they/eat dinner/for an hour*
   >
   > *He's been talking on the telephone for twenty minutes.*

GRAMMAR NOTES

1. To contrast the present perfect and simple past tense, have students write sentences about where they live, work, and study, now and in the past.

2. To elicit examples for Grammar Note 3, ask students about their accomplishments during the past year. Tell them not to mention a specific point in time. Point out that the *X* in the timeline is above the line instead of on the line. This indicates an unspecified point of time.

   > *I've moved into a new apartment.*
   >
   > *I've learned how to use Lotus 1-2-3.*

EXERCISES

Exercise 9, page 19. Explain that in the United States and Canada, wedding stories such as this one appear in a special section of the newspaper. Ask about customs regarding public wedding announcements in countries students know about.

Vocabulary (optional): Explain as necessary: *justice of the peace* (someone who acts as the judge in less important courts of law, such as traffic courts. A justice of the peace has the authority to perform wedding ceremonies), *rehabilitation nurse* (a nurse who works with people who must relearn functions such as walking or taking care of themselves).

Exercise 12, page 21. Have students write a response to Haven't Said a Word Yet's letter.

Exercise 13, page 22. Vocabulary (optional): Explain as necessary: *undercover detective* (a police detective who does not wear a uniform and who pretends to be a civilian in order to solve a crime), *counterfeiter* (a criminal who prints money that is not real), *show biz* (show business), *first laid eyes on each other* (saw each other for the first time), *christening* (a ceremony in some Christian denominations in which a baby is named), *mellowed* (became softer).

Exercise 16, page 26. Before listening, have students look at the pairs of pictures, noting the differences.

Exercise 18, page 29. This is the first Quotable Quotes exercise in the book. Point out the use of *man* and *he* in the Hazlitt and McLuhan quotes. The writers use the so-called "generic" noun *man* to refer to all people (male and female) and *he* to refer to any person (male or female). You may wish to point out that this practice is in a state of change and that many people today prefer to use true gender-neutral terms. However, since many famous quotations were said a long time ago, before sexism in language became an issue, students should expect to find occurrences of *he* and *man* referring to both men and women.

Exercise 20, page 30. Explain that the items shown are examples of memorabilia—things we keep to remind us of special times in the past. Before they begin the exercise, have students look carefully at the items. Elicit what some of the items are, what events took place related to them, and when the events occurred.

UNIT 2: Past Perfect

INTRODUCTION

CULTURE NOTE: Talk shows are television shows in which people discuss controversial personal and social issues such as runaway children, sexual abuse, and divorce. Sometimes celebrities appear on the show, but often the guests are ordinary people who have experienced these problems. Talk-show hosts question the guests, and there is usually a lot of interaction with the audience.

Establish the context: The context is a biographical article about the talk-show host Oprah Winfrey. You may want to bring in an issue of *People Magazine, TV Guide,* or other popular magazines to show students the type of article.

If you are teaching in the United States or Canada, have students look at the photograph of Winfrey and talk about what they know of her and their opinions of her show. If you are teaching outside North America, discuss talk shows with which students are familiar. Talk about the personalities of the talk-show hosts and the types of topics that their guests discuss. Ask your students: *What kind of personality should a talk-show host have?*

Focus questions:

When did Winfrey start speaking publicly? (when she was two)

By 1989, did many people recognize Winfrey's name? (Yes, they did. Her name was a household word.)

Comprehension questions:

Main idea: *Why did Winfrey become so successful as a talk-show host?* (She loves to talk; she has the right kind of personality; she makes people feel comfortable.)

Details: *Did she decide on her career before or after her twelfth birthday?* (She decided before she was twelve.)

When did she get her first TV talk show? (in 1986)

What kind of working experience led up to this job? (She was a TV news reporter and an actress.)

Inference: *What kind of personality did Oprah have as a child?* (Possible answer: She was friendly and outgoing.)

Opinion: *Are talk shows only entertainment, or do they also help people understand problems?*

Vocabulary (optional): Explain as necessary: *acting debut* (first appearance as an actor), *household name* (a name that everyone knows).

Grammar in context:

1. Put a timeline on the board.

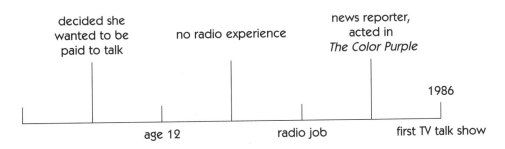

2. Explain that we use the past perfect to describe an event that happened before another event in the past: *When Oprah was age twelve, she had already decided she wanted to be paid to talk. When she got her radio job, she hadn't had any radio experience.* Elicit and write other examples of the past perfect from the text and show their relation to times in Oprah's life.

GRAMMAR CHARTS

1. Use the sentences from the explanation of the grammar in context, and ask students to produce the rule for forming the past perfect. Elicit or point out that the auxiliary (helping) verb *had* is always in the past, and does not change with different pronouns.
2. Write the grammar labels on the board above the sentence as students produce the rule: Subject, *Had*, Past Participle
3. Review past participles and refer students to Appendix 1 on page A1 of the Student's Book.

GRAMMAR NOTES

1. Use the timeline from the explanation of grammar in context and review the meaning of the past perfect.
2. Using other examples from the opening text, point out the use of the past perfect to show which of two events happened first. Elicit additional examples from students or make up your own.

    Kim Sook had studied English in Korea before she enrolled in this class.

    Rohana had already worked as a nurse's aid by the time she entered the nursing program.

3. Give additional examples of the past perfect for repeated action:

    Katie had already heard the same music many times by the time she went to the concert.

    Phil had knocked on the door several times when the teacher opened it.

4. For Grammar Note 6 point out that the words *before, after,* and *as soon as* explain the time relationship, so the past perfect is not absolutely necessary.

5. With students, act out some additional examples of the Be Careful note, for example:

> *When I came into the room, George erased the board.*
>
> *When I came into the room, George had erased the board.*
>
> *When Sylvie came into the room, she turned on the lights.*
>
> *When Sylvie came into the room, Sam had already turned on the lights.*

EXERCISES

Exercise 1, page 35. Have students work in pairs to complete the exercise. Go over the answers with them. Use a timeline and refer back to relevant grammar notes for sentences students have problems with.

Exercise 2, page 36. Students should be familiar with the timeline from the explanation of the grammar in context. Introduce the information briefly by asking questions: *When did Oprah Winfrey give her first speech? When did she begin Tennessee State University?* Have them work alone or in pairs to complete the exercise.

Exercise 3, page 37. Discuss the meaning of *troubled teen* (a teenager with emotional problems). Point out or elicit that this type of difficulty is a typical talk-show topic. Elicit the meaning of *psychologist* (a professional who works with people who are experiencing emotional problems). Establish the time frame: The mother and son came to see the psychologist some time in the past. The psychologist is describing events that had occurred before that visit.

When students complete the exercise, have them read it aloud.

Exercise 4, page 37. Elicit the connection between this context, an interview with a troubled teen, and the previous one. Do the first one or two items with students, and then have them complete the exercise in pairs. Go over the answers with the class. At this point you may want to give students a chance to respond to the material. Ask some discussion questions: *Is this a common problem in other cultures or countries? Why do children leave home?* After a short discussion, have pairs of students take the parts and read the interview.

Exercise 5, page 38. Explain the context and ask questions about the schedule: *What time does he arrive at the studio? What is he doing at 3:00?* Have students complete the exercise in pairs, and then read their answers aloud.

Exercise 6, page 39. Ask students to read the events. Ask them to speculate about which events occurred before others. Then play the cassette or read the interview twice. Have students compare their answers. Then have them listen again to confirm their answers.

Exercise 7, page 40. Have students look again at the schedule in exercise 5 and then write a similar schedule about their own day yesterday. They can use their schedules as a reference for this activity. Elicit some adjectives to use for item 7. Ask students how they feel after they've had a busy day or a slow day: tired, exhausted, frustrated, good about accomplishing so much, and so forth.

Have students complete the task individually and then work with a partner to compare their day. Partners can report to the class about each other's day:

> *Yesterday wasn't a busy day for Steve. By 9:00 he hadn't eaten breakfast yet.*

Exercise 8, page 40. Write the topics on the chalkboard, and ask a few questions to get the class started:

> *Had you ever seen an American football game before you came here?*
>
> *Had you ever ridden on a subway?*

Have one or more students come to the front and write some of the results of the class discussion on the chalkboard.

Exercise 9, page 40. Optional writing exercise. Have students write an autobiographical paragraph. Ask students to go back and reread the reading in the Introduction. Review the main idea and the detail questions about Oprah Winfrey. Ask students to come up with a general statement about their own lives or personalities. Then ask them to use that statement at the beginning of their paragraph and some of the information from their timeline as supporting details. If students agree, you may wish to "publish" their autobiographies in a class newsletter.

Optional activity: Decide on a talk show that everyone can watch outside class. Have a class discussion about the show and the talk-show topics.

UNIT 3: Past Perfect Progressive

INTRODUCTION

CULTURE NOTE: The marathon, a footrace of about twenty-six miles, was one of the Olympic games in ancient Greece. It commemorated the first marathon runner, a messenger who ran twenty-six miles with news of a victory and then died of exhaustion after he had delivered his message. Completing a marathon is a symbolic as well as a physical achievement. It's a symbol of victory over one's own limitations. Modern marathons, which are held in many cities of the world, have developed in popularity during the last twenty years. In the United States, more than 50,000 people participate in them every year. The New York City Marathon, which is featured in this article, attracts about 10,000 runners.

Establish the context: The context is a news report following the New York City Marathon. Have students look at the picture and guess what the event is. Elicit information about a marathon: *How long is the race? Who participates? Why do people become so excited about it?* Find out if anyone in the class has ever run in a marathon or knows someone who has. After the students have shared their own knowledge, present additional information from the Culture Note.

Focus questions:

Was it raining at the beginning of the race? (No, it wasn't. The weather was clear.)

Was Mtolo leading when the reporter first saw him? (No, he wasn't.)

When did spectators gather at the finish line, before or after Mtolo crossed the line? (before)

What did Mtolo do in South Africa while he was waiting to compete internationally? (He worked to improve conditions.)

Comprehension questions:

Main idea: *Why was this race a dream come true for Willie Mtolo?*
(He had waited for years to compete.)

Details: *Where does the reporter usually stand to watch the marathon?* (in Central Park, near the finish line)

Where is Willie Mtolo from? (South Africa)

Why was South Africa banned from international races for twenty-one years? (because of its policy of apartheid)

Before the ban was lifted, did Mtolo leave his country to compete? (No, he didn't.)

Inference: *What does the writer mean by a "tunnel of spectators" at the finish line?* (Possible answer: Because there were so many spectators at that place, there were no open spaces along the street. Running along the street at that place felt like passing through a tunnel.)

Opinion: *Why do people become so emotional about marathon races?*

Vocabulary (optional): Explain as necessary: *spectators* (people who watch an event such as a race), *overtake* (pass), *Central Park* (a large park in the center of Manhattan in New York City. The New York Marathon ends there), *deafening* (extremely loud; loud enough to cause deafness), *apartheid* (South Africa's former policy of separation of the races. Blacks and members of other races had been oppressed economically and politically by this policy), *banned* (not permitted), *compatriot* (a person born in or a citizen of the same country as another), *emigrate* (to leave one's own country to go to live in another).

Grammar in context: Point out that the story first focuses on the most dramatic moment of the race, the moment when Willie Mtolo passed Espinosa, just a few minutes before the end of the race. After mentioning this important moment, the writer goes back and tells about events leading up to that moment. (Mtolo had been running for almost two hours.) Events that were in progress before a particular moment in the past are often in the past perfect progressive.

On the chalkboard, write examples of the past perfect progressive from the story. Elicit from students the important moment and the activity before that moment. Underline the past perfect progressive.

> It <u>had been raining</u> hard the night before the race.
>
> By the time he passed Espinosa, Mtolo <u>had been running</u> for almost two hours.
>
> The crowd <u>had been gathering</u> at this spot for hours.
>
> He <u>had been waiting</u> for this chance to compete internationally.

GRAMMAR CHARTS

1. Note what several students had been doing just prior to the beginning of class. Write verbs and phrases on the chalkboard: *read, talk, finish homework, look for a pen, walk around.* Write sentences such as the following:

   > Before class started, Phan had been reading the textbook.
   >
   > Fabiana and Maria had been talking.
   >
   > Joiana had been looking for a pen.

   Ask students to supply the rule for forming the past perfect progressive and label the parts of the sentences on the chalkboard: *had been + -ing* form of the verb.

2. Note that the form is the same for all the pronouns.

GRAMMAR NOTES

1. Point out that in Grammar Note 1, the broken line in the timeline indicates that the action may or may not continue after the specific point that is mentioned.

2. After students read the grammar note, write a time on the board: *6:00.* Ask students to state what they'd been doing or what other family members had been doing up to that time. Write examples on the chalkboard:

   > It was 6:00.
   >
   > I'd been preparing dinner.
   >
   > My husband had been reading the newspaper.
   >
   > Our daughter had been doing her homework.

   Have students practice questions by asking one another:

   > **A:** *I called you at 5:00 yesterday. What had you been doing before I called?*
   >
   > **B:** *I'd been taking a shower.* OR *I'd been washing the dishes.*

3. Act out the difference between clauses with the past perfect progressive and clauses with the past progressive.

> *When I came in, Mimi had been erasing the chalkboard.* (Mimi stops before you come into the room.)

> *When I came in, Mimi was erasing the chalkboard.* (Mimi is still erasing it when you come in.)

4. Practice Grammar Note 3 by bringing in magazine pictures and having students ask and answer questions:

> **A:** *I saw these people at 3:00 last Tuesday. They were soaking wet. What had they been doing?*

> **B:** *They'd been walking in the rain.*

> **A:** *This woman was carrying several shopping bags. What had she been shopping for?*

> **B:** *She'd been buying new school clothes.*

EXERCISES

Exercise 1, page 44. After students complete the exercise, have them practice the interview in pairs.

Exercise 4, page 46. *Optional activity.* Before starting the exercise, ask students to think of something they accomplished that took effort and teamwork to achieve. Tell them to write it down on a piece of paper. Elicit some answers and write them on the chalkboard. Ask students to describe what they had been doing before the event to reach their goal, for example:

> *Last March, my friend and I both took the college entrance exam.*

> *We'd been studying together all winter.*

> *We'd been going to a coffee shop near school to review the lessons.*

> *We'd been giving each other quizzes.*

Tell the class that the exercise is about two people who had trained for the marathon together.

After they complete the exercise, ask students to write some sentences about their own experiences. They can exchange their sentences with a partner and discuss their achievements.

Exercise 6, page 47. Have pairs of students report their answers to the class. Write them on the chalkboard.

Exercise 7, page 48. Follow the general procedure for information-gap exercises on page 4 of this Teacher's Manual. Have students read the entire selection first; then have one pair model the first two questions and answers for the class.

Have a class discussion about the follow-up questions. After the discussion you may wish to ask students to write a paragraph telling who the man and woman are, and what their relationship is.

Exercise 8, page 49. *Optional Writing Exercise.* After the discussion, have students write a story using some of their guesses about the party. You may want to start them off with an opening sentence or two, for example:

> *When I saw the room the next morning, it all came back to me. We'd all been sitting on the floor and eating pizza, and the empty pizza box was still on the floor...*

Optional activities.
1. Have students agree on a popular talk show to watch before the next class meets. Have a class discussion of the topic. Talk about what the guests had done or had been doing that was the topic of the talk show.
2. Have students write down one or two important events from their lives. Have them tell a partner what the events are and then ask and answer each other's questions.

> **A:** *I was married in February 1988.*

> **B:** *How long had you and your fiancé(e) been seeing each other?* OR *Where had you been working when you met him (or her)?*

UNIT 4: Future Progressive

INTRODUCTION

CULTURE NOTE: Futurists are scientists who analyze current trends in order to predict the future. Their function is to help prepare for changes. Because the twenty-first century is approaching, the predictions of futurists are being aired more frequently.

Establish the context: This is a magazine article predicting future trends in major categories such as education, employment, and transportation. Have students make a list of categories suggested by the illustration (clothing, transportation, robots, computers). Write the list on the chalkboard. Ask the class to predict changes that might occur in their daily lives in the next millennium.

Focus questions:

What are two good effects of people working at home? (They'll be able to spend more time with their families, and air pollution caused by automobiles will be reduced.)

What kind of transportation will people use for middle-distance trips? (mass transit)

In 1992 what did radio antennas start to look for? (life in other galaxies)

Comprehension questions:

Main idea: *Which of these is <u>not</u> a category in the article?*

a. work   b. clothing   c. family   d. transportation

(Answer: c)

Details: *What communications equipment do telecommuters use?* (telephones, faxes, and computers)

How will people travel short distances in the future? (They'll still use the family car.)

Will winter and summer clothing be made of different materials? (Not necessarily. The same material will be cool in summer and warm in winter.)

How will students of the future be able to experience a battle that was fought in the nineteenth century? (with virtual reality technology)

Which planet are scientists planning to colonize? (Mars)

Inference: *Why will job skills become obsolete quickly?* (Possible answer: Because technology is developing very rapidly, people will have to constantly learn new skills in order to use the technology on their jobs.)

Opinion: *What other changes will we see?*

Will scientists find other civilizations in the universe?

Will the new technology improve everyone's lives?

Vocabulary (optional): Explain as necessary: *Millennium* (Remind students of *decade* and *century*. Write the date January 1, 2000 on the chalkboard. Tell them: This is when the new millennium will start. Ask them to guess the meaning of *millennium* [1,000 years]), *era* (period of time that begins with a particular event, for example, the Christian Era, which began with the birth of Jesus, or that is marked by an important development such as the space era, when humans began to explore places outside Earth), *telecommuting* (working at home, using communications equipment such as a fax, a computer, and a telephone [Have students find the definition that is in the text]), *fax* (a piece of equipment that transmits images such as print or pictures over telephone lines. *Fax* comes from *facsimile*), *cut down on* (reduce), *mass transit* (transportation systems for carrying large numbers of people), *Bullet Train* (a train capable of speeds of more than 140 mph [225 km]. The Bullet Train between Tokyo and Osaka was one of the first, and most famous), *Star Trek* (a very popular television series about space exploration. The crew of the spaceship includes people from other planets; their adventures involve encounters with civilizations from different parts of the universe. The series has attracted a large following of "trekkies" who enjoy dressing in the Star Trek uniforms), *body suit* (a one-piece garment that covers the whole body [Refer students to the illustration]), *high tech* (a product that uses the most recent technology), *etched* (a pattern made by cutting lines into a hard surface), *interactive* (a situation in which two things have an effect on each other [Refer students to the example. In interactive entertainment, the player actually takes one of the roles in the situation, and his or her actions influence what happens]), *shoot the rapids* (rapids are dangerous places in a river where water runs very swiftly over rocks. *To shoot the rapids* means to ride through the rapids on a raft or in a boat), *Battle of Waterloo* (battle in which Napoleon was finally defeated. It was fought near the Belgian village of Waterloo), *blur* (to become less distinct or sharp [Refer to the context—the difference between work and home won't be clear anymore when more people work at home]), *apprenticeship* (system in which a person learns a skill or a profession by working at it, rather than in school), *obsolete* (out-of-date, not used anymore), *scan* (to examine in order to search for something), *visionary* (having the power to imagine the future), *shuttle* (transportation that moves back and forth over a short distance on a regular schedule), *iron out* (to find a solution to).

Grammar in context: On the chalkboard, write examples of sentences from the text of the future progressive with *will* and *be going to*.

> *Where will we be working in this new era?*
>
> *In the twenty-first century, more and more people will be telecommuting.*
>
> *Small, intelligent robots are going to be doing all the household chores.*

Point out that the future progressive emphasizes that these actions will take place over a period of time *(in the new era, in the twenty-first century).*

GRAMMAR CHARTS

1. Using these same sentences, elicit the rule from the class, and write the grammar labels above the sentences.
2. Give students additional practice in forming questions. Write some activities and time expressions on the chalkboard. Have students form the questions, and write them on the chalkboard. Then have them ask and answer questions, either as a whole class, or in pairs.

study	*tomorrow morning/afternoon/evening*
shop	*next week/weekend*
visit friends	
work	
do housework	

A: *Will you be studying tomorrow evening?*

B: *No, I won't. I'll be doing housework.*

A: *Are you going to be visiting friends next weekend?*

B: *No, I'm not. I'm going to be studying.*

GRAMMAR NOTES

1. Write a timeline on the chalkboard and give examples of the future progressive from the text. Use the timeline to point out that the future progressive describes an action in progress before and after a specific point of time in the future.

   Give personal examples of things you expect to be doing at this time next year. Elicit examples from students:

   > *At this time next year, I'll be teaching English.*
   >
   > *Mary Lou will be opening her own business.*
   >
   > *An Tsu will be starting computer classes.*

2. To practice time clauses, have students think of some situations in which people share tasks. Then elicit paired verbs, for example:

   > *sweep the floor*   *wash the dishes*
   >
   > *mow the lawn*   *work in the garden*
   >
   > *erase the chalkboard*   *put the chairs in rows*

   Have the students form sentences with time clauses, for example:

   > *I'll be sweeping the floor while you wash the dishes.*
   >
   > *Chong will be mowing the lawn while Roxanna works in the garden.*

3. After students read Grammar Note 3, play a game with the class. Hand out slips of paper with tasks written on them. Tell students to try to get someone in the class to do that task for them, for example: *return a library book, buy some stamps at the post office, make a photocopy,* or *give a message to the teacher.*

   > **A:** *Will you be going to the library tomorrow?*
   >
   > **B:** *Yes, I will. Why?*
   >
   > **A:** *Would you mind returning this book for me? It's overdue.*

EXERCISES

Exercise 1, page 58.

1. Have students read the instruction line and look over the calendar.
2. Elicit a description of Professor Granite's profession. (She's a futurist. She predicts future trends.)

Vocabulary (optional): Explain as necessary: *seminar* (a small group of people working on an advanced [academic] subject and sharing their results), *energy* (give or elicit examples: solar, nuclear, fossil fuel. Point out or elicit that one of the major issues the world faces is safe and reliable sources of energy).

Exercise 2, page 59.
Have students read the instruction line and look at the schedule. Before they start the exercise, elicit opinions from the class: *Will household robots improve life or not? What will people be doing instead of household chores?*

Exercise 3, page 60.

1. Remind students about the meaning of *underground* and *shuttle.*
2. After they complete the exercise, have students practice the dialogues in pairs.

Exercise 4, page 61.
Discuss the title of the exercise. Elicit or explain that *the sky's the limit* is an idiom that means there are almost no limits; almost anything is possible. Give some examples:

A: *How much can we spend on vacation this year?*

B: *The sky's the limit! We just won the lottery.*

After they complete the exercise, elicit students' reactions. Tell them: *Imagine you won a ticket for the Mars Shuttle. Would you go? Why or why not?*

Exercise 5, page 62.

1. Play the cassette or read the tapescript as many times as necessary for students to complete the exercise.
2. Have them compare their answers with a partner's before going over them with the whole class.

Optional activity.

1. Ask students: *What will you be doing ten years from now?* Have them think about the question and write sentences in answer for about ten minutes. Circulate and help them write accurately.
2. When students finish writing, have them work in groups and discuss their predictions.
3. Groups should report to the whole class.

UNIT 5: Future Perfect and Future Perfect Progressive

INTRODUCTION

CULTURE NOTE: Since the economic recession that began in the 1980s, many people in the United States have become more frugal and have started to save for purchases rather than use credit.

Establish the context: The context is a newsletter, a regular publication for a group with a special interest. Note that the newsletter is the January 1 issue. People often make New Year's resolutions to improve their lives. Draw students' attention to the illustration of the hand and the piggy bank. Elicit that the picture illustrates the concept of saving small amounts of money consistently. Talk about the term *penny pincher,* a frugal person. Have students speculate on why we use that term. Have a cross-cultural discussion about the value of frugality. Is it a positive value in other cultures or are frugal people considered to lack generosity?

Focus questions:

Does the editor of this newsletter believe that it's possible to save money these days? (Yes, she does.)

How much does Janice need to make a down payment on a used car? ($780)

What is one thing Janice plans to stop buying? (paperback books)

How did Anne Marie Dupont manage to save for her daughter's piano lessons? (She started to pack inexpensive lunches for herself and her daughter.)

How long will it take Don Caputo to pay off his credit-card debt? (a year and a half)

Comprehension questions:

Main idea: *The newsletter explains how to*

a. occasionally save a large sum of money

b. save small sums of money over a long period of time

(Answer: b)

Details: *What is the annual take-home pay of a word processor?* ($20,000)

What are the essential costs of living? (food, clothing, rent)

According to Hubbard, is it safer to invest money or just save it? (save it)

How is Don Caputo going to save money? (by writing letters instead of making long distance phone calls)

When will Tom Lu be able to buy his CD player? (next holiday season)

Inference: *Will the people mentioned in the newsletter make big sacrifices to save for their goals?* (Possible answer: Probably not. They'll save by giving up small luxuries.)

Opinion: *Is it better to save for things you want or to buy on credit? Why? Are there any exceptions?*

Vocabulary (optional): Explain as necessary: *takes home* (has left after taxes and other deductions), *down payment* (the first payment on a large item such as a house or a car that one plans to buy over time), *avid* (eager), *sacrifice* (the loss of something very valuable), *keep up with* (to go as fast as; not fall behind), *double your money* (to cause something to become twice as great or as valuable; to fold in half), *pay off* (to pay an entire debt), *costly* (expensive), *a long haul* (the act of pulling a heavy burden for a long distance), *disposable income* (the amount of income one can use for optional expenses), *accumulate* (to save), *bang for the buck* (an idiom meaning value for the money).

Grammar in context: Put a timeline on the chalkboard:

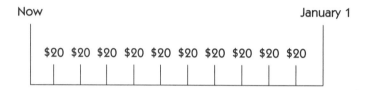

Write examples from the text on the chalkboard, for example:

> *Janice will have saved $200 by the end of the year.* (Explain that Janice will reach her goal before December 31; by the end of the year, she'll have $200.)

The future perfect and the future perfect progressive are used to talk about things that will be completed at a particular time in the future.

> *On the fifteenth of this month, Jennifer will have been studying piano for six months.* (Explain that Jennifer started before the fifteenth, she'll complete six months on the fifteenth, and the lessons will continue after that.)

GRAMMAR CHARTS

1. Use the examples from the grammar in context explanation and elicit the rule for forming the future perfect.

2. Write the grammar labels above the sentences:

> *Will (not)   Have + Past Participle*

3. Set up a grammar drill. Ask students what they hope to accomplish by next year. Write phrases on the board:

> *By next year: learn the future perfect*
>
> *get a driver's license*
>
> *move to a new apartment*
>
> *learn word processing*

4. Have students produce sentences using these cues or their own ideas. *By next year I'll have learned the future perfect.*

5. Practice questions using the same cues. Have students ask one another:

A: *Will you have gotten your driver's license by next year?*

B: *Yes, I will (have). OR No, I won't (have).*

A: *When will you have learned word processing?*

B: *By June.*

6. Repeat the procedure for the present perfect progressive. For the drill, supply verbs along with time periods:

> *play piano/ten years*
>
> *driving this car/two months*
>
> *speaking English/three years*
>
> *By next year I'll have been playing the piano for ten years.*

A: *By next year, will you have been playing the piano for ten years?*

B: *Yes, I will (have). OR No, I won't (have).*

A: *By next year how long will you have been driving this car?*

B: *Three years.*

GRAMMAR NOTES

1. Give more examples from the text:

> *By next January Janice will have bought a car.*
>
> *Tom will have bought his CD player.*
>
> *Don will have paid a lot of money on his credit card debt.*

Ask students to talk about what they hope to accomplish and give examples.

> *Phan will have cleaned out her attic.*
>
> *Mark will have finished his term paper.*

2. After they read about the future perfect progressive, ask students to talk with a partner about how long they will have been living in their town, working at their jobs, and studying at their school by the end of the year. Then have partners report to the class about each other. Write additional examples on the chalkboard.

> *Goia will have been living in Miami for five years.*
>
> *Fran will have been working at Reynolds for six months.*
>
> *Sandy will have been studying here for a year.*

3. For additional practice with the future perfect and future perfect progressive, invent a character and put his or her schedule for the following day on the chalkboard.

> *7:00   get up and shower*
>
> *7:30   get dressed*
>
> *7:45–8:15   eat breakfast*
>
> *8:30   leave for work and so forth*

Ask questions:

> **A:** *Will Sam have gotten dressed by 7:30?*
>
> **B:** *No, he won't have.*

> **A:** *It's 10:00. Will he have left for work already?*
>
> **B:** *Yes, he will.*

Have students make their own schedules and work with partners to ask and answer questions. Circulate and help students practice the structure.

4. After students read about time clauses, write paired phrases on the chalkboard and have them make sentences with time clauses.

> *the library close   study three hours*
>
> *catch the bus   get dark already*
>
> *graduate from school   work at my job for eight years*
>
> *When the library closes, I'll have been studying for three hours.*
>
> *When I catch the bus, it'll have gotten dark already.*
>
> *When I graduate from school, I'll have been working at my job for eight years.*

Elicit other examples from students and write them on the chalkboard.

EXERCISES

Exercise 2, page 69. Have students read over the items in the timeline and ask for their comments about the sequence of events in Tom's life. *Tom's going to get married before he starts college. He's going to move to another town before he graduates. Will that be difficult? Has anyone experienced something similar?*

Optional activity. Have students make their own timelines with things they hope to have accomplished before and after five years from now. Then have them write sentences about what they will and won't have accomplished by then. They can share the information with a partner or a group.

Exercise 3, page 70. If students did the optional activity for exercise 2, they can continue it now. Have them work in pairs and read each other's timelines and sentences. Then ask students to write about their partner's timeline using time clauses.

> *By the time Eva starts her business, she'll have already become a parent.*
>
> *May won't have visited her family in Singapore by the time she graduates.*

Exercise 4, page 71. Remind students to use the future perfect with specific amounts ($5.00, seven books) and the future progressive with lengths of time (seven weeks).

Optional activity. Have groups of students make up similar questions. Groups can exchange questions with each other and work out the answers.

Exercise 5, page 72. Have students make other suggestions for vacations for each amount saved.

Exercise 7, page 73. Optional writing activity. Have the class collect the tips and publish a class Penny-Pinchers Newsletter. Using real products, students can make up Penny-Pincher Problems similar to the one in the newsletter in the Introduction.

UNIT 6: Tag Questions

INTRODUCTION

CULTURE NOTE: Magazines often compare the quality of life in various United States cities, and there is a rivalry among major cities and regions regarding how they are ranked as places to live. The rivalry between New York City and Los Angeles, or the East Coast and the West Coast is typical. Weather, traffic, crime statistics, and availability of jobs, housing, and health care are aspects that are considered when cities are evaluated. There are several distinctive regional accents in the United States that identify where a speaker is from. These include accents of people from New England, New York, the South, Texas, and other southwestern states. Students may have heard speeches made by John F. Kennedy of by Jimmy Carter. Kennedy was from Boston, and Carter is from Georgia. Their accents are good examples of New England and southern accents.

Establish the context: The context is a person-in-the-street interview, a format for which a reporter asks the opinions of ordinary people, chosen randomly. Ask if anyone in the class has ever taken part in such an interview. Would they object if asked? Have a discussion about what the class members would say about their own city in a magazine or a television interview. Talk about the climate, traffic, schools, restaurants, entertainment, jobs, and connections to Europe, Latin America, and Asia.

Focus questions:

> *Why does Tom Moffett end the interview?* (to talk to his agent)
>
> *Did Marta Aguirre move to L.A. recently?* (No, she moved to L.A. twenty years ago.)
>
> *Which person is from L.A. originally?* (Roberta Wilson)

Comprehension questions:

Main idea: *Why do people move to L.A.?* (The movie industry in Hollywood, the weather, business connections in Asia, and quality of life: "It's a nice city to live in.")

Details: *Is it still easy to sell scripts in Hollywood?* (No, it's not.)

                    Does L.A. have a problem with air pollution? (Yes, it does.)

                    What kind of business does Kato work for? (the computer business)

                    Why is Wilson moving to New York City? (She got laid off from her job in L.A., and she found a job in New York City.)

Inference: *Why did Wilson decide not to have a car in New York?* (Possible answer: After living in L.A., she was tired of driving in traffic.)

Opinion: *What makes a city a good place to live? Where would you live if you had the choice? Why?*

Vocabulary (optional): Explain as necessary: *screenplay* (story written for the movies), *script* (a play or a speech in its written form), *agent* (someone who represents artists. An agent finds work for artists and represents them in their business affairs), *smog* (air pollution formed by a mixture of smoke, fog, and the waste gases from cars, trucks, and factories), *laid off* (released from a job when there is not enough business), *small world* (an idiom that people use to comment on a coincidence: *I just found out that Gerry and I went to the same college. Small world, isn't it?*) *freeway* (a very wide road built for fast vehicles traveling long distances and from which one may get on and off only at certain places).

Grammar in context: Write examples of the text on the chalkboard and explain them:

> *You're Jackie LaCosta, aren't you?* (Moffett has seen LaCosta on television, and has good reason to believe that the interviewer is LaCosta.)
>
> *You're not from California, are you?* (Because of Moffet's regional accent, LaCosta is certain that Moffet isn't from California.)

In the first example, the tag question is used to check information that the speaker already has some idea about. Point out that LaCosta confirms the information. In the second example, the tag question is a conversation strategy and not a question at all. Point out that LaCosta does not respond to the tag question. Play the cassette or read the tapescript again and discuss other examples in the text. Try to decide whether the speaker is checking information or is just making conversation.

GRAMMAR CHARTS

For statements with auxiliaries, give additional examples with different auxiliaries.

We should move to L.A., shouldn't we?

They could speak French, couldn't they?

On the chalkboard, write information about one of the characters from the reading in the Introduction. Have students practice asking and answering questions:

He's from New York City.	*He's not from L.A.*
He's a screenwriter.	*He's not a singer.*
He likes to write mysteries.	*He didn't sell his last script.*
He'll be famous some day.	*He doesn't have any children yet.*

Students can work in pairs and continue the activity with examples based on the other characters.

GRAMMAR NOTES

1. Practice the two intonation patterns. Choose another character from the story, and make a list of things you know and things you want to check. For example, for Roberta Wilson, the list might be:

know	want to check
from L.A.	*found a good job*
got laid off	*knows some people there*
is moving East	*lived there during college*
found a job in New York City	*doesn't want to stay in New York City*
isn't going to buy a car there	

Have students make up statements with tag questions and use the appropriate intonation to ask the questions.

Roberta's from L.A., isn't she?   *She found a good job, didn't she?*

2. Have students work with a partner and write questions with auxiliaries *be, have, will, should,* and *can.* Tell them to write questions to ask their partners, for example:

You're studying engineering, aren't you?

You've been here for several years, haven't you?

You'll go back to Singapore when you graduate, won't you?

3. Give students present and past tense verbs and have them write questions to ask their partners, such as *like, want, saw, go, went, know,* and so forth:

You like Mexican food, don't you?

You want to move, don't you?

You saw Batman Returns, *didn't you?*

4. Tell them to write several negative statements with tag questions using the same verbs, for example: *You don't like sports, do you?*

5. Have students use the questions that they have written to interview each other.

        A: *You like sports, don't you?*

        B: *Yes I do.* OR: *No, I don't.*

EXERCISES

Exercise 1, page 82. After students complete the exercise, have them mark the intonation patterns (⌣ for rising, ⌢ for falling) and then act out the conversation with a partner. Possible answers:

Nice day, isn't it?

You don't know of any apartments, do you?

It's not furnished, is it?

He doesn't need a furnished apartment, does he?

I guess he can always rent some, can't he?

Exercise 3, page 83. Explain or elicit the meaning of *invisible* (can't be seen) and *visible* (can be seen).

Exercise 4, page 84. Teach unfamiliar vocabulary as necessary: *Burbank* (a city in Los Angeles County in California. Two famous film companies, Walt Disney Productions and Warner Brothers-Seven Arts, are located there).

Exercise 6, page 85. Brainstorm some questions with the class before students start to work with partners. Remind them that falling intonation indicates that they are quite certain of their information. Rising intonation indicates that they are asking a real question and expect an answer.

You're an architect, aren't you?

You can't play the piano, can you?

You like Chinese opera, don't you?

You've been to Hollywood, haven't you?

Exercise 7, page 86.

1. Have students choose their partners and decide which one is A and which one is B. Tell them they are going to learn more about L.A. and New York City.

2. Tell the A students to complete the statements and question tags about Los Angeles. Tell them that they do not need to know the information to complete the statements because they are going to check their information with Student B. Remind them that if they are not sure of the information, they will use rising intonation.

    Los Angeles is one of the largest cities in the United States, isn't it? (The speaker isn't sure; he or she is asking a real question to check the information.)

    Los Angeles is one of the largest cities in the United States, isn't it? (The speaker is quite sure of the information.)

3. Tell the B students to read the paragraph about Los Angeles.

4. When both partners are ready, have them do the information gap about Los Angeles.

5. When students have finished talking about Los Angeles, tell the B students to complete the statements and question tags about New York City. As you did with the questions about Los Angeles, tell students that they do not need to know the information to complete the statements because they are going to

check their information with Student A. Remind them that if they are not sure of the information, they will use rising intonation.

New York City is the largest city in the United States, isn't it? (The speaker isn't sure. He or she is asking a real question to check information.)

New York City is the largest city in the United States, isn't it? (The speaker is quite sure of the information.)

6. Tell the A students to read the paragraph about New York City.
7. When both partners are ready, have them do the information-gap exercise about New York City.

Exercise 8, page 87. Have groups perform their role-plays for the class.

UNIT 7: Additions and Responses with *So, Too, Neither, Not either,* and *But*

INTRODUCTION

CULTURE NOTE: In the U.S., families with twins often face difficulties because they do not have the support of extended families. These families face severe strains as they try to cope with the economic, physical, and emotional demands of multiple births. There are several national organizations that help families of twins deal with these demands. Local groups help families find assistance with housework, organize yard sales where people can buy clothing and toys cheaply, and arrange for speakers who discuss parenting issues. These groups also keep in touch with large research projects that follow the life history of twins.

One of the important issues among U.S. parents of twins is that of the individual identity of each twin. Parents are taught to recognize and nurture individual differences as well as their unique situation as twins.

Establish the context: The context is a magazine article about identical twins. Ask students to discuss their own experiences and observations. Is anyone in the class a twin, or does anyone know twins, either identical or fraternal? Would anyone like to have a twin? Why or why not? How are twins raised in different cultures—do they dress in identical clothes, have rhyming names, and so on, as they sometimes do in North America?

Focus questions:

Did Mark and Gerald grow up in the same family? (No, they didn't.)

When did they meet? (when they were thirty-one)

What was surprising about Mark and Gerald? (Their lifestyles were so similar.)

What jobs had Jim Springer and Jim Lewis had? (They both had been gas station attendants and law enforcement agents.)

Where did Barbara grow up? (in the United States)

Who was outgoing, Barbara or Andrea? (Andrea)

According to this article, does heredity alone govern our lives? (No, it doesn't.)

Comprehension questions:

Main idea: *Which question are researchers trying to answer?*

a. When twins are separated at birth, can they lead normal lives?

b. Which affects us more, heredity or environment?

(Answer: b)

Details:	*What did Mark and Gerald do for a living?* (They were both firefighters.)
	When identical twins grow up together in the same family, what two things do they share? (environment and genetic factors)
	Which of these aspects of the Springer brothers' lives does the story <u>not</u> tell about?
	a. their names b. their hobbies c. their occupations d. their pets
	(Answer: b)
	Where did Andrea grow up? (in Germany)
	Did Barbara stay married to the same man? (No, she didn't.)
Inference:	*Why were Andrea and Barbara so different from each other?* (Possible answer: They grew up in different cultures and in different families; their different environments affected them.)
Opinion:	*Mark and Gerald didn't know about each other, and they met accidentally. Barbara's parents didn't tell her she had a twin either. Is it better for adoptive parents to tell or not tell their adopted child about a twin?*
	Which plays a greater role in people's lives, nature or nurture?

Vocabulary (optional): Explain as necessary: *nature or nurture* (a common expression that refers to the question mentioned in paragraph 3: *Which has more effect on our lives, heredity (nature) or environment (nurture)?*), *gene* (the material in the center of a cell that controls how a human being develops), *genetic* (refers to the information in genes, which is inherited from one's parents), *coincidence* (events or situations that were accidental, but that seemed planned [Have students find examples of coincidences from the story of the two Jims]), *tonsillectomy* (a surgical operation for removal of the tonsils, small organs near the throat), *heritage* (something passed down within a family), *suggest* (to offer for consideration or as an explanation [In this context *suggest* does not mean *give advice*]).

Grammar in context: On the chalkboard write examples of additions from the text. Point out that these statements express similarity. Have students find other examples in the text. Identify the similarities that the examples point to.

Write examples of additions with *but.* Point out that these statements show a contrast. Have students find other examples in the text and identify the differences that these statements point to.

GRAMMAR CHARTS

1. Point out the different word order within the sentence additions.

   So and *neither* precede the second noun (i.e., the one that is being compared with the first noun). The verb comes after *so* and *neither.*

            1.   2.
   *Andrea is a twin, and **so is** Barbara.*

            1.   2.
   *Andrea isn't very tall. **Neither is** Barbara.*

   Too and *not either* follow the second noun (i.e., the one that is being compared with the first noun). The verb comes before *too* and *not either.*

            1.   2.
   *Andrea is a twin, and Barbara **is too**.*

            1.   2.
   *Andrea isn't very tall, and Barbara **isn't either**.*

2. Use information about students from the class to practice the forms with *be*.

> *Aster is from Ethiopia, and so is Mabel.*
>
> *Aster is studying nursing, and Mabel is too.*

3. Point out that a main verb other than *be* is not repeated. Instead, the form of *be* or the auxiliary that is used in the main sentence is repeated in the addition.

   Use the appropriate form of *do* if there is no auxiliary or form of *be*.

> *Marta is wearing a scarf, and **so is** Ana.*
>
> *Tom has already finished. **So has** his brother.*
>
> *Erik forgot his book. **So did** Wanda.*

GRAMMAR NOTES

For additional practice, find pictures of similar products and have students work in pairs or groups to write sentences comparing the two.

> *The Lexus has four doors, and the Taurus does too.*

You can also elicit topics and questions from the class and then do a survey, for example:

> *Who can speak French?*
>
> *Who has visited . . .* (a local museum or other attraction)?
>
> *Who saw . . .* (the name of a popular movie)?

Write the answers on the chalkboard. Have students work in groups and use the information to produce more examples.

EXERCISES

Exercise 3, page 94. After the students complete the exercise, ask the class: *Do the husbands of the twins have a lot in common? If so, is this just a coincidence?*

Exercise 4, page 95. Optional activity. Ask students to bring in pictures of family members whom they resemble. Have them work in groups and discuss the similarities and differences with these family members.

Exercise 7, page 97. Have pairs of students report to the whole class. Have a class discussion about the questions.

Exercise 10, page 99. If students did the optional activity in exercise 4, they can use information from that discussion in their writing. If they did not do it, you may want to ask students to bring in pictures and have the discussion at this time, as a prewriting activity.

UNIT 8: Gerunds and Infinitives: Review and Expansion

INTRODUCTION

CULTURE NOTE: The Second Amendment to the U.S. Constitution states in part: " . . . the right of the people to keep and bear arms shall not be infringed." Those who oppose gun control usually point to this amendment in their arguments, since it is very difficult to change the Constitution. The most powerful group that opposes any kind of gun control is the National Rifle Association. This is a lobbying organization, a group that spends large sums of money to influence voters and lawmakers.

Establish the context: The context is a magazine editorial. In an editorial, the editor expresses his or her opinion (viewpoint) on an issue rather than simply giving information. Discuss the information in the Culture Note and elicit students' opinions on the issue.

> *Should citizens have the right to own a weapon for self-protection or for sport? How is the possession of weapons controlled in other countries? Do people use guns for sport (target practice and hunting), and if so, how are they controlled? What are some arguments against selling guns to private citizens?*

Focus questions:

> *How many people die of gunshot wounds in the United States every year?* (more than 34,000)
>
> *Do a majority of the voters support more laws to control handguns?* (Yes, they do.)
>
> *What does the Brady Law require?* (Would-be gun owners must wait for five days before purchasing a gun.)
>
> *What is the position of the National Rifle Association?* ("Guns don't kill people. People kill people.")
>
> *What percent of U.S. children in a recent survey said it was easy for them to acquire a gun?* (59 percent)

Comprehension questions:

Main idea:
> *How does the author of this editorial feel about gun control? Is he for or against it?* (He's for it.)

Details:
> *How does the murder rate in the United States compare with that in Europe and in Japan?* (six times higher than in Europe, seven times higher than in Japan)
>
> *What is the purpose of the five-day waiting period that the Brady Law imposes?* (to give police a chance to find out whether the prospective customer has a criminal record and prevent people from committing impulse crimes)
>
> *What other proposals have been made to control guns?* (banning certain kinds of ammunition, and taxing ammunition at a rate of $10,000, making it more difficult to get a license to sell guns)
>
> *In what ways are Vancouver and Seattle similar? In what one way are they very different?* (Similar: economically, ethnically, socially, culturally, and in all crime statistics except one. Different: Chances of getting shot are eight times greater in Seattle than in Vancouver.)
>
> *In a recent year, how many gun murders occurred in Munich?* (75)
>
> *How many in the same year in Miami?* (1,480)

Inference:
> *Why do people in Seattle have a much greater chance of getting shot than people in Vancouver?* (Vancouver has strict gun control legislation, whereas guns are easily accessible in Seattle. One can infer that gun control works in Vancouver to prevent gun violence.)

Opinion:
> *In places where there is a high crime rate, should people have the right to own a gun for self-protection?*

Vocabulary (optional): Explain as necessary: *viewpoint* (opinion), *epidemic* (so many cases of a disease that it is out of control), *Congress* (the lawmaking body of the United States), *firearms* (guns), *the Brady Law* (a law controlling the purchase of handguns; named after an official of the Reagan administration who was seriously injured when someone used a gun in an attempt to assassinate former President Reagan), *would-be* (prospective), *prospective* (expected or probable), *impulse* (a sudden desire to do something; *impulsive* describes an action that someone takes before thinking about it), *rashly* (without thinking enough about the results), *curbing* (controlling), *imposing* (establishing), *ammunition* (bullets; something shot from a weapon), *arsenal* (building where weapons and explosives are made or stored), *frontierspeople* (the people who explored and settled new areas of North America from about 1725 to 1900), *bear arms* (to carry weapons).

Grammar in context: Gerunds and infinitives are formed from verbs but function as nouns. Write some statements on the board and underline the verbs:

> *In the United States, many people <u>become</u> victims of gun violence.*

> *Recently, Congress <u>passed</u> a law to control handguns.*

Then rewrite the sentences with gerunds and infinitives.

> *They are fed up with <u>becoming</u> victims of gun violence.*

> *They're urging Congress <u>to pass</u> a law to control handguns.*

Point out that with gerunds and infinitives, we can make statements about activities. Give other examples from the text.

GRAMMAR CHARTS AND GRAMMAR NOTES

As you go through the Grammar Notes, refer to the appropriate example in the grammar chart.

EXERCISES

Exercise 1, page 108. Have students look over the survey and petition. Point out that this material is sent out by a group that supports gun control. The survey and petition are used to influence the votes of members of Congress. Elicit the function of a survey (to collect information about people's opinions) and the petition (to make a formal request of one's representative in Congress).

Point out that the petition is in a formal, legal style.

Vocabulary (optional): Explain as necessary: *priority* (something of the highest importance), *concealed weapons* (weapons that are hidden [e.g., under a coat or in the glove compartment of a car]), *Whereas* (a formal way to introduce the reasons for making a request of a congressmember; it means *because ...*), *crucial* (necessary).

Tell students that they will be completing the survey and discussing their opinions in exercise 7. At this time, you may wish to have an informal discussion to check students' understanding of the material.

Exercise 2, page 109. Readers often respond to editorials with letters expressing their own opinions. Magazines publish letters giving opposing viewpoints in order to give a balanced view of an issue.

After students complete the letters, ask for their reactions to the writer's views. Are they reasonable? Should people be encouraged to protect themselves with guns? Will solving complex social problems get rid of the problem of gun violence?

Exercise 3, page 110. CULTURE NOTE: Violence in schools has become a major problem in the United States. Although urban areas have the biggest problems, violence also occurs in suburban and even rural areas.

Vocabulary (optional): Explain as necessary: *suspended* (a punishment in which a student is not allowed to attend school for a period of time).

Exercise 5, page 112. After students do the exercise, elicit their opinions about the student's essay. Do they agree or disagree with the writer's point of view?

Exercise 6, page 113. After students complete the listening task, have them work in groups of four or five to discuss their own opinions about these measures. They can record opinions for and against as in the exercise.

Exercise 7, page 113. Have students complete the survey. If they do it in class, circulate and help out with vocabulary or comprehension problems. Have students work in small groups to discuss their answers. After the groups discuss their surveys, send a couple of students to the front of the class. Have one student ask for the information and count hands, and have the other tally the information on the chalkboard.

Optional writing activity. After their discussion, have students write a letter to the editor about their own opinions. They can use the letter in exercise 5 as a model.

UNIT 9: Verbs Followed by Objects and the Base Form: Make, Have, Let, Help

INTRODUCTION

Establish the context: This is a magazine article about two styles of teaching. Have the students look at the two pictures and describe the differences between them. For example, in the first picture, the teacher is seated among her students; in the other picture, the teacher is standing at the front of the class. In the first picture, students are talking spontaneously, and in the second, a student is raising his hand before speaking. Have a class discussion about which type of classroom students prefer. Is one or the other better depending on the subject matter being taught? Ask students to describe a good learning experience. Was it teacher-centered or student-centered?

Focus questions:

> *How do Ms. Jacobson's students choose topics to write about?* (by keeping a journal)
>
> *Who selects the writing that is published in the class newsletter?* (a committee of students)
>
> *At 8:05, where is Mrs. Quintana?* (at the front of the class) *Where are her students?* (in their seats, ready for class to begin)
>
> *What is one possible objection to Mrs. Quintana's choosing her students' writing topics for them?* (Students may be writing about topics that do not interest them.)

Comprehension questions:

Main idea: *Write* S *next to the student-centered techniques and* T *next to the teacher-centered techniques*

> _____ *students use an assigned textbook* (T)
>
> _____ *students choose their own topics* (S)
>
> _____ *group discussions* (S)
>
> _____ *teacher-led class discussions* (T)
>
> _____ *papers corrected by the teacher using red ink* (T)
>
> _____ *revisions made with the help of peer tutors* (S)

Details: *What subjects do Ms. Jacobson and Mrs. Quintana teach?* (writing)

> *Which approach uses the teacher as a facilitator?* (student-centered)
>
> *What is one cooperative learning technique?* (peer tutoring; group discussions)
>
> *Which teacher plans to test her students on a textbook assignment?* (Mrs. Quintana)
>
> *Do most teachers use a purely teacher-centered or a purely student-centered approach?* (No. Most use a combination of the two approaches.)

Inference: *Why does Sandra Jacobson use* Ms. *as a title while the other teacher uses* Mrs.*?* (Possible answer: Ms. Jacobson is less traditional than Mrs. Quintana.)

Opinion: *Which method would you prefer for a writing course? Why?*

> *Which method would you prefer for a computer course in WordPerfect for Windows? Why?*

Vocabulary (optional): Explain as necessary: *approach* (a manner of doing something), *facilitator* (a helper [point out that the word is defined in the same sentence as someone who assists students in reaching their educational goals]), *peer* (someone equal in status or age: *Peer tutoring* is tutoring done by other students), *pursue* (to follow).

Grammar in context: Point out that with both teaching styles, teachers have to motivate students to learn and develop skills. Elicit from students how they do this: by persuading students to study, by helping students, by encouraging them, and by requiring them to do things that will help them learn.

Write several examples of the structure on the chalkboard and underline the structure.

> *You should <u>let</u> students choose.*
>
> *She <u>has</u> her students keep journals.*
>
> *The committee <u>makes</u> the writers revise.*

Point out that we often use this structure to express things that go on in a relationship with someone in authority such as a teacher or a parent.

GRAMMAR CHARTS

Use the sentences from the explanation of the grammar in context, and ask students to produce the rule for using *make, have, let,* and *help.*

GRAMMAR NOTES

1. Explain or elicit the meaning of each word and give additional examples. *Make* means to require or force: *The teacher made an unruly student leave the room.*

   Have means to cause someone to do something, often part of a procedure or a method: *The customs officers had us fill out forms before they inspected our luggage.*

   Let means to permit: *The judge would not let witnesses speak to journalists.*

   Help means to assist: *Small group discussions help students feel more confident about expressing their opinions.*

2. Ask students to think of someone whom they have had some authority over, or who has had authority over them, and write examples with *make, have, let,* and *help.* They can discuss their examples in pairs. Elicit some and put them on the chalkboard. Show both the base form and the infinitive after *help.*

3. Give additional examples for *get,* meaning to manage to persuade someone to do something, but with difficulty. *Jim got a plumber to come on a Sunday and fix the kitchen sink. I don't know how Jim did it.*

4. Give more examples of *make,* meaning to cause, for example:

   > *Rain makes the flowers grow.*
   >
   > *Your card made me feel better when I was sick.*
   >
   > *Sad movies make Mina cry.*

EXERCISES

Exercise 2, page 118. After students have completed the exercise, elicit other examples for the different authority figures.

Exercise 4, page 121. Elicit students' opinions about the composition: *Were these parents too strict? What were their own home and school responsibilities? What did their parents have them do and let them do regarding homework and helping around the house?* Point out the use of *On the one hand,* in the second paragraph; to introduce one side of an argument. Ask students to find the other side of the argument in the paragraph (*But I wish . . .*).

Exercise 5, page 122. Elicit the origin of the expression *Let them eat cake:* When Marie Antoinette was told that the poor people of France had no bread to eat, she replied, "Let them eat cake."

Exercise 6, page 122. Encourage students to support their ideas with reasons and examples, for instance:

> *I don't think parents should make a teenager take care of younger children in the family. My parents made me take care of my two younger sisters. I never had time to play with my own friends.*

Optional writing exercise. Have a discussion with the whole class after students discuss the list with a partner. Elicit reasons and examples for some of the items and write them on the chalkboard. Ask students to write two or three paragraphs expressing an opinion about one of the items. Tell them to use examples that they have heard in class to support their opinions.

Exercise 7, page 123. Optional writing exercise. After students finish discussing the situations, ask them to choose one and write a letter to an advice columnist about the situation. Bring in an example of a Dear Abby or other advice column as a model. Students can exchange letters and write answers to one another's letters.

UNIT 10: The Passive: Overview

INTRODUCTION

BACKGROUND NOTE: *Reader's Digest* is a monthly publication that reprints condensations, or shortened versions, of articles from popular books and magazines. Inspirational stories and practical how-to articles are often published. Stories about miraculous rescues and other adventures are often reprinted as well. Besides reprints, *Reader's Digest* includes special features such as ... My Most Unforgettable Character ... jokes, and quotations.

Establish the context: Bring in a copy of *Reader's Digest* to show the class. Show titles of typical articles and features such as the quotations and jokes. Elicit students' experiences and opinions: *Have they read the magazine in their own languages? In English? What articles do they like?* Ask them to look at the advertisement. *Which languages in the ad do they recognize?*

Focus questions:

> *How many editions of* Reader's Digest *are there?* (forty-six)
>
> *How many people read it last year?* (more than 100 million)

Comprehension questions:

Main idea:	*Do all the foreign-language editions publish the same material?* (No. Editions are tailored for their audiences.)
Details:	*How many years has* Reader's Digest *been appearing?* (It's been published since 1922, so the answer will vary depending on the current year.)
	Who reads it today? (people in every country in the world)
	How many languages is the magazine published in? (eighteen)
Inference:	*Is the magazine suitable only for adults?* (Possible answer: The picture suggests that young people can read it also.)
Opinion:	*Why is* Reader's Digest *so popular?* (Possible answers: The articles are tailored to the audiences; they're condensed, so they're easier and faster to read than the original versions; the size of the magazine makes it easy to carry; people enjoy the humor; all ages can enjoy it.)

Vocabulary (optional): Explain as necessary: *founded* (started, established), *tailored* (created especially to fit the interests of a particular audience), *subscribe* (to pay ahead of time for a year's magazines).

Grammar in context: Ask the class: *In an advertisement, what is the most important information?* (the name of the product). Write some examples of the structure on the chalkboard and elicit or supply the agent in each sentence:

> Reader's Digest *was founded in 1922.* (by its founders)
>
> *It is read by people all over the world.* (by people)
>
> *Each foreign-language edition is tailored.* (by writers and editors)

Ask students: *In each sentence, which is more important,* Reader's Digest *or the agent?* The focus of each sentence is *Reader's Digest.* The passive structure keeps the focus on the magazine.

GRAMMAR CHARTS

1. Give several more examples of sentences in both active and passive. Use only the simple present and simple past tenses.

<u>Active</u>	<u>Passive</u>
Supermarkets sell it.	*It's sold in supermarkets*
A lot of commuters carry it.	*It's carried by a lot of commuters.*
It published an article about smoking last month.	*An article about smoking was published last month.*
My high school English teacher used it.	*It was used by my high school English teacher*

2. Elicit the rule for forming the passive, and write grammar labels above the sentences: Subject, and *Be* + Past Participle.

3. Point out that *Be* changes with different pronouns and tenses.

GRAMMAR NOTES

1. Point out that the same information can be given a different focus, for example:

> In an article about Abner Doubleday: *Abner Doubleday invented baseball.*
>
> In an article about baseball: *Baseball was invented by Abner Doubleday.*

2. Emphasize that the agent is usually not mentioned in passive sentences. The agent may be unknown: *John's car was stolen last week. The police haven't found the culprits.* The agent may be unimportant, especially when impersonal processes or large public events are involved:

> *In Japan, the Tanabata Festival is celebrated in July.*
>
> *Rice is grown on the island of Honshu.*

3. Elicit information from students about their countries' agriculture, manufacturing, sports, and festivals. Write some examples on the chalkboard.

> *Oats are grown in the north.*
>
> *Soccer is played in schoolyards.*
>
> *New Year is celebrated in January or February.*
>
> *A big plastics factory was founded a few years ago.*

Students can work in groups to produce more examples.

4. Point out that we sometimes use the passive to talk about a problem without assigning blame. Give some examples of classroom or school problems and have students make passive sentences.

The teacher doesn't erase the chalkboard after class. The chalkboard isn't erased after class.

Students leave the lights on. The lights are left on.

The secretary didn't do the photocopying. The photocopying wasn't done.

EXERCISES

Exercise 1, page 134. If students have trouble identifying active and passive forms, have them underline the verb in each sentence. Remind them of the form of the passive.

Vocabulary (optional): Explain as necessary: *proofreader* ([Ask students to infer the meaning] someone who corrects spelling, punctuation, and other mistakes in a text), *condensed* (made shorter, but keeping the original meaning).

Exercise 2, page 134. Ask students to look over the list of languages. Discuss where Arabic, English, Japanese, and Spanish are spoken. Ask students about other languages they speak or know about and where they are spoken. Ask them to estimate the number of speakers of these languages, using the passive.

Exercise 4, page 136. Ask students to read the chart. Before the students start the exercise, talk about the changes that have occurred in each category.

Exercise 5, page 138. Explain that a copyeditor reads material before it is published and questions information that seems incorrect. Remind students about the interview in exercise 3. You may want to have students act out the interview to remind the class of the information.

Exercise 9, page 141.

1. Have students find Luzon and Mindanao on the silhouette map so that they can see the islands in relation to the whole country.
2. If you have students from the Philippines or students who have visited the Philippines, elicit information about the country.
3. Review the verbs for each type of material in the key to the product map: *grow* (for plants), *raise* (for animals), *mine* (for ore and minerals), *produce* (for manufactured goods). Pronounce names of the plants, animals, and products for the students.
4. Have the students work in pairs to complete the exercise.
5. When they finish, put the key to the map on the chalkboard. Have one student complete the information as students report the results.

Exercise 10, page 142. Optional activity. Collect the trivia questions and divide the class in teams. Ask the teams questions as in a quiz show.

Exercise 11, page 143. Follow the procedure for Quotable Quotes on page 4 of this Teacher's Manual. Encourage students to supply examples to illustrate the meaning of the quotations.

Exercise 12, page 143. You may want to take your students to the library and help them locate information in encyclopedias or other reference books. Encourage students to bring in pictures or articles from their countries. Display the reports.

UNIT 11: The Passive with Modals

INTRODUCTION

Establish the context: Ask students to look at the picture of the space station and ask them: *Would you like to live on a space station? What problems will there be for people who stay there a long time?*

Focus questions:

> *What is* Freedom? *(a space station; an international project)*
>
> *What do Lozano and Wong want to avoid?* (cross-cultural problems)
>
> *What TV show do Lozano and Wong suggest watching?* (Star Trek)

Comprehension questions:

Main idea: *Which sentence best states the main idea of the article?*

> *a. People from different cultures should learn to get along.*
>
> *b. People from the United States sometimes make decisions too quickly.*
>
> *c. The success of space station* Freedom *may depend on cross-cultural tolerance.*
>
> (Answer: c)

Details: *Who will operate* Freedom? (a crew of astronauts from different countries)

> *At first, how often will the crew change?* (every ninety days)
>
> *Partners who don't know American slang may feel like* _____ . (outsiders)
>
> *Is using a textbook always the best way to teach cross-cultural sensitivity?*
> (No. Experience and observation are often better.)

Inference: *Why should astronauts watch* Star Trek? (Possible answer: Since it is a drama, astronauts can actually observe people solving misunderstandings, rather than just read about problems in textbooks.)

Opinion: *Is cross-cultural training really necessary? If so, what skills should crew members learn?*

Vocabulary (optional): Explain as necessary: *close quarters* (crowded living accommodations that have little privacy), *apprehension* (anxiety), *launched* (sent into the sky), *trapped environment* (an environment such as the space station that people can't leave), *anthropologist* (a scientist who studies human beings, including their beliefs, social behavior, and physical characteristics), *religious dietary restrictions* (limitations that a religion sets on what its members may eat. For example, Jews and Muslims may not eat pork, and many Buddhists are vegetarians. Some Christians have dietary restrictions during Lent—the forty days before Easter), *tolerance* (acceptance of customs and behavior different from one's own), *harmony* (relations marked by peace and tolerance), *eons* (very long periods of time).

Grammar in context: Review the use of the passive: We use it when the focus is not on the agent. This article is about a large international project. In most cases, the agent is either unknown or is an impersonal procedure. The object of the action is the focus of the sentence:

> Freedom *will be launched from the space shuttle.* (The agent is the entire project, not a single person.)
>
> *The crew will be replaced every ninety days.* (The agent is a procedure.)
>
> *What time should meals be served?* (This is a question about a procedure.)
>
> *Tolerance can't be taught. It must be observed.* (The agent is too vague to name.)

GRAMMAR CHARTS

Elicit the rule from the sentences on the chalkboard and write the grammar labels.

Give some sentences with the impersonal *they* as the subject and ask students to transform them into the passive.

They should serve lunch at 12:00.	*Lunch should be served at 12:00.*
They should prepare more international dishes.	*More international dishes should be prepared.*

They can't describe the view of Earth.   *The view of Earth can't be described.*

They have to recycle their water.   *Their water has to be recycled.*

They could ask astronauts to extend their stay.   *Astronauts could be asked to extend their stay.*

They ought to use other languages socially.   *Other languages ought to be used socially.*

GRAMMAR NOTES

1. Point out that the meaning of the modals is the same in passive or active sentences.

2. Tell students to imagine that they are setting up an apartment with several other students. Ask them to establish house rules with *will, must, have to,* and *have got to.* If necessary, supply cues:

   > *meetings/hold/every week* (will)
   >
   > *rules/change/at house meetings* (may)
   >
   > *dishes/wash/after every meal* (must)
   >
   > *rules/follow/by guests* (have to)
   >
   > *loud music/play/after 10:00 P.M.* (must not)

3. Then ask students to use *ought to, should,* and *don't have to* to talk about things that would be a good idea.

   > *Food ought to be shared by everyone.*
   >
   > *Phone calls shouldn't be allowed after midnight.*

EXERCISES

Exercise 1, page 147. After students complete the exercise, have a short class discussion about the issues raised in the article. Ask the students:

> *Is food important to them? Why? What food would they want to have on a long mission?*
>
> *Will different styles and colors of uniforms help people feel better? What would they not want to wear?*
>
> *What should be done about privacy?*
>
> *What kind of recreation could be provided?*

Exercise 2, page 147. Vocabulary (optional): Explain as necessary: *flight simulation* (an experience that tries to copy the real experience. Astronauts practice underwater, for example, in order to experience weightlessness).

Exercise 4, page 150. Vocabulary (optional): Explain as necessary: *restraints* ([ask students to infer the meaning from the information in the sentence] hands and feet float around at zero gravity—the restraints hold them in place).

Exercise 5, page 151. Have students read the dialogue. Make sure they understand the story.
Tell them that they are to listen carefully and choose the correct word. Explain that either word is possible in the context.

Exercise 6, page 152. Have students review the unit and talk about some of the problems that are anticipated on space missions, for example: tasteless food or too little of a popular dish, the need for clothing that can be adjusted to temperature changes, crew members feeling like outsiders because they don't know American slang.

Exercise 8, page 153. Have students convert the cost of $16,000 an hour to local currency where appropriate. After students discuss the question, have them write an opinion essay or a letter to the editor about it.

UNIT 12: Passive Causatives

INTRODUCTION

CULTURE NOTE: Anyone who earns more than a certain amount of income in the United States must complete a federal income tax form. Taxpayers may calculate their own taxes, or they can hire an accountant to do them. There are also large companies such as H & R Block that perform this service inexpensively. The form (or a request for an extension of time) must be filed by midnight, April 15. By that time, the envelope must be postmarked (stamped with the date and time) at the post office. If it isn't, you may have to pay a penalty and interest on the money you owe. At post offices that stay open for last-minute filers, the deadline has become a public event. Patrons often find music, soft drinks, pizza, assistance in filing, and even free stamps in some places.

Establish the context: The context is an on-the-spot news broadcast at New York City's main post office in Manhattan. Ask students: *How are taxes filed in other countries? Are taxes difficult to calculate? Is there a deadline? If so, when? Do people usually figure out their own taxes, or do they hire professionals to do them?*

Focus question:

> *Why is the second man filing so late?* (He lost his W-2 form because his apartment was being painted.)

Comprehension questions:

Main idea:	*Why is there a big crowd of people at the main post office at 11:35 P.M.?* (They're filing their taxes right before the deadline.)
Details:	*Did the woman do her taxes herself in past years?* (No, an accountant did them for her.)
	Did the first man wait until the last minute before he brought his taxes to H & R Block? (No, but he lost his completed taxes for a while.)
	What did the second man ask his former employer to do? (send him a new W-2 form)
Inference:	*Did Ken Watanabe believe the second man's excuse?* (Possible answer: Probably not. He said, "You can do better than that!")
Opinion:	*Does the carnival atmosphere help people file by the deadline? If so, how?*

Vocabulary (optional): Explain as necessary: *postmarked* (stamped with the date and time by the post office; the postmark proves when a letter was mailed), *file* (to send in officially, as required by law), *mobbed* (very crowded), *federal income tax returns* (the forms on which someone's taxes are calculated and reported), *the eleventh hour* (the last minute), *stuff* (informal word for a collection of things), *W-2 form* (the form that an employer uses to report an employee's income; one part goes to the employee, and one part goes to the federal government's Internal Revenue Service), *the bottom line* (the most important fact; the last amount on a profit and loss calculation, shows the amount of profit or loss after everything has been taken into account).

Grammar in context: Write examples of the structure on the chalkboard:

> *You must have your return postmarked by midnight.*
>
> *You can even get your back rubbed at the post office.*
>
> *Sheila has always had her taxes prepared by an accountant.*

Point out that we use this structure to talk about things that someone arranges for someone else to do.

GRAMMAR CHARTS

Underline the structure in the example sentences and point out or elicit the rule for forming it. Label the example sentences with the grammar labels:

Have/Get   *Object*   *Past Participle*

Construct a drill by inventing a character (a famous Hollywood star, perhaps) who is so busy that he or she has no time to do all of life's small daily chores. Elicit the tasks that this person has done for him or her and write them on the chalkboard as cues.

clothes/select	*dog/walk*
lawn/mow	*house/clean*
children/take care of/nanny	*meals/prepare/cook*
telephone calls/return/by a personal secretary	*hair/cut*

Ask students to make sentences using the cues. Elicit different verb tenses.

A: *What's Sam going to have done this afternoon?*

B: *He's going to have his telephone calls returned by his personal secretary.*

C: *He's going to have his hair cut.*

D: *He's going to have his dog walked.*

Use the cues to practice questions and answers.

How often does he have his house cleaned?

Is he having his hair cut today?

GRAMMAR NOTES

1. Use cues from the drill and ask students to work in pairs to produce examples of things they have done and things they do themselves.

2. Give more examples of contrasts between the past perfect and the passive causative with *have* and *get*. Ask students to tell you whether you did it or arranged to have it done, for example:

   I had washed the car before I left. (I did it myself.)

   I had it washed before I left. (Someone did it for me.)

   I had walked the dog in the morning. (I did it myself.)

   I had the dog walked in the morning. (Someone did it for me.)

3. Bring students' attention to the *Be careful!* note. Then have them look at the end of the reading in the Introduction on page 155. *When the reporter says, "These folks my be filing at the last minute, but the bottom line is, they got it done," does he mean that they did it themselves or that someone did it for them?* (They did it themselves.)

EXERCISES

Exercise 2, page 158. In this exercise, it's April 19. Have students locate the date on the calendar and then look over the notes on the calendar to see what has been done and what remains to be done. Remind them to use the appropriate verb tense for each sentence.

After they finish, elicit some other services people often have done when they move and add them to the calendar at appropriate spots. Possible additions:

get the children signed up for school

have their records transferred to the new school

get the car registered

have mail forwarded

Exercise 4, page 160. Remind students that Art appeared in exercise 2, where he was moving to California. Have them read the five sentences and guess why this work was done in Art's new home. Ask them to speculate about what kind of work Art does.

Exercise 5, page 161. Circulate and help students with vocabulary they need to talk about the pictures, for example:

porch	*shingles*	*bushes*
antenna	*paving stones*	
to weed	*hanging plant*	

After they finish, have one student go to the front and write on the chalkboard as students report what has been done. Ask what else they could do in addition, for instance:

They could have more trees planted.

They could have a basketball net or some play equipment put up.

UNIT 13: Advisability and Obligation in the Past: Should have, Ought to have, Could have, Might have

INTRODUCTION

BACKGROUND NOTE: Many popular psychology books and articles stress that the way people interpret a situation affects them more than the situation itself. According to cognitive psychologists such as the ones mentioned in this article, most situations are neutral, neither good nor bad. It is one's interpretation of a situation and the resulting reaction that makes an event good or bad. These psychologists suggest strategies to help people change the way they think about situations and consequently become happier and more effective.

Establish the context: The context is an article from a popular magazine such as *Psychology Today, Health,* or *Prevention Magazine*. You may want to bring in an issue of one of these magazines to show the class.

Ask the students to look at the lines by John Greenleaf Whittier (U.S. poet, 1807–1892) and the title of the article. The words *It might have been* mean that something was possible but didn't happen. Many times people have feelings of regret about things that seemed possible but didn't occur. Elicit types of missed opportunities that people regret (not necessarily personal experiences).

Focus questions:

What does the title suggest about these psychologists' opinion of regretful feelings? (They are useless.)

What happens when people dwell too much on past mistakes? (They can't move on with their lives.)

Did the mother go to the football game? (No, she didn't.)

According to cognitive psychologists, which is easier—thinking about the past or solving the problems of the present? (It's easier to think about the past.)

Comprehension questions:

Main idea: *According to cognitive psychology, what is Paul's problem?*

                              a. He didn't go on to college.

                              b. He believes that not going to college was a terrible mistake.

                              (Answer: b)

Details: *Is Paul a doctor?* (No, he isn't.)

                     Is he rich and famous? (No, he isn't.)

                     Is it always wrong to think about past errors? (No. We learn that way.)

                     According to Freeman and DeWolf, was it really possible for most people to act differently in the past? (No, it wasn't. Feelings of regret are often not based on fact.)

                     Why should people record and listen to their "woulda/coulda/shoulda thoughts"? (This practice helps people see the illogic of these thoughts.)

Inference: *Why might Paul be spending so much time dwelling on past mistakes?* (Possible answer: According to the last paragraph, it's easier to do that than solve present problems.)

Opinion: *Do you agree that people's interpretation of events has more impact than the events themselves? Are there any exceptions?*

Vocabulary (optional): Explain as necessary: *dwell on* (think about too much), *paralyzed* (unable to move), *woulda/coulda/shoulda* (the spelling reflects informal pronunciation of the phrases we often use to express feelings of regret, e.g., *I shoulda gone to college = I should have gone to college. I regret not going.* Although we often pronounce these phrases this way, it is not correct to write them this way.), *disorder* (a physical or mental illness), *challenging* (fighting), *lament* (to express deep regret), *jerk* (a fool [Warn students that this is an impolite slang term]), *speculate* (to guess; to make theories).

Grammar in context: Write examples from the text on the chalkboard:

         I ought to have applied to college.

         I could have become a doctor.

         I shouldn't have missed that opportunity.

Remind students of the title of the article. This grammatical structure expresses actions that were advisable or obligatory in the past. Since these actions were usually not taken, there is often a feeling of regret or blame attached to the statements.

Give a scenario in which someone would tend to have regrets or self-blame, for example:

         Carol didn't have much change, so she didn't put quite enough money into the parking meter for the time she was going to be in class. When she came out of class, she was five minutes over the time, and the meter attendant was writing a ticket. Carol accepted the ticket, but she forgot to pay it. Now she owes twice as much money.

Help students make sentences about this situation, and write them on the chalkboard, for example:

         She shouldn't have parked at the meter.

         She should have gotten change before she tried to park.

         She could have left class a little early.

         She might have argued with the meter attendant.

         She ought to have paid the ticket right away.

GRAMMAR CHARTS

1. Underline the relevant structures in the examples on the chalkboard. Elicit or point out the rule for the form, and label the structures:

Modal   Have   *Past Participle*

2. Point out that *have* does not change for the different pronouns. Since it follows a modal, the base form is always used.

3. Use the situation about the parking ticket to practice questions or develop another scenario from your own experience. Write cues on the chalkboard:

when/come back	*When should she have come back?*
argue with the meter attendant	*Should she have argued with the meter attendant?*
where/park instead	*Where should she have parked instead?*
paid the ticket right away	*Should she have paid the ticket right away?*

GRAMMAR NOTES

1. Emphasize that these phrases sound like *could of* or *coulda,* and so forth but that it is not correct to write them this way.

2. Point out that statements like *She could have at least called me,* and *You might have told us* strongly suggest blame of the person who did not do the expected thing. People say these things when they are angry.

EXERCISES

Exercise 2, page 170. After students complete the exercise, have a class discussion about the students' own ideas regarding the situation.

Exercise 6, page 173. Explain that S.O.S. (in the survey title) is also the Morse code signal for an emergency. A sense of obligation is a feeling of being responsible for something. Ask students to think about whether they have a strong sense of obligation. Point out that there are no right or wrong answers in the survey.

Exercise 7, page 174. After the groups discuss the dilemmas, have a discussion with the whole class about them.

Exercise 8, page 174. After their discussion, students can respond to one another in writing.

UNIT 14: Speculations and Conclusions about the Past: May have, Might have, Could have, Must have, Had to have

INTRODUCTION

BACKGROUND NOTE: The Nazca culture flourished around 1000 B.C. in what is now southern Peru. The Nazcans are known for their beautiful pottery and textiles as well as for the mysterious Nazca lines.

Easter Island is a small, isolated island, a member of the Polynesian group in the Pacific. It is 2,200 miles from Chile, which controls it politically, and 1,100 miles from the nearest Polynesian island. Europeans first visited the island in 1722, the day before Easter. Its name in the language of its native people is Te-Pit-o-te-Henua (navel of the world). The colossal statues for which Easter Island is famous have been studied by archaeologists since 1914.

Establish the context: Ask students to look at the first picture and speculate about what the Nazca lines represent and what they are made of. Ask students to talk about why they were created. Then ask students to look at the picture of the Easter Island statues on the next page. Ask them if the statues were difficult to make. Tell students that they are going to read about one man's interpretation of these achievements.

Focus questions:

> *According to von Däniken, what was one possible use of the Nazca lines?* (to mark a landing strip for spacecraft)
>
> *Does von Däniken believe that there were a lot of people living on Easter Island when the statues were carved?* (No. He believes that the island had a very small population.)
>
> *In von Däniken's theory, were mythological creatures really gods?* (No. They were creatures from outer space.)
>
> *Have many people read von Däniken's books?* (Yes. His theories fascinate millions of readers.)

Comprehension questions:

Main idea: *According to von Däniken's theories, who is responsible for many of the great achievements of ancient civilizations?* (civilizations from outer space)

Details: *Where does a viewer have to be in order to recognize the shapes in the Nazca lines?* (about 600 feet in the air)

How did the Nazcans build them without airplanes, according to von Däniken? (with instructions from a spacecraft)

What examples of advanced technology does von Däniken see in ancient art? (rocket ships, robots, and wristwatches)

Why are scientists skeptical of von Däniken's theories? (They prefer to look for answers closer to home.)

Inference: *Does von Däniken have a high opinion of the ancient civilizations he writes about?* (Possible answer: No, he doesn't. He doesn't believe that the people of these civilizations were able to make great achievements on their own.)

Opinion: *Could von Däniken's theories be true?*

Vocabulary (optional): Explain as necessary: *close encounters* (meetings with beings from other planets), *chariot* (a two-wheeled horse-drawn vehicle used in ancient times in battles and races), *creation myths* (stories that explain how the the earth and its creatures were first made), *assert* (to state firmly), *cosmos* (the universe), *compiled* (assembled; information put together from several different sources), *cartographers* (map makers [Ask students to infer the meaning from the context, which describes a map]), *skeptical* (not believing; asking for more or better proof).

Grammar in context: Refer students to the pictures again and ask: *Do we know for certain why these things were built and how they were built?* Elicit that no one knows for certain, and that most of what we say about many ancient structures is speculation. Write examples on the board from the text.

> *The drawings might have marked a landing strip for spacecraft.*
>
> *The island could only have supported a small population.*
>
> *Mythological gods must actually have been space creatures.*

Point out that von Däniken is speculating about these possibilities based on his interpretation of the evidence. Remind students that *may, might,* and *could* express possibilities. *Must, had to,* and *couldn't* express more certainty on the part of the speaker.

GRAMMAR CHARTS

1. Elicit the rule from the sentences on the chalkboard and write the grammar labels above the sentences:

   Subject   Modal   Have   Past Participle

2. Point out that we often use this structure in short answers to *yes/no* questions:

   A: *Did Mehmet finish writing his résumé?*

   B: *He couldn't have. He only started a few minutes ago.*

GRAMMAR NOTES

1. If possible, bring in one or more of von Däniken's books and show students photographs of the artifacts that von Däniken writes about. Use them to cue speculations.

   Could this have been a spaceship?

   The artist might have used a robot as a model for this face.

2. Tell students that they may hear *have to have* + past participle (instead of *had to have* + past participle) and *can't have* + past participle as well as *couldn't have* + past participle. The forms they have just practiced are the most commonly used ones.

EXERCISES

Exercise 1, page 180. When students complete the exercise, ask them to make other speculations or come to additional conclusions about some of the information, for example:

   Number 2: *He must have taken his research very seriously.*

   Number 6: *A lot of people may have had similar ideas.*

Exercise 2, page 180. Point out that in items 17 and 19 it is not necessary to repeat the words *could have* because in both cases they are close to an earlier occurrence of *could have* + past participle. Only the past participle need be repeated.

Ask students if their opinions have changed after reading this new information.

Exercise 3, page 182. Students may be interested in hearing that the photo of the Loch Ness monster was a fraud. The photographer recently confessed on his deathbed.

Optional activity. Tabloid newspapers like the *National Enquirer* often publish stories about UFO sightings and strange, supernatural events. Students might enjoy reading and discussing one of these stories, and then speculating about what really happened.

Exercise 4, page 183. Point out the use of quotation marks for incorrect naming in Item 4. The person calling the Nazcan lines "streets" knows that they really aren't streets, but is calling them that for lack of a better word.

Exercise 5, page 184. Before students listen to the tape, have them discuss the pictures of artifacts and speculate about what they might have been used for. Take notes and compare their answers with the speculations on the tape.

Exercise 7, page 186. If possible, bring in a map to show the location of the Yucatán Peninsula and the Yenisey River in Siberia.

Optional activity. Have students choose a topic from the unit and do some library research. Possible topics are:

   Nazca civilization   *Bigfoot and yeti*

   the Nazca lines   *the disappearance of the dinosaurs the Easter Island statues*   *the explosion on the Yenisey River in Siberia*

Mayan culture

Students can write reports and present them to the class. They should discuss the speculations and conclusions that have been made about their topic.

UNIT 15: Factual Conditionals: Present

INTRODUCTION

Establish the context: Have students look at the pictures and headings, and ask them about their own experiences as travelers. Discuss some problems such as airline regulations, food, getting tired, motion sickness, traveling with children. Ask students what they do when they face these situations; don't limit the discussion to airline travel. Then tell students they are going to read an article that contains tips for traveling by plane.

Focus questions:

How can you avoid getting stiff during a long flight? (by moving around the cabin every hour and by doing stretching exercises in your seat)

Do airlines have the right to refuse to carry people with disabilities as passengers? (only under very special circumstances)

Comprehension questions:

Main idea: *Which sentence best states the main idea of this article?*

a. Jet lag, dehydration, and delays are usually unavoidable on long flights.

b. With the information in this article, you can avoid a lot of the discomfort of air travel.

(Answer: b)

Details: *Are the following statements true or false?*

Because of the new electronic reservation systems, you don't have to reconfirm an international reservation. (false)

People who don't check in at the gate are sometimes bumped from a flight. (true)

You don't have to order a low-cholesterol meal ahead of time. (false)

Getting to their destination at night helps travelers get to sleep at the right time. (true)

Passengers with disabilities don't have to be concerned about their rights as passengers. (false)

Airlines will sometimes provide electric cars for families making connecting flights. (true)

Inference: *What's the problem with many airline meals?* (Possible answer: They're not fresh, and they don't taste good.)

Opinion: *What's the biggest hassle about traveling long distance by air?*

Vocabulary (optional): Explain as necessary: *hassles* (problems), *bumped from a flight* (have your seat given to another passenger), *kosher* (food prepared in accordance with Jewish religious law), *dehydration* (loss of fluids; [Tell students to read about how to avoid this problem, and then ask them to look at the picture of the clock and infer the meaning.]), *jet lag* (the discomfort that occurs after a long airplane trip, when the body has not yet adjusted to the change in time zones), *paraplegic* (a person who does not have the use of his or her arms or legs).

Grammar in context: The article discusses what airplane passengers should do under certain conditions, or what happens under certain conditions. On the board, write examples similar to those in the text:

If you don't check in at the gate, you could be bumped from the flight.

Whenever people fly long distances, they suffer from jet lag.

Passengers get stiff if they don't move around the cabin.

The *if* clause talks about the condition. The main clause talks about what you should do, or what usually happens under that condition.

GRAMMAR CHARTS

Point out that the simple present tense is used in both the *if* clause and the main clause.

Note that in questions, question word order is used in the main clause, but not in the *if* clause.

GRAMMAR NOTES

1. Give additional examples of general truths and scientific facts.

    Water expands if it freezes.

    If water vapor cools, it becomes liquid.

    If children don't receive enough attention, they behave badly.

    If people don't drink milk, they often don't get enough calcium.

    Elicit examples from students.

2. Refer to the reading in the Introduction, and ask students to produce examples of things that generally occur from their own experience. Ask them questions such as:

    Can you sleep if the plane's crowded?

    Do you get motion sickness if you read?

    What do you do if there are noisy children in a seat near you?

    Should you drink soda if you're thirsty?

    How do you get seats together if you travel with a big group?

    A: *What do you eat if you take a long flight?*

    B: *If I take a long flight, I usually eat the regular food.*

    C: *I always order a vegetarian meal if I take a long flight.*

3. Give examples of sentences opening with the *if* clause and with the main clause. Ask students to punctuate them.

4. To practice factual conditionals with modals, ask students to give some tips about visiting a city that they know well.

What should you do if	*you want to find some good bargains?*
	you like to try different kinds of food?
	you want the best view of the city?
What can you do if	*you don't have a lot of money?*
	you have a lot/only a little time to spend there?
	the weather turns bad?
What might happen if	*you drive too fast?*
	you don't tip your server?

you get lost?

you lose your passport?

5. Tell students to imagine that someone is taking over their jobs for one day. Write a list of instructions about what to do under certain conditions.

> *If Mr. Jones calls, ask for his telephone number.*
>
> *If the new shipment arrives, don't open the packages.*
>
> *If you want a good lunch, try Harmon's.*
>
> *If there's a problem with the computers, call this number.*
>
> *If you can't find a wrench, use pliers.*

6. Rewrite examples from Grammar Notes 4 and 5 using *then*.

> *If you want to find some good bargains, then you should go to the department stores.*
>
> *If you want a good lunch, then try Harmon's.*

7. Rewrite some examples from step 2 with *when* and *whenever*:

> *Whenever I read in a car, I get motion sickness.*
>
> *When there are noisy children in a seat near me, I try to move.*
>
> *You shouldn't drink soda when you're thirsty. You should drink water.*

EXERCISES

Exercise 1, page 195. Have a discussion about students' experiences with very delayed or overbooked flights. Has anyone been awarded compensation for delays? What did they do to receive it? What are their rights as passengers?

Vocabulary (optional): Explain as necessary: *compensate* (to pay for some loss or damage), *unduly* (more than normal or expected), *upgrade* (a change from a lower- to a higher-class ticket, e.g., from business to first class), *toiletries* (products for personal grooming such as toothpaste, deodorant, and hair spray).

Exercise 2, page 196.

1. Explain that the title of the exercise refers to tourists who travel to so many places in a short time that they have trouble remembering where they are.
2. Have students work in groups and write similar questions and answers about their own city. Groups can exchange questions and answers with another group and do the sentence combining.

Exercise 3, page 197.

1. Discuss the title, which also refers to programs airlines offer that award free miles after a passenger has flown a certain number of miles on that airline.
2. Point out that in this exercise, students must decide which is the condition and which is the result.
3. Note that in number 5, *you* is the impersonal *you*. The flight attendant is not referring to the interviewer.

Exercise 4, page 198. After students complete the exercise, ask them to explain the results, using *if*, for example: *A fire goes out if there's no oxygen.*

Exercise 5, page 200.

1. Have students read the boarding passes, and elicit information about them, for example: who is traveling, where they are going, and their flight number and seat numbers.

2. Then have students read the statements in the exercise before you play the cassette or read the transcript.

Exercise 6, page 201.

1. Remind students about the examples they wrote when they were working on the grammar notes, and the sentences they wrote for exercise 2.

2. Pairs of students can create brochures, drawing pictures or bringing in postcards or photographs of the city.

UNIT 16: Factual Conditionals: Future

INTRODUCTION

CULTURE NOTE: Before an election in the United States, voters' groups such as the League of Women Voters publish brochures giving information about the candidates. The brochures give the candidates' backgrounds and descriptions of their platforms. The two major political parties in the United States are the Democratic and the Republican parties. Traditionally, Democrats have emphasized social programs, while Republicans have taken a more conservative approach that stresses punishing criminals and developing businesses. Baker and Ibarguen are mayoral candidates and they are addressing problems of a U.S. city—housing, education, crime, and unemployment. Campaign speeches sometimes exaggerate the candidates' power to make certain changes. For example, Ibarguen promises to enforce mandatory prison sentences for violent crime, but, in fact, mayors have no power to do this.

Establish the context: Ask students to think about the city or the town you are in. What problems does the mayor, or government head, have to address? Which are the most important problems? What should a candidate promise to do in your town? Tell students that they are going to read about the political platforms of two candidates for mayor in a U.S. city.

Focus questions:

How can Baker's city help its citizens get some of the 16 million new jobs?
(by preparing them with a good education)

Under Ibarguen's administration, what will happen to someone who commits a violent crime? (He or she will go to jail and will serve the full sentence.)

What will people lose if they don't vote? (a say in the future of their city)

Comprehension questions:

Main idea: Write B (Baker) *or* I (Ibarguen) *to show which candidate made each promise*

improve the school system (B)

fight crime in neighborhoods (I)

bring jobs back to the city (I)

provide better housing (B)

Details: *Which candidate served as district attorney?* (Ibarguen)

Which candidate is now the mayor? (Baker)

Which candidate believes that education is the most important issue? (Baker)

Who wants more police officers on the streets to fight crime? (Ibarguen)

According to Baker, what will be the result of having an educated work force?
(Businesses will thrive.)

Why does Ibarguen want to lower taxes? (If taxes are lowered, businesses will return.)

Inference:	*Does this city have a healthy economy and a good quality of life?* (Possible answer: It seems to have a lot of crime and bad housing.)
	Does Baker believe that more police will solve the crime problem? (Possible answer: No. He emphasizes housing instead.)
Opinion:	*Which is the better approach to solving the problem of crime, Baker's or Ibarguen's?*

Vocabulary (optional): Explain as necessary: *city clerk* (the official who keeps the records of a city and issues marriage and other licenses), *state assembly* (the lawmaking body of a state), *LL.B.* (Bachelor of Laws, an undergraduate degree), *B.S.* (Bachelor of Science, an undergraduate degree) *cum laude* (with distinction), *city comptroller* (the official who controls the finances of a city), *district attorney* (a government lawyer who brings charges against people arrested for crimes), *United States House of Representatives* (one of the two houses of Congress, the lawmaking body of the United States government), *U.C.L.A.* (University of California at Los Angeles), *U.S.C.* (University of Southern California), *B.A.* (Bachelor of Arts, an undergraduate degree), *backbone* (the basic part; the part that supports everything else), *priority* (something that is judged to be more important than other things), *a say* (some influence; voting gives citizens a say in government), *plagued* (to be the victim of a widespread and harmful situation), *administration* (the part of the government under the control of the mayor), *do time* (to spend time in prison), *mandatory* (required; when a prison sentence for a particular crime is mandatory, the judge has no choice, but must impose the sentence on someone convicted of that crime).

Grammar in context: Point out that the candidates are making campaign promises about what they will do if they are elected. They also are making predictions about the future of the city under conditions that they will create. Write examples on the board:

> *If I am elected, I will help you fight for every street, for every house.*

> *If our citizens have decent homes, then our neighborhoods will become healthy again.*

Point out or elicit the tenses in each clause:

| *If clause:* | present tense |
| *Result clause:* | future |

Write a condition on the chalkboard, such as: *It's probably going to rain tomorrow.* Have students build a chain of consequences, for example:

> *If it rains tomorrow, I won't go to class.*

> *If I don't go to class, I won't know the assignment.*

> *If I don't know the assignment, I won't be able to do my homework.*

> *If I don't do my homework, . . .*

GRAMMAR CHARTS

1. Note that you can use either *will* or *be going to* in the result clause.
2. Point out that question word order is used only in the result clause.

GRAMMAR NOTES

1. If an election campaign is going on or has gone on recently, bring in material that students can use to develop examples. Campaign ads in newspapers and magazines, letters to the editor, and short news stories about speeches would be helpful. Have students read the material and make predictions about what will happen if each candidate is elected.

> *If Rush wins, he's going to be tough on crime.*

> *If Young is elected, she won't know how to manage foreign policy.*

2. Explain that *unless* expresses a condition that prevents the action in the main clause:

> *I'll be home early <u>unless I work overtime</u>.* (Working overtime is the only condition that will prevent my coming home early.)
>
> *We'll shop tomorrow <u>unless the stores are closed</u>.* (The stores being closed will prevent us from shopping tomorrow; otherwise, we'll do it.)

Ask students to write two or three sentences about their future plans. Put some of them on the board:

> *I'm going to start my own business.*
>
> *I'll study computer programming.*
>
> *I'm going to graduate next year.*

Then ask them to think about a condition that could prevent this from happening, and write sentences with *unless*. Elicit sentences and put them on the chalkboard.

> *Unless the bank refuses my loan application, I'm going to start my own business.*
>
> *I'll study computer programming unless there are more jobs in teaching.*
>
> *Unless I drop out next semester, I'm going to graduate next year.*

EXERCISES

Exercise 1, page 206. Vocabulary (optional): Explain as necessary: *sanitation workers* (city employees who pick up the garbage).

Exercise 2, page 206. Vocabulary (optional): Explain as necessary: *polls* (in this context *polls* refers to opinion polls, in which a number of people are questioned about their preferences in order to predict the outcome of an election; also, giving votes at the election itself).

Exercise 5, page 209. Explain that these conversations are occurring at the place where people have come to cast their votes. When people register to vote, they are usually issued voter registration cards, and their names are recorded in a book or entered into a computer. At the polling place, the names are checked in the book or on a computer printout.

Exercise 6, page 210. Vocabulary (optional): Explain as necessary: *recreation centers* (neighborhood centers where young people come to play sports or take part in other activities. [Students can probably infer the meaning from the interview]).

Exercise 9, page 211. Optional activities. This activity can be expanded in a number of ways. Groups can choose a candidate and then write a speech outlining problems and making campaign promises. Candidates can debate issues.

Possible writing activities include writing a brochure such as the one in the reading in the Introduction introducing their candidates. Groups can also write campaign advertisements and letters to the editor.

UNIT 17: Unreal Conditionals: Present

INTRODUCTION

BACKGROUND NOTE: In the nineteenth century, the brothers Jacob and Wilhelm Grimm made the first scholarly collection of folk stories. They collected the stories from German peasants, who had passed them orally from generation to generation. In English the stories are known as *Grimm's Fairy Tales*. "The Fisherman and his Wife" is one of the most famous of these stories, which include the favorites "Hansel and Gretel," "Cinderella," and "Snow White and the Seven Dwarfs." Like many other fairy tales, "The Fisherman and

His Wife" shows a sympathetic communication between people and animals as well as magic. (*Source: Encyclopedia Americana.* Danbury, Conn.: Grolier, Inc., 1987.)

Establish the context: Ask students to look at the illustration and the first sentence and say what kind of story this is. After students read the story, ask if they know a similar folk story from their own cultures.

Focus questions:

Why did the fisherman let the fish go? (Because it was really an enchanted prince. It wouldn't be good to eat.)

What is the wife's second wish? (to live in a big stone castle)

What is her last wish? (She wants to be like the Lord of the universe.)

Comprehension questions:

Main idea: *One moral of this story is:*

a. It is better to live in a pigsty than to be an emperor.

b. If you demand too much, you might lose everything.

c. You should always demand the best for yourself.

(Answer: b)

Details: *How does the sea change each time the fisherman's wife wants something?* (It becomes darker and more stormy.)

Why isn't the wife happy after she gets the little cottage? (It's too crowded.)

Why does she want to be King? (She wants to own all the land.)

Why does she want to be like the Lord of the universe? (So she can make the sun rise and set.)

What does the fish do after her last wish? (He takes everything away and gives them back the pigsty.)

Inference: *Why does the fish take everything away at the end?* (Possible answers: to punish the wife's greediness; because the wife wanted to be as powerful as a god)

Opinion: *Do you think the fisherman's wife should have asked for anything from the fish?*

Grammar in context: Explain that we use the simple past tense in conditional sentences to show that a condition is unlikely or impossible. Write an example of a true situation from the story, for example: *I'm not a regular fish—I'm an enchanted prince.*

The simple present tense is used here because the situation is true.

Write an example of an unreal condition: *If you <u>ate</u> me, I <u>wouldn't</u> even <u>taste</u> right.* The fish believes that it's unlikely that the fisherman will kill him and eat him.

The simple past tense *ate* in the *if* clause and *would* + base form of the verb in the result clause express this sense that the situation is unreal or unlikely.

For wishes, point out that the fisherman's wife uses the simple present tense to express their real situation: We *live* in a pigsty.

She uses the simple past tense to express the unreal situation that she wishes for: I wish we *lived* in a cottage.

Write more examples from the text on the chalkboard.

GRAMMAR CHARTS

Point out or elicit the rule and write the grammar labels above the sentences.

Ask students about unlikely or unreal conditions, for example:

What would you do if you won the lottery?

What would you do if you could fly?

How would you make friends if you didn't know anyone here?

Where would you live if you could live anywhere in the world?

How would you practice English if you didn't have time to come to class?

Write examples on the chalkboard as students produce them. Point out that in each clause, the situation is untrue at the moment, for example:

If I won the lottery, I'd buy a big house. (You are not a lottery winner. You aren't buying a big house.)

If I didn't have time to come to class, I wouldn't be able to practice English. (You do have time to come to class. You are able to practice English.)

The verb forms (simple past tense in the *if* clause, *would* + base form in the result clause) indicate that these situations are unreal or untrue. The simple past tense form does not refer to past time. Its use here is really subjunctive and refers to an unreal situation. The students' first languages may have a distinctive subjunctive verb form to express unreal situations, unlike English, which uses the simple past tense for this function.

Ask students what they would wish for if they each had three wishes. Write examples on the chalkboard.

GRAMMAR NOTES

1. Point out that you can use the modals *might* or *could* instead of *would* in the result clause. Give additional examples by transforming examples you have given with *would*, for example:

   If I won the lottery, I might not stay here.

   If I didn't have time to come to class, I could practice English by reading or watching television.

2. Read one or two situations from a newspaper advice column. Ask students to give the person some advice. *If I were you, I would apologize.* Note that *were* in this sentence is really a subjunctive form of *be*.

EXERCISES

Exercise 2, page 216. After students do the exercise, tell them to imagine that they are friends of Marta and that she is asking them for advice about her situation. Tell them to give advice using *If I were you . . .*

   If I were you, I'd rent a hall.

   If I were you, I'd invite all your relatives to a picnic when the weather gets warm.

Exercise 6, page 219. Tell students that Philip Wiley was an American writer who wrote very controversial books of social criticism.

Vocabulary (optional): Explain as necessary: *sexist* (describes the attitude that one gender is inferior).

Exercise 7, page 220. Ask students to look at the picture and read the list of eight statements. Ask them if they know a fairy tale about a princess and a frog. Elicit other traditional stories that students might know. After students listen to the story and do the exercise, ask them to compare this story with other traditional stories.

Exercise 9, page 221. Newspaper advice columns are good sources of problems that students will enjoy commenting on.

UNIT 18: Unreal Conditionals: Past

INTRODUCTION

CULTURE AND BACKGROUND NOTE: Watching *It's a Wonderful Life*, a movie directed by Frank Capra, has become a holiday tradition in the United States. There is a videotape available that includes an interview with Capra and a book with photographs from the movie. The story is especially appropriate for the holiday season since it confirms the value of the life of an ordinary man, George Bailey. Capra, who was born in Italy, emigrated with his family to the United States in 1906. Capra became a film director in 1921, and a number of his comedies won Academy Awards. He had a strong feeling for the lives of ordinary people during the difficult times of the Great Depression and World War II. His own immigrant background probably inspired his sympathetic portrayals in *It's a Wonderful Life* of immigrants who were struggling to build their own homes and escape the exploitation of the villain landlord, Mr. Potter.

If possible, rent or borrow from a library a copy of *It's a Wonderful Life*. Show it to the class after you have completed the unit, and then have a class discussion about the film.

Establish the context: This movie review gives four stars, the highest rating, to *It's a Wonderful Life* and recommends it for the holiday season. Ask the students to look at the picture and guess what is going on with the two characters. Ask them: *What has just happened? How does the seated character feel at this moment? Why is the other man dressed as he is?*

Focus questions:

What is George Bailey's problem at the beginning of the story? (He's in desperate trouble with his business.)

What does the audience see just before George jumps off the bridge? (a flashback of his life)

Who rescues him? (Clarence, a second-class angel)

Why did George stay in Bedford Falls? (Whenever he was ready to leave, somebody needed him.)

When he is rescued, does George believe that his life has value? (No, he doesn't.)

What kind of life did Mary have because of George? (She had a happy family life.)

Comprehension questions:

Main idea: *Is the following statement about George true or false?*

Before Clarence saved him, George had fulfilled his dreams by staying in Bedford Falls. (False)

Details: *What is George's job?* (He's the president of a building and loan association.)

How did George help his brother Harry? (He saved him from drowning as a child.)

Why does George want to commit suicide? (His business is in ruins, and he faces a possible jail sentence.)

When Clarence shows him life in Bedford Falls without George, what does George find at the site of his mother's home? (a depressing boardinghouse)

What is the last scene that Clarence shows George? (the graves of hundreds of soldiers who died because George's brother had not been there to save them)

Inference: *Why does George sound happy about going to jail?* (Possible answer: He's so happy to return to his own life, that he's willing to accept all of his problems.)

Opinion: *Was George's life more valuable as a small town building and loan officer than as a great architect and world traveler?*

Vocabulary (optional): Explain as necessary: *a building and loan association* (a company that lends individuals money for mortgages), *flashback* (in a movie or a book, a part of the story that goes back in time to show what happened earlier), *genial* (friendly and kind), *episodes* (events in a story), *boardinghouse* (a private home in which people can rent rooms), *vignette* (a picture of a typical scene).

Grammar in context: Remind students about the previous unit on present unreal conditionals. Elicit that the simple past tense in present unreal conditionals indicates that something in the present is unreal or untrue. In past unreal conditionals the past perfect indicates that something in the past is unreal or untrue. Discuss the premise of the film: When George wishes that he had not been born, Clarence shows him life in Bedford Falls as if he had never lived. These scenes show an unreal or untrue situation in the past. Give examples:

> *If George hadn't been there, his brother would have drowned.* (George was there. His brother didn't drown.)

> *If Harry had died, he wouldn't have saved hundreds of other lives.* (Harry didn't die. He saved hundreds of other lives.)

GRAMMAR CHARTS

After labeling example sentences, help the students produce more examples. Ask, for example, *What did you do last weekend?* Write answers on the board, for example: *I studied.   I worked.   I went to the beach with my family.*

Then ask, *What would you have done if you hadn't studied?* Write answers, using past unreal conditionals. *If I hadn't worked, I would have gone to the park.*

Help students ask and answer questions about these statements.

> *If you had gone to the park, would you have played softball?*

> *How long would you have stayed if you had gone to the beach?*

GRAMMAR NOTES

1. Point out that in past unreal conditional sentences, the past perfect and *would have* + past participle express that the situation is unreal or untrue.

2. Use some of the example sentences from Grammar in Context to practice with *might have* and *could have*: *If we hadn't worked all weekend, we could have gone to the beach.*

3. Ask students to think of things that they regret in the past and write sentences.

> *I didn't go to college when I was young.*

> *I never learned how to drive.*

> *I didn't participate in sports in high school.*

Ask them to exchange their sentences with a partner and write what their partner wishes were true:

> *Karina wishes she had gone to college when she was young.*

> *Theo wishes he had learned how to drive.*

EXERCISES

Exercise 4, page 227. After students finish the exercise, ask them what Lauren should have done. What would they have done if they had found the wallet?

Exercise 8, page 229. Before doing this exercise, you may want to show the film *It's a Wonderful Life* to your class. The pictures can then be used to stimulate a class discussion about the film.

Exercise 9, page 231. *Optional writing exercise.* After discussing their sentences with a partner, students can write a short, two- or three-paragraph essay about their lives. They should first write a summary about important events and achievements in their lives, and then speculate about what would have happened if they hadn't been born.

UNIT 19: Adjective Clauses with Subject Relative Pronouns

INTRODUCTION

CULTURE NOTE: The *Psychology Today* survey on friendship that is mentioned in the reading contradicts other studies that have found that Americans rarely form deep friendships in which the two friends become interdependent. One study finds that Americans form their friendships in shared activities, either work, childrearing, or sports, and usually keep the friends in each category separate. They tend to avoid becoming deeply involved with others, and prefer to get help from professionals such as lawyers or psychotherapists when they need help or support. While it is difficult to generalize across cultures, it can be said that friendship in other cultures may involve the whole person rather than just one category of activity. Friends may also accept obligations to each other and expect relationships of long duration, sometimes across several generations.

BACKGROUND NOTE: Margaret Mead (1901–1978) was an American anthropologist who wrote about the relationship between individual personality and culture. Her work took her to Samoa, the Admiralty Islands, New Guinea, and Bali, where she observed the cultures she wrote about. Mead, who believed that culture largely determines personality, also wrote about the "national character" of modern nations such as the Soviet Union. She expressed her views openly on many contemporary subjects.

Establish the context: The context is an article about definitions of friendship in different cultures. Have the students look at the picture and read the title. Ask them to think of a definition of a friend in a culture they are very familiar with. What do they expect of their friend? How often do they see each other? Can they maintain the friendship over a long period of time, or a long distance?

Focus questions:

Do all people from the same culture have the same definition of the word friend? (No, it varies within the culture.)

According to Margaret Mead, whom could you comfortably disagree with—a French friend or a German friend? (a French friend)

Among what nationality are friends like dancing partners? (among the British)

Comprehension questions:

Main idea: *According to Mead, which country's cultural pattern is represented by each statement?*

1. *She was my best friend in college, but we don't see each other anymore.* (United States)

2. *He's been like a second son to my parents.* (German)

3. *We love to argue about politics.* (French)

4. *When we saw each other after ten years, it was as though we had never been separated.* (British)

Details: *Do all friends share their deepest secrets?* (No. Ideas of friendship vary.)

Are there many studies of friendship in different cultures? (No, there aren't.)

Among the French, how does friendship affect one's best qualities? (It draws them out.)

When do Germans often make their important friendships? (when they are young)

Can Americans distinguish friends from acquaintances? (Yes, they can.)

Inference: *Why would someone from another culture be confused to hear an American say, "I just made a new friend yesterday."* (Possible answer: In many cultures, friendships take time to develop; people do not use the term to mean acquaintance.)

Opinion: *What is the most important quality in a friend?*

Vocabulary (optional): Explain as necessary: *assumes more depth* (becomes deeper, more thoughtful and philosophical), *vice versa* (the opposite. What A calls a friend, B calls an acquaintance, What A calls an acquaintance, B calls a friend.), *accentuated* (made sharper), *intensified* (made stronger), *incorporate* (to include, make a part of), *bonds* (connections), *congeniality* (natural agreement), *mutuality* (having in common, shared), *tentatively* (not definite or decided).

Grammar in context:

1. The article discusses the definition of *friend* in a number of cultures. Adjective clauses are often used to write definitions, for example:

    A friend is someone who plays cards with you every Friday night.

    A friend is someone who chooses and is chosen.

2. They are also used to identify which ones of a category are meant, for example:

    Americans <u>who answered the survey</u> find it easy to distinguish between close and casual friends. (The sentence applies only to some Americans. The clause identifies which Americans are meant.)

    Americans <u>who have made English friends</u> often comment . . . (Again, the sentence applies only to certain Americans. The clause identifies which ones are referred to.)

3. Adjective clauses may give more information about a noun that is already identified:

    Germans, <u>whose friendships are based on mutual feelings</u>, regard important disagreements as a tragedy. (The sentence refers to all Germans. The adjective clause gives more information about all Germans.)

GRAMMAR CHARTS

1. Explain that adjective clauses can describe any noun in the sentence. The first grammar chart shows adjective clauses that describe a noun in the predicate.
2. When the adjective clause describes the subject of the sentence (as in the second grammar chart), the clause comes between the subject and verb of the main clause.
3. When you use an adjective clause, you are embedding another sentence in the main sentence. The relative pronoun is the link that relates the embedded clause to the main clause. Show this graphically on the chalkboard:

    A friend knows you.

    A friend   can give you advice = A friend who knows you can give you advice.

    His sister writes books.

    My friend   lives in Boston = My friend whose sister writes books lives in Boston.

GRAMMAR NOTES

1. Practice combining sentences by playing a variant of "Button, Button, Who's Got the Button?" First, write at least one identifying sentence about each student, for example:

She speaks Persian.

His bag is on the floor.

He always sits in the front row.

Give a button (a coin or any other small object) to different students in the class, and have other students tell you who has it without mentioning the person's name.

The woman who speaks Persian has it.

The man whose bag is on the floor has it.

2. If your students know one another fairly well, have them write one sentence each about several classmates. Choose someone to be It. It gives a clue, for example:

I'm thinking of someone whose son is in the second grade.

I'm thinking of a man who works as a mechanic.

Students guess the identity. (*Source:* Celce-Murcia, Marianne, and Hilles, Sharon. *Techniques and Resources in Teaching Grammar.* N.Y.: Oxford University Press, 1988.)

3. Use some of the sentences from these games to illustrate the difference between identifying and nonidentifying adjective clauses.

Faiza, who speaks Persian, has the button. (We already know who Faiza is. The adjective clause gives additional information about her, but we don't need the information in order to identify her.)

The woman who speaks Persian has the button. (We can't identify the woman without the information in the adjective clause.)

Point out that proper nouns and nouns that have superlative adjectives usually have nonidentifying adjective clauses, for example:

Dominique, who is leaving in November, will take the final exam early.

The tallest student, who always sits in the back, needs a lot of leg room.

Have students practice the intonation patterns. Ask them to make up a sentence about a cousin, a sister, or a brother. Tell them to say the sentence with the correct intonation, pausing slightly before and after nonidentifying adjective clauses. Have the rest of the class guess whether the students have more than one of that relative.

My cousin, who lives in Caracas, is coming to visit us soon. (probably only one cousin)

My cousin who plays the piano keeps me awake at night with his practicing.
(more than one cousin)

EXERCISES

Exercise 1, page 244. Vocabulary (optional): Explain as necessary: *warts and all* (an idiom that means "even with all our faults"), *paths often cross ours* (we often meet at the same places [Point out the examples in the next sentence of the text]).

Go over the four comprehension questions carefully.

1. Because there are no commas around the adjective clause, the writer is using the clause to identify which of several colleagues is your acquaintance.

2. Because there are commas around the adjective clause, the speaker may have only one next-door neighbor. He or she therefore doesn't need to identify which one, and is only giving more information about the neighbor.

3. The phrase *My table tennis partner* identifies the person clearly. The adjective clause gives only more information about this person.

4. Since there are no commas around the adjective clause, it is an identifying adjective clause. There are several vice presidents and the clause identifies which one is meant.

Exercise 2, page 245.

1. If students are not sure of the meaning of some of the words, have them match the ones that they are sure of and then try to guess the meanings of the others. Explain that *alter ego* means "another I." Pronounce *confidant* /ˈkɑnfə.dænt/, and point out that it is different in meaning and pronunciation from confident. /ˈkɑnfədənt/

2. Remind students that identifying adjective clauses are often used to create definitions. This kind of definition refers first to the general category (a person . . .) and then, in the adjective clause, gives the identifying characteristic (who knows you but is not a close friend).

Exercise 3, page 246. If possible, bring in a copy of *Psychology Today* magazine to show students the kind of articles it contains.

When students have completed the exercise, have a class discussion about how they feel about these survey results. Are they true for them or other people whom they know?

Exercise 5, page 248. After students complete the exercise, ask them why the writer's friendship with Bob is unusual (Bob is older than the writer and as a teacher has a different status). Ask them whether they feel that this friendship is appropriate or possible.

Exercise 6, page 249. CULTURE NOTE: Remind students about the meaning of *reunion,* which they learned in exercise 2 ("a meeting after a long separation"). In the United States, people often have school reunions (high school and college) at ten-year intervals.

Ask students if they have ever been to a reunion. If so, what was it like? Had people changed a great deal? Were they able to recognize former classmates?

Exercise 10, page 252. *Optional writing activity.* Have students look again at exercise 2, and then write definitions of *friend, acquaintance, best friend, colleague,* and *buddy,* using adjective clauses.

UNIT 20: Adjective Clauses with Object Relative Pronouns, When, and Where

INTRODUCTION

CULTURE NOTE: Researchers have described four stages of the acculturation process that many people experience when they move to a new culture. In the first, or *honeymoon* stage, the person feels excitement about being in the new culture. In the second stage, he or she moves into *culture shock.* At this stage frustration and fear reach their highest points, especially among those who cannot return to their native lands. This stage has been referred to as *anomie.* In the third stage, the immigrant begins to cope with situations that had formerly seemed insoluble. At this stage, language students are very receptive to mastering the language. During the fourth stage, complete acculturation occurs. In the United States, this process happens most fully with young immigrants who attend schools and who look forward to taking their places in the mainstream culture. Acculturation happens less completely for older immigrants and for those whose stake in the new culture is not strong because of their plans to return to their homelands. (*Source:* Scarcella, Robin. *Teaching Language Minority Students in the Multicultural Classroom.* Englewood Cliffs, N.J.: Prentice Hall, 1990.)

Establish the context: The context is a book review of two autobiographical accounts of the experiences of immigrants in Canadian and U.S. cultures. One was a first-generation immigrant and one was a second-generation immigrant. Ask students to look at the pictures of Eva Hoffman and Ben Fong-Torres and speculate about the kinds of experiences they have had getting used to North American culture. Discuss culture shock with your students. Ask them if they have ever experienced culture shock themselves. If so, what aspects of the new culture were most different or most difficult to deal with?

Focus questions:

When did Hoffman move to Canada? (when she was thirteen)

Why does Eva feel no connection to English when she moves to Vancouver?
(All her memories and feelings are still in her first language, Polish.)

Where was Ben Fong-Torres born? (in the United States)

Why does Fong-Torres still have trouble communicating with his parents? (English is still a second language for them; he has never really learned Chinese.)

What is Fong-Torres's job? (He's a broadcaster and a journalist.)

Comprehension questions:

Main idea: *What was the central problem for both authors?*

a. their parents   b. language   (Answer: b)

Details: *In Cracow, how often did Eva see her friend Marek?* (almost daily)

What place in Cracow does Eva most regret leaving? (her music school)

Why does her teacher in Vancouver call her Eva instead of Ewa? (because Eva is easier for the teacher to pronounce)

Where were Fong-Torres's parents born? (in China)

Why does Fong-Torres speak baby talk when he speaks Chinese?
(He doesn't know enough words.)

Who does Fong-Torres most want to communicate with? (his parents)

Inference: *What did Eva Hoffman lose in translation?* (Possible answers: Her identity, her connection with Cracow, and her childhood)

Opinion: *Is it more difficult to be a first-generation or a second-generation immigrant?*

Vocabulary (optional): Explain as necessary: *escapades* (adventures), *Cracow* (a major city in Poland located on the Vistula River), *uproot* (to tear up a plant, roots and all; to move to a new place, leaving one's family and culture behind), *cramped* (small and crowded), *bear* (to tolerate), *come to terms with* (to accept), *reconcile* (to find agreement between two different things), *grapple with* (to struggle with), *laser* (a device that produces a very intense, narrow beam of light), *barrier* (something that blocks or limits: A language barrier limits communication), *Watergate* (an office building in Washington, D.C., where the Democratic National Committee had its offices. A scandal involving electronic eavesdropping by the Republicans led to investigations of the Nixon administration that eventually forced Nixon to resign), *annuity* (a sum of money paid to a person for a certain number of years or until death), *concoct* (to make something new by mixing or combining parts), *ironic* (a result opposite of what one would expect), *eloquently* (expressing ideas and opinions well), *bridge the gap* (to fill an empty space).

Grammar in context: The descriptions of people, places, and times in these two autobiographies include many examples of adjective clauses. Give examples from the reading in the Introduction of adjective clauses with object relative pronouns, and show how they are derived from two sentences.

She had visited cafes with <u>her father</u> + She watched <u>her father</u> in lively conversations with his friends.

= She had visited cafes with her father, who she watched in lively conversations with his friends.

Her friendship with <u>Marek</u> deepened. + She visited <u>Marek's apartment</u> almost daily.

= Her friendship with Marek, whose apartment she visited almost daily, deepened.

When and *where*, although technically not relative pronouns, function the same way. Give examples of adjective clauses with *when* and *where*:

The barrier had stood through countless moments. + We needed to talk with each other then.

= The barrier had stood through countless moments when we needed to talk to each other.

I'm filled with images of the sun-baked villages. + We had taken summer vacations there.

= I'm filled with images of the sun-baked villages where we had taken summer vacations.

GRAMMAR CHARTS

Point out how the arrows show that relative pronouns, *when,* and *where* describe nouns.

GRAMMAR NOTES

1. Remind students that adjective clauses can describe any noun in the sentence. The first grammar chart shows adjective clauses that describe a noun in the predicate.
2. When the adjective clause describes the subject of the sentence, the clause comes between the subject and verb of the main clause.
3. When you use an adjective clause, you are embedding another sentence in the main sentence. The relative pronoun is the link that relates the embedded clause to the main clause, and it comes at the beginning of the clause. Show this graphically on the chalkboard:

   Cindy is talking to the student.

   The student   comes from Vietnam. = The student Cindy is talking to comes from Vietnam.

   I borrowed his class notes.

   My friend   needs his notebook tonight. = My friend whose class notes I borrowed needs his notebook tonight.

4. To give students more practice, elicit statements from them about things they've done recently. On the chalkboard write statements that contain a direct object, for example:

   I went to the state fair.

   I studied for a math test.

   I baked a cake.

   We looked at a new apartment.

Have students make sentences in the following pattern, using all the variants.

   Let me tell you about the state fair that I went to last weekend.

   which I went to last weekend.

   I went to last weekend.

5. To practice all the object relative pronouns, *when* and *where*, give students statements and have them complete them with adjective clauses, for example:

> **A:** *You're reading a newspaper.*
>
> **B:** *Yes. The newspaper I'm reading is very interesting.*
>
> **A:** *You're going to the bank.*
>
> **B:** *Yes. The bank that I'm going to is nearby.*
>
> **A:** *You once had a wonderful vacation.*
>
> **B:** *I once had a wonderful vacation, when the weather was perfect for two weeks.*
>
> **A:** *You used to live in an old house.*
>
> **B:** *We used to live in an old house where the roof leaked whenever it rained.*

EXERCISES

Exercise 1, page 258. Vocabulary (optional): Explain as necessary: *anonymous* (without a name or individual identity), *oblique* (slanted; not perpendicular to the line), *eccentric characters* (odd or unusual people).

After students complete the second part of the exercise, ask them to supply relative pronouns for the adjective clauses that they've underlined.

> *overdress (that or which) we are required to wear*
>
> *eccentric characters (who or whom or that) I know*
>
> *the shapes (that or which) icicles make*
>
> *poems (that or which) we've memorized*

Have a brief discussion about the content of these two excerpts. Ask students to describe life in the Hoffmans' apartment building. Does it sound as if Hoffman was happy living there? Why did students in her school wear a school uniform? Have your students worn uniforms? How did they feel about them? Did the schoolwork that Hoffman remembered sound interesting and enjoyable?

Exercise 3, page 260. Vocabulary (optional): Explain as necessary: *siblings* (brothers and sisters), *reminisce* (to talk about the old days).

Exercise 5, page 262. Before students listen to the cassette, or hear a reading of the tapescript, have them look over the three pictures and discuss the differences that they see.

Exercise 6, page 263. (See page 4 of this Teacher's Manual for general procedures for information-gap exercises. Have students find a partner and decide who is A and who is B. Before they begin, have them read the information. You may want students to write their questions before they begin the information-gap activity. Circulate and help students with the reading and with writing their questions.

Vocabulary (optional): Explain as necessary: *Exclusion Act* (a law passed in 1882. It was passed because of the opposition in California during the 1860s and 1870s to immigration of Chinese workers), *Deems Taylor* (a U.S. composer and music critic who was well known from 1936 to 1943 as a radio commentator on the broadcasts of the New York Philharmonic Orchestra), *DJ* (disk jockey; the host of a show that plays recorded music).

Exercises 7 and 8, page 264. These activities can be combined, and students can use photographs that they have discussed to illustrate their essays about a childhood place.

You may also want to have students listen again to the woman's description of her childhood room in exercise 5.

UNIT 21: Direct and Indirect Speech

INTRODUCTION

CULTURE NOTE: Notions of honesty differ within a culture and across cultures. This topic lends itself well to cross-cultural comparisons.

Establish the context: Ask students to look at the picture and identify the machine that the man is hooked up to (a lie detector). Ask them to interpret what is happening. (The man is telling a *whopper*—a big lie.) Have a cross-cultural discussion about lying. When is it acceptable? When is it necessary? Give examples of situations, and ask students whether it is acceptable or necessary to lie under those circumstances, for example:

You are late for an appointment, but you don't have a good excuse.

You have a social engagement, but you're too tired to attend.

You don't like a gift that someone has given you.

Your friend just bought some new shoes, and you don't like them.

Your boss asks for your opinion about an important issue, and you know that his or her opinion is different from yours.

Focus questions:

How did Dick Spivak feel about his fiancée's new dress? (He hated it.)

What are white lies? (harmless untruths)

Do people get more or less honest as they get older? (more honest)

Is lying a new problem? (No, it's not.)

Comprehension questions:

Main idea: *Which of the following is <u>not</u> one of the most frequent reasons that people tell lies?*

a. to get something more quickly

b. to do someone harm

c. to appear more acceptable

d. to protect someone's feelings

    (Answer: b)

Details: *What did Dick say to his credit card company?* ("The check is in the mail.")
Is Dick an especially dishonest person? (No, he's not. He's ordinary.)

Who is more likely to tell a lie: Mary Lou, 68 years old, from Baton Rouge, Louisiana, who has a high school diploma, OR Tom, age 28, from Boston, Massachusetts, who has a master's degree? (Answer: Tom)

Do most people feel that we have high standards of honesty today? (No, they don't.)

Opinion: *Is it always wrong to lie?*

Vocabulary (optional): Explain as necessary: *whopper* (a big lie), *gender* (state of being masculine or feminine), *white lies* (harmless untruths. [Refer students to the definition in the text]).

Grammar in context: Tell students that there are two ways of showing what someone has said. Give examples from the text: *He said, "It looks great on you." He said that it looked great on her.*

Point out the differences between direct and indirect speech:

Direct Speech	Indirect Speech
quotation marks	*no quotation marks*
a comma between the direct speech and the reporting clause	*no comma*
The reported sentence in direct speech begins with a capital letter.	*The reported sentence in indirect speech does not begin with a capital letter.*
the pronoun <u>you</u> because that was the speaker's exact word	*the pronoun <u>her</u> to keep the original meaning*
simple present tense (<u>looks</u>)	*simple past tense (<u>looked</u>)*

Give other examples from the text.

GRAMMAR CHARTS

Point out that *that* is optional in indirect speech.

GRAMMAR NOTES

Write some short dialogues, or have students write them. Use only statements with verbs in the simple present or simple past tense, for example:

Lin: *We didn't receive your check last week.*

 Your payment is late.

Retha: *My check is in the mail. I mailed it yesterday.*

Distribute the dialogues to pairs of students. Have them enact them for the class and have other students report what was said, for example:

 Lin said that they hadn't received Retha's check.

 He said that her payment was late.

 Retha said that her check was in the mail. She said that she had mailed it yesterday.

EXERCISES

Exercise 1, page 272. Vocabulary (optional): Explain as necessary: *management consulting firm* (experts on management work for this type of firm, which is hired by other companies to evaluate management practices and to recommend improvements), *discrepancies* (differences, especially differences that suggest that something dishonest has occurred), *landed the new job* ([ask students to infer the meaning] to succeed in getting hired for the new job), *eventually* (after some time).

Exercise 3, page 273. Have students talk about the real situation as well as the lie, for example:

 She said that it looked great on her, but it really looked terrible.

 It was an ugly dress.

 She said it was her own recipe, but she had bought the cake.

Exercise 4, page 276. Tell students that they are reporting a conversation that took place very recently, and that Biodata hasn't hired anyone for the job yet. Answers will vary, since some of the indirect statements either can have tense changes or can remain in the present.

Remind or elicit from students why some sentences can be reported either way, for example:

> *Lisa said that they wanted someone with experience as a programmer.*
>
> *Lisa said that they want someone with experience as a programmer.* (They still want someone because they haven't hired anyone yet.)

Exercise 9, page 279. Optional writing exercise. Have students choose one quotation and write a paragraph about it. In the paragraph, students should explain the quotation, and then state whether they agree or disagree with this idea. To support their opinions, they can use examples from their own or others' experiences that they discussed in exercise 6.

UNIT 22: Indirect Speech: Tense Changes

INTRODUCTION

BACKGROUND NOTE: The largest and most dangerous storms on earth are hurricanes. In the United States, the hurricane season on the Atlantic and the Gulf coasts is from June to November, with peak occurrences in September. At the National Hurricane Center in Miami, Florida, meteorologists collect data using satellites, weather balloons, and reports from observers. They look for signs such as rain, strong winds, and spiral clouds. When they spot a hurricane, meteorologists sometimes fly into the hurricane to collect data.

A trailer is a vehicle that can be pulled by a car or a truck, and that is furnished for living. Some trailers, called mobile homes, are quite large and have bathrooms, kitchens, and bedrooms. Trailer parks rent space for mobile homes and provide hookups for water and cooking gas. Trailers are vulnerable to hurricanes and tornadoes.

Establish the context: Have students look at the picture and comment. Ask if anyone has ever experienced a hurricane or other extreme weather condition. Talk about the kinds of preparations people make for this kind of storm and how the reports of weather forecasters can help people get ready.

Focus questions:

> *Where did the storm start?* (off the coast of West Africa)
>
> *What problems did stores and gas stations have as people got ready for Hurricane Andrew?* (They couldn't keep up with the demand for gas, canned food, and bottled water.)
>
> *Who suffered the most?* (people in private homes and trailer parks)
>
> *Before the storm, did Jim Jenkins know what a force-five hurricane was like?* (No, he didn't. If he had known, he would have left.)

Comprehension questions:

Main idea:　　　*Put these events in the correct order.*

> _____ *The government provided emergency relief.* (5)
>
> _____ *Meteorologists named the storm Andrew.* (2)
>
> _____ *Weather advisories warned people to get ready for a force-four hurricane.* (4)
>
> _____ *The storm became a hurricane.* (3)
>
> _____ *Meteorologists spotted a small tropical storm.* (1)

Details:　　　*When did meteorologists name the tropical storm Andrew?* (when it grew stronger and moved west)

> *Why did Lixion Avila call his boss at 3:00 A.M.?* (because Andrew had turned into a hurricane)

What did people who lived near the coast have to do? (leave their homes)

What damage did Hurricane Andrew do to the National Hurricane Center?
(It tore the radar off the roof.)

What happened to the Jenkins's house? (A trailer blew through it.)

What was the predicted cost of rebuilding after Hurricane Andrew? ($20 billion)

Inference: *Is it possible to avoid damage when a hurricane like Andrew strikes?* (Possible answer: No, it isn't. Even though Floridians had received a lot of warning, Andrew still caused great damage.)

Opinion: *What should the government do to help people before and after a disaster like Hurricane Andrew?*

Vocabulary (optional): Explain as necessary: *tropical* (related to the tropics, the hot area of the earth between $23\frac{1}{2}$ north latitude and $23\frac{1}{2}$ south latitude), *track* (to follow closely), *go on the air* (to announce on radio and television), *dazed* (confused after an accident or a blow).

Grammar in context: This news article reports what people said before and after Hurricane Andrew. Give some examples of indirect speech and show or elicit the direct speech, for example:

Avila told his boss that they had a hurricane. "We have a hurricane."

Gas stations reported that they could not keep up with demands for gas. "We can't keep up with demands for gas."

The Center reported that the electricity had gone out during the storm. "The electricity went out during the storm."

GRAMMAR NOTES

1. Remind students of the tense changes that they learned about in Unit 21: In indirect speech, present tense often changes to past tense, and past tense often changes to past perfect.

2. To give additional practice in changing present progressive and present perfect to past progressive and past perfect, tell students to work in pairs and do the following role-play:

Imagine that you are talking on the telephone to a relative who lives in another town. You haven't seen this relative for a while. Tell him or her what you are doing at this moment and this semester. Then tell what you have accomplished since you've last seen him or her.

A: *Hi. This is Aunt Agatha. Are you busy?*

B: *Oh, no. I'm just watching television.*

A: *So, how's your semester going?*

B: *Great. I'm taking a computer course.*

A: *Really? What have you learned so far?*

B: *I've already learned how to use a spreadsheet.*

After they practice, they should perform the role-play for the class. Students can report what B said:

She said she was watching television.

She told her aunt that she was taking a computer course this semester.

She said she'd already learned how to use a spreadsheet.

3. To practice modals, list the modals on the chalkboard, and ask students to think of what they would say to someone who was going to study abroad. Write sentences on the chalkboard as students dictate them, for example:

You'll learn English very quickly.

We can write to each other every week.

You may get homesick at first.

You must get a lot of rest.

Then ask the class to imagine that someone had given them that advice. Report what was said to them. Write the indirect speech on the chalkboard next to the direct speech, for example:

She said I'd learn English very quickly.

EXERCISES

Exercise 2, page 285. Point out or elicit that rumors, or unofficial reports, are very common when there's an emergency and people want information.

Exercise 3, page 286. Vocabulary (optional): Explain as necessary: *upside* (the good points), *weather satellite* (a satellite that orbits the earth and sends back information about weather conditions).

Exercise 4, page 287. Vocabulary (optional): Explain as necessary: *eye of the hurricane* (the center of the hurricane, where winds are usually quiet. When the eye passes over, it may seem for a while that the storm is over).

Optional exercise. For additional practice, bring in some cartoons from the newspaper. Have students work in pairs or in groups to write indirect speech from the direct speech. You can also white out the direct speech in the speech bubbles and give the students the indirect speech. Have them write the direct speech in the speech bubbles.

Exercise 5, page 289. Emphasize to students that they will be listening to a great deal of information, and that they do not have to catch everything. They will have a chance to get together with other students and compare information in order to fill in what they missed.

UNIT 23: Indirect Instructions, Commands, Requests, and Invitations

INTRODUCTION

CULTURE NOTE: Some experts attribute a rise in sleep disorders to U.S. lifestyles. They point to the existence of night shifts for workers, all-night television, and twenty-four-hour shopping at supermarkets and drugstores, all of which support irregular sleep habits. People who suffer from insomnia can be diagnosed at a sleep center. Sleep centers in the United States are accredited by the American Sleep Disorders Association, which keeps a list of accredited centers around the country. At a sleep center, sophisticated equipment is used to find the exact source of a sleep disorder.

Establish the context: Have the students look at the picture and instruction line and guess where the sleeping man is, and what the equipment and wires are for. Discuss students' knowledge of sleep disorders. What remedies do they know about or use for insomnia? Is it a serious problem?

Focus questions:

Who is Connie Sung? (the host of "Here's to Your Health!")

Who is Dr. Ray Thorpe? (her guest; the director of the U.S. Sleep Disorders Clinic)

When patients have a problem with sleep cycles, what does Dr. Thorpe often ask them to do? (spend a night at his sleep clinic)

Comprehension questions:

Main idea: *Which of these should you <u>not</u> do right before going to sleep?*

         a. eat a high carbohydrate snack

         b. exercise vigorously

         (Answer: b)

Details: *In his book, what does Dr. Thorpe advise people to do?* (pay more attention to sleep disorders)

         How many car accidents are caused by drowsy drivers every year? (up to 200,000)

         Why should people with insomnia stop smoking and drinking? (They are bad for general health and they interfere with sleep.)

         Is it a good idea to eat a heavy meal before bedtime? (No, it's not.)

Inference :   *Why does fatigue cost U.S. businesses about $70 billion a year?* (Possible answer: When people are tired, they make mistakes and they don't produce as much.)

         Why should people do unpleasant tasks when they can't sleep? (They might go to sleep just to avoid the task.)

Opinion: *Is lack of sleep really a big problem?*

         What's the best way to get a good night's sleep?

Vocabulary (optional): Explain as necessary: *insomnia* (inability to sleep), *night shift* (a shift is a scheduled time to work. The night shift is the 4:00 P.M. to midnight schedule), *deprivation* (condition of not having something), *drowsy* (sleepy), *fatigue* (extreme tiredness), *remedy* (something that cures a disease or relieves its symptoms, for example, a cold remedy), *cycle* (a series of events that repeats itself), *slumber* (peaceful sleep), *monitor* (to watch carefully).

GRAMMAR CHARTS

The first two sentences in the charts illustrate instructions or commands (depending on how they are said). The third sentence is a request, and the last sentence is an invitation. Point this out or elicit the information from students.

GRAMMAR NOTES

For additional practice, have students work in groups. Give each group a situation and have them write dialogues with invitations, commands, requests, and instructions. Have students role-play the situation, and then ask the class to report what was said.

Invite someone to a party. Tell the guest what time to come. Give instructions on how to get to the party. Ask the person to bring some food.

Lisa: *I'm having a party on Saturday night. Can you come?*

Jerry: *I'd love to. Thanks.*

Lisa: *Please come around 8:00. Take the Number 6 bus to Forest Hill Avenue. Don't take the express bus. My house is near the corner of Forest Hill and Lake.*

Jerry: *That sounds easy.*

Lisa: *Oh, and I'm asking everyone to bring something. Could you bring some potato chips?*

Jerry: *Sure.*

Possible report:	*Lisa asked Jerry to come to her party. She told him to come around 8:00. She said to take the Number 6 bus. She told him not to take the express bus. She asked him to bring some potato chips.*

EXERCISES

Exercise 1, page 294. After students have done the exercise, have them change the indirect speech to direct speech, for example: *Please arrive at 8:30. Bring your nightshirt and toothbrush.*

Exercise 2, page 295. Ask students if they know of any other remedies for the ailments mentioned.

Exercise 5, page 298. Have students review exercise 2 on page 295 for ideas. Ask them whether they use similar remedies for these ailments.

UNIT 24: Indirect Questions

INTRODUCTION

CULTURE NOTE: Equal employment opportunity laws in the United States forbid employers from discriminating on the basis of age, sex, race, religion, and national origin. For this reason, they are not permitted to ask questions about these things during an interview. In exercise 5 on page 309, there is a list of illegal questions.

Establish the context: Ask students about their own experiences at job interviews. What kinds of questions have they been asked? Do they find interviews stressful? If so, how do they deal with the stress? Tell students the information in the Culture Note. Then ask them to look at the picture and say which questions are OK to ask and which are not.

Focus questions:

What kind of interview had Melissa Morrow had? (a stress interview)

During a stress interview, what can the interviewer observe? (how the candidate reacts to pressure)

Do you have to answer improper questions? (No, you don't.)

Comprehension questions:

Main idea: *For which job is a stress interview appropriate?*

a. public relations officer for a nuclear power plant

b. accountant

(Answer: a)

Details: *Who ended Melissa's interview?* (She did.)

What are three features of a stress interview? (tough, tricky questions, long silences, negative evaluations of the candidate)

Choose which question is <u>not</u> OK for an employer to ask a job candidate.

a. How fast can you type?

b. How much money do you owe?

(Answer: b)

Inference: *In Melissa's case, did the company benefit by conducting a stress interview?* (Possible answer: No. She was successful at the interview, but she decided, because of the interview, that she didn't want to work for that company.)

Opinion: *Are stress interviews really useful?*

Vocabulary (optional): Explain as necessary: *tricky questions* (refer students to examples of tricky questions in Melissa's interview. These are questions that may trap the candidate into revealing negative things about himself or herself.), *poised* (having a calm and self-confident manner), *hostile* (unfriendly), *news anchor* (a newscaster who coordinates a news program that is being broadcast from several places), *merit* (to be worth), *warrant* (to justify something, to make it necessary), *backfire* (to have an effect that is opposite the desired one), *alienate* (to make unfriendly or hostile), *come through with flying colors* (to succeed particularly well), *legitimate* (meeting established standards), *composure* (poise).

Grammar in context: The article reports types of questions that are asked in job interviews. Give some examples of indirect questions from the text and elicit the direct questions:

> *He asked if she had cleaned out her car recently. "Have you cleaned out your car recently?"*
>
> *An interviewer should not ask how old you are. "How old are you?"*

Point out that statement word order, not question word order, is used in indirect questions. Also note that the tenses change in indirect questions just as they do in other indirect speech.

GRAMMAR NOTES

For additional practice, have students work in groups to write questions that could be asked at a job interview, both by the interviewer and by the candidate. Have students role-play job interviews and then ask the class to report what was said.

> **A:** *She asked him if he had studied computer programming.*
>
> **B:** *He asked her if the company had health insurance benefits.*

EXERCISES

Exercise 1, page 305. After students complete the exercise, have them produce direct questions.

Exercise 3, page 307. Point out that it's appropriate for the job candidate to ask questions about the position and about the company.

Vocabulary (optional): Explain as necessary: *major layoffs* (a period in which a large number of people lose their jobs because business has been poor).

Exercise 6, page 310. Have students review the questions in exercise 3 for ideas. Point out that most résumés list experience in chronological order, beginning with the most recent job.

UNIT 25: Embedded Questions

INTRODUCTION

CULTURE NOTE: Tipping is customary in the United States and Canada. However, as the interview points out, even natives of these countries need information about whom and how much to tip. It's important to realize that cab drivers, restaurant servers, people who make deliveries, and others do not receive the normal minimum wage. Their salaries are lower because the tips they receive are considered part of their wages.

Establish the context: Have a cross-cultural discussion about tipping in different countries. Is tipping customary in countries your students know about? Are people within a country very familiar with tipping practices? Do the people who receive tips depend on their tips or are their salaries sufficient?

Focus questions:

Are Americans sure about tipping practices in their own country? (Many are not sure.)

What did TIP stand for in the seventeenth century? (To Insure Promptness)

Should you leave pennies for a restaurant server as part of your tip? (Yes, if they are part of the change you received when you paid your bill.)

Comprehension questions:

Main idea: *Is tipping international?* (No, it isn't.)

Does Frankel's book discuss tipping internationally? (No, it gives information on tipping in the United States.)

How can one get information on tipping in other countries? (from books, travel agents, and consulates)

Details: *Who was Frankel working with when she decided to write her book on tipping?* (people living in the United States from abroad)

Do people in the United States tip everyone who serves a meal? (No. They don't tip flight attendants.)

In the seventeenth century, when did people tip? (before a meal, to insure prompt service)

According to Frankel, should you tip when someone has given you bad service? (Yes, but you should not tip the ordinary amount.)

True or False: The rules for tipping are very logical. (false)

Inference: *Why do Americans have questions about U.S. tipping customs?* (Possible answer: Tipping is customary for many different services and the rules are not logical.)

Opinion: *Is tipping a good custom, or should service people simply be paid a wage for their work?*

Vocabulary (optional): Explain as necessary: *insure* (to guarantee), *promptness* (the quality of doing something without delay), *inequities* (situations that are unfair [Refer students to Fuchs's example in the previous question: tips are tied to the amount of the bill, rather than the amount of labor involved]).

GRAMMAR CHARTS

Point out the different end punctuation.

GRAMMAR NOTES

Write the beginnings of polite embedded questions on the chalkboard. Give situations for role-plays, and have students practice asking one another polite questions, such as:

You're on the bus. Your watch has stopped. What time is it?

You're at a movie theater, and you think you're late. Has the movie started?

You're lost. Where is Boulevard Street?

A: *Do you know what time it is?*

B: *Yes. It's ten after eight.*

A: *Can you tell me if the movie has started yet?*

B: *No, it hasn't. It starts in ten minutes.*

A: *Pardon me. Could you tell me where Boulevard Street is?*

B: *Sure. It's two blocks in that direction.*

EXERCISES

Exercise 1, page 316. Point out that the ad includes a coupon that readers can use to order the book. When sending away for products, residents of certain states have to include the sales tax in the price.

Exercise 2, page 317. Explain that Down Under is a slang term for Australia. It refers to the fact that the whole continent is in the Southern Hemisphere.

Exercise 3, page 318. Students may have to be reminded that the end punctuation depends on whether the main clause is a statement or a question. Refer them to Grammar Note 5 if necessary.

CULTURE NOTE: The Smithsonian is a scientific and cultural institution located in Washington, D.C. It is sponsored by the U.S. government and includes fourteen museums and a zoo. It conducts numerous public service programs. Many of the museums are located on the Mall in Washington, and this is where the two tourists are going when they ask where the Smithsonian is.

Williamsburg, Virginia, used to be the capital of the Virginia colony. The town, with its seventeenth- and eighteenth-century buildings, has been restored to its original condition. Shopkeepers wear colonial dress and sell goods typical of the period.

Exercise 5, page 321. Before they listen, have students read the answers and predict the questions.

Exercise 8, page 323. Optional writing exercise. Ask students to write a paragraph explaining their opinions about one of the questions that they discussed. Tell them to use information from their discussion to support and illustrate their opinions.

Optional activity. Call on student volunteers to act as "experts" on any topic they choose (e.g., their jobs, countries, cooking, raising children). The rest of the class can ask them for information, using embedded questions.

UNIT 26: Reflexive and Reciprocal Pronouns

INTRODUCTION

BACKGROUND NOTE: Recently, psychologists have been studying the effects of hope and optimism in people's lives. Studies indicate that positive attitudes have pervasive effects on many aspects of life, including physical and emotional health and success on the job. One study indicates that when college freshmen show a high degree of hopefulness, their grades are better than the grades of students who have similar ability but a more pessimistic outlook. Self-talk, one's dialogue with oneself, is an indicator of whether a person is optimistic or pessimistic. Optimists do not blame themselves, and they tell themselves that bad situations are temporary and limited. Pessimists, on the other hand, take the blame for bad outcomes and see them as permanent and pervasive. (*Source:* Goleman, Daniel, Ph.D. "What hope can do for you." *Self,* June 1992, p. 112.)

Establish the context: After students listen to the cassette or hear the tapescript, have them look at the thought bubbles and say which ones Sara might be thinking and which ones Tom might be thinking. Discuss whether or not thoughts like these have any effect on how people act or what happens to them.

Focus questions:

What happened to both Sara and Tom last fall? (They both lost their jobs.)

According to Sara, why did she get her job back? (Her employers finally realized that they needed her.)

Comprehension questions:

Main idea: *Why is self-talk important?* (It can affect our performance and even our health.)

Details: *Who continued leisure time activities during the winter?* (Sara did.)

Who got sick? (Tom did.)

Can the job loss be blamed for Tom's problems? (No, because Sara got laid off too, and she acted quite differently.)

How did Tom view his own situation? (He was helpless and permanently unemployed.)

Inference: *If they hadn't gotten their jobs back, who would have found a new job sooner?* (Possible answer: Sara might have, since she didn't feel helpless or see her situation as permanent.)

Opinion: *Does self-talk really influence how people act and feel?*

Is self-talk useful when you're learning a new language?

Vocabulary (optional): Explain as necessary: *deprived* (prevented from doing), *optimist* (someone who believes that things will turn out fine).

Grammar in context: The article is about the way people explain problems to themselves. Write examples on the chalkboard and explain them.

They explained the problem to themselves. (Tom explained it to Tom; Sara explained it to Sara.)

Tom isolated himself. (Tom kept Tom away from other people.)

Sara told herself that her problem was temporary. (Sara explained this to Sara.)

They took each other's telephone numbers. (Tom took Sara's number and Sara took Tom's number.)

GRAMMAR CHARTS

Point out that reflexive and reciprocal pronouns often refer back to the subject of the sentence.

GRAMMAR NOTES

1. For additional practice, give students slips of paper with instructions, for example:

Read to yourself out loud.   *Talk to a classmate about the lesson.*

Read to a classmate out loud.   *Pat yourself on the back.*

Talk to yourself about the lesson.   *Pat a classmate on the back.*

Act out one instruction yourself, and ask questions.

Teacher: *I'm reading to myself. Anna, what am I doing?*

Anna: *You're reading to yourself.*

Teacher: *Van, ask Lee what I'm doing.*

Van: *What's the teacher doing, Lee?*

Lee: *She's reading to herself.*

Have students come to the front and act out the instructions. Ask questions to elicit the different reflexive pronouns.

A: *What are you and Sabrina doing?*

B: *We're talking to each other about the lesson.*

A: *What are Chong and Sabrina doing?*

B: *They're talking to each other about the lesson.*

A: *What are you doing, Rigoberta?*

B: *I'm reading to myself.*

A: *What's Rigoberta doing, Stefan?*

B: *She's reading to herself.*

2. Call students' attention to Grammar Note 3 on page 331. Have students reread the Introduction to find the example of a reflexive pronoun used to emphasize a noun. *The job itself can't explain Tom's problem.*

EXERCISES

Exercise 1, page 332. Have students come up with possible examples of athletes' self-talk. *"Come on. You can do it. You can win this race."* Have other students report back. *She told herself that she could win the race.*

Exercise 5, page 335. Point out that both pronouns are possible in each context, and that students must listen carefully to distinguish the correct pronoun.

After doing and checking the exercise, ask students to interpret the two choices for each question.

Optional writing exercise. Have students work with a partner or in a small group and brainstorm ways to use positive self-talk for language learning. Have individuals or groups write a how-to paper based on their discussion. It should give instructions and examples.

Examples:

Encourage yourself often. Stefan reminds himself that he couldn't speak English at all last year.

Reward yourself for your achievements. Marissa sometimes buys herself a little gift when she has done well on a test.

Find a pen pal. Sal has been writing to his pen pal for more than a year.

They write to each other at least once a month.

UNIT 27: Phrasal Verbs

INTRODUCTION

Establish the context: Tell students that they are going to read and listen to an article about invention. Ask them to look at the pictures and identify each invention if they can. Ask them how they think each one was invented. Find out if anyone in the class has invented a new way to do something or a new device or tool. If so, how did it happen?

Focus questions:

Where are new things usually invented, and by whom? (everywhere, and by all kinds of people)

What happened to de Mestrel's dog? (Burrs got stuck in his coat during his walks in the mountains.)

What does imagination help inventors do? (put things together in a new way)

Did Chester Greenwood's friends keep making fun of him? (No. They soon wanted earmuffs too.)

Why did Borden's invention probably save lives? (At that time there was no way to refrigerate milk.)

Comprehension questions:

Main idea: *Which quality is <u>not</u> part of inventiveness?*

curiosity	*imagination*	*pessimism*
problem solving	*tenacity*	*self-confidence*

(Answer: pessimism)

Details: *Why did de Mestrel examine the burrs under a microscope?* (He wondered why they were so hard to remove.)

What is Velcro® used for today? (everything from sneakers to space suits)

How did Walter Morrison think of the idea for the Frisbee®? (He saw two truck drivers playing with a pie pan.)

What problem did Greenwood's earmuffs solve? (frostbitten ears)

Did Eastman develop his camera and film quickly? (No, he spent years researching chemicals and photography.)

Inference: *Why do inventors sometimes seem strange to others?* (Possible answer: They often try out new ideas.)

Opinion: *Which quality of an inventor is most important? Why?*

Vocabulary (optional): Explain as necessary: *creativity* (the ability to produce new ideas and things), *universal* (for all people; very widespread), *potential* (having the possibility for developing something), *burrs* (the seed bearing parts of certain plants; burrs cling to animal fur or clothing, which allows the plant to be spread to new territory), *solar-powered* (having the sun as a source of energy), *frostbitten* (an injury to the skin caused by great cold; frostbitten parts of the body become swollen and discolored), *earmuffs* (coverings for the ears that keep them warm [See the picture on page 338]), *patented* (A patent is a document from a government patent office. It gives the holder the exclusive right to make and sell an invention, an invention that is protected by a patent is patented), *tenacity* (persistence; the ability not to quit), *condensing* (a process for removing water from milk).

Grammar in context: Tell students that phrasal verbs are extremely common in English. They consist of a verb plus a particle. The particle is usually a word such as *up, down, on,* or *over* that is used as a preposition in other contexts. However, when it is combined with a verb to make a phrasal verb, the combination often has a meaning quite different from the separate meanings of the verb and of the particle. Put examples on the chalkboard from the first paragraph and ask students to reread the paragraph and guess the meanings of the phrasal verbs from the context.

dream up	*imagine*
put together	*assemble*
drop out	*quit*

GRAMMAR CHARTS

Point out that two of the three verbs have direct objects. However, with *turn on,* the direct object (if it's a noun) may come between the verb and the particle.

GRAMMAR NOTES

1. Point out that phrasal verbs are much more commonly used in spoken English than one-word verbs with similar meanings, for example: *Here's the bus. Let's get on* is much more natural than *Let's board.* In order to understand spoken English, students must understand phrasal verbs. They must also use them if they wish to sound idiomatic.

   Because they are so common, and because there is no way to tell whether a phrasal verb is separable or inseparable, it's a good idea for students to keep a list of phrasal verbs and to learn their meaning and whether they are separable or inseparable. Refer students to Appendices 15 and 16 in the Student's Book.

2. To give more practice with pronouns as the objects of phrasal verbs, write two lists on the chalkboard, one for separable and one for inseparable phrasal verbs, for example:

inseparable	separable
take after	*take off*
call on	*call back*
drop out of	*figure out*
get over	*hand out*
look out for	*look up*

   Begin a sentence with each verb, and have students complete the sentence using a pronoun. For example:

   Sara and her sister are just like their father in many ways. They really take _____.

   It's too hot for that coat. Why don't you take _____.

   My math teacher told me to figure out the problem, so I'm trying to figure _____.

EXERCISES

Exercise 1, page 342. Before students read the article, elicit their own knowledge about the invention of the personal computer. If they do know about it, ask them what qualities they think the two inventors had.

Vocabulary (optional): Explain as necessary: *prototype* (the first one; the one from which all later models are developed).

Exercise 3, page 344. Vocabulary (optional): Explain as necessary: *Bunsen burner* (a small gas burner used in a laboratory), *goggles* (protective glasses worn over the eyes).

Exercise 5, page 346. BACKGROUND NOTE: Inventors often keep notebooks to keep track of the development of their ideas. Witnesses sign and date the notebook at different stages of the invention's development. The notebook provides a record that can be used in case there is a dispute over a patent.

Exercise 6, page 347. Before starting the exercise, elicit from students what they know about the structure of a camera and how it works.

Exercise 7, page 349. BACKGROUND NOTE: Rube Goldberg was born on July 4, 1883 in San Francisco. Although he is best known for his *Crazy Inventions* cartoons, he drew political and editorial cartoons as well, and spent the last years of his life as a sculptor. His awards include a 1948 Pulitzer Prize for political cartoons, and the Reuben, an award of the National Cartoonists Society, in 1968.

If possible, bring in a book of Rube Goldberg cartoons to show your class. Let students look through examples before they design their own "Rube Goldberg."

Tapescript

UNIT 1 Section One

Introduction (Student's Book, page 2). *Read and listen to this book review.*

What's in a Baby Name?

So, you're expecting a baby, and you're still putting off choosing a name. Perhaps you've read some of those studies that claim that teachers give better grades to David and Karen than to Elmer and Gertrude. Or that people find a Bertha less pretty than a Lisa—even when both women are equally attractive.

You're right—it is a big decision, and you don't want to make a mistake. Now there's help and solace for the anxious parent-to-be, in the form of Sue Browder's *The New Age Baby Name Book* (New York: Warner Books, 1987). Browder explores the psychological effects of names and assures us that those studies about teachers are probably flawed. On the other hand, she believes a distinctive name helps a child develop self-esteem. (Distinctive, not weird—a name like Ima Pigg doesn't do much for anyone's self-confidence.)

What are some of today's naming trends? Most Americans still choose names that already exist, but many are taking them from different sources. People are using yesterday's nicknames as today's formal given names. For example, Carrie is becoming more popular than Caroline. The distinction between male and female names is blurring somewhat, too. More and more people are selecting unisex names such as Dana, Leslie, or Marty. And many parents are turning to their roots and choosing names that reflect their ethnic background. Names like Kachina (Native American: "sacred dancer"), Lateef (North African: "gentle"), and Jonina (Hebrew: "dove") are becoming more and more common.

Whether you are considering traditional names like Mary and John, or you prefer more contemporary ones like Megan and Jared, this book has them all along with their place of origin, meaning, and—where necessary—pronunciation. The *New Age Baby Name Book* presents a wealth of information and makes fascinating reading—even if you aren't becoming a parent.

Exercise 3 (Student's Book, page 6). *Listen to two classmates discuss these pictures. Then listen again and label each picture with the correct name from the box.*

A: Hi, Janine. What are you doing?

B: Looking at photos. Wanna see?

A: Sure. I love photos. Oh, who's that?

B: My nephew, Michael. But everyone calls him Bozo.

A: Bozo? As in Bozo the clown? Gee, that's kind of insulting, isn't it? I bet he hates it.

B: Not really. He knows we mean it affectionately. Anyhow, he just makes a joke out of it—like with everything else.

A: Oh. Does he always act like this?

B: Yep. He's always fooling around. Just like in this picture.

A: Who's that?

B: That's my niece, Alex. Isn't she cute?

A: Alex! Isn't that a boy's name?

B: Not anymore. Well, maybe some people still consider it a boy's name, but more and more parents are giving girls names like Alex, too.

A: Now, <u>he's</u> really cute.

B: Uh-huh. That's my friend Mehmet.

A: Mehmet? What kind of name is that?

B: Well, he comes from Turkey, so I guess it's Turkish. I don't know what it means, though.

A: What's he doing <u>here</u>?

B: He's studying photography. [laughs] Can't you tell?

A: Does he <u>always</u> walk around with all that equipment?

B: Actually he usually has even more. In fact, he gave me one of his cameras to take this picture with.

A: And who's that?

B: That's my cousin. We call her "Sunshine."

A: Sunshine? How come?

B: Because she smiles so much.

A: But she's <u>not</u> smiling in the <u>picture</u>! In fact, she looks pretty serious.

B: You're right. She doesn't look happy at all.

A: Well, so much for nicknames!

A: That guy looks familiar. Who is he?

B: Oh, you know who that is! That's my brother, Karl.

A: Karl! I didn't recognize him. Doesn't he wear glasses?

B: Yeah. Usually. But he doesn't like how he looks in them, so he's wearing contact lenses for the picture.

B: Guess which one is Bertha.

A: Bertha? That's easy. Bertha's the woman who's looking directly at the camera.

B: Wrong! That's my Aunt Vicki.

A: You're kidding! She looks more like a Bertha to me!

B: Why?

A: I don't know. The name Vicki sounds like it belongs to someone young and sexy—like the other woman.

B: Nope. Bertha's her daughter!

A: Strange.

Section Two

Introduction (Student's Book, page 8). *Read and listen to this excerpt from a journal article about naming systems.*

Louisa Horvath was following tradition when she named her daughter Doris. "We were going to name her Amanda, but my great Aunt Dorothy died just before she was born, so we decided to name the baby after her." Many cultures honor older family members by naming children after them. The Horvaths were adhering to an old Jewish custom which forbids naming a child after a living relative. However, in other western cultures, parents frequently name children after living relatives, especially parents and grandparents. "Before my son was born, the oldest boy was always named Walter," recalls one man. "As a boy, I knew I was going to break this tradition. I was just too uncomfortable with my father's name."

The practice of naming children after another person, living or deceased, has been frowned upon by different groups of people at different times. Believing that everyone should have a unique name, many Native American cultures even kept registers of available names and appointed officials who gave or withheld permission to use a name. As a result, Native Americans never adopted relatives' names. Instead, they often used names that referred to an event in someone's life. Sometimes they chose a name that recalled what was happening at the beginning of the mother's labor. A Miwok woman, for example, was gathering seeds for jewelry when her labor began. She named her child "Howotmila." (Howotu means "beads," and Howotmila means "running hand down the branch of a bush to find seeds for beads.")

Incident naming, as this practice is called, is still used in many places, including modern Africa. "The sun was shining brightly when I came into the world," explains Ayadele. "In Swahili, my name means 'sunshine in the house.'"

The practice of incident naming may at first glance seem strange to Westerners. However, it is not unlike the derivation of some nicknames. One woman recalls: "In fourth grade, one of the boys sneaked a baby turtle into my lunchbox. It crawled out while I was eating lunch, and I screamed and cried. After that, everyone called me 'Turtle.'"

Incident naming and naming children after relatives are only two of many naming systems. Throughout history hopeful parents have also named children for some quality which they want their child to embody. This practice abounds all over the world. One East African man recalls: "My parents named me Jahi, which is a Swahili name meaning 'dignity.' They wanted me to get more education. Whenever I was going to give up, my name always reminded me of their hopes."

Exercise 7 (Student's Book, page 14). *Listen to a woman explain how she got her nickname. Then listen again and circle the letter of the series of pictures that illustrate her story.*

Interviewer: So, how did you get your nickname?

Woman: Well, actually it's a pretty romantic story. John and I were both working for a newspaper. We didn't know each other well at the time, but one day we got an assignment together. (I was a photographer, and he was a writer.) Well, we were doing this story outside when it started to storm. I mean, it was *really* coming down hard. When it started lightning and thundering too, we ran into the nearest coffee shop we could find. As soon as we sat down, lightning struck nearby and the place lost its electricity. When the lights went out, the coffee-shop owner brought out candles.

Interviewer: Oh. So while it was thundering and lightning outside, the two of you were sitting there and talking by candlelight. How long did the storm last?

Woman: Oh, I guess about an hour.

Interviewer: So you both got to know each other pretty well.

Woman: Yes. You know at work there was never enough time to talk—we were always working against some deadline. So, anyway, John was just beginning to tell me a little about his childhood when the lights went back on. We were going to leave and get back to work, but then we just sat there another two hours talking. When we finally left, the sky was clear and the sun was shining. It all seemed so symbolic. A month later we were married.

Interviewer: So the storm brought the two of you together.

Woman: Uh-huh. And that's how I got my nickname "Thunder."

Interviewer: Is John's nickname "Lightning," by any chance?"

Woman: [laughing] How'd you guess?

Interviewer: It just struck me.

Section Three

Introduction (Student's Book, page 16). *Read and listen to the newspaper advice column.*

Times Have Changed

Dear John:

My son and his girlfriend have been making wedding plans. At first I was delighted, but last week I heard something that changed my feelings. It seems that our future daughter-in-law has decided to keep using her maiden name after the wedding. Her reasons: She doesn't want to "lose her identity." Her parents named her 21 years ago, and she's been Donna So-and-so (I won't use her real name) since then. She sees no reason to change now. Secondly, she's been performing with the Rockland Symphony Orchestra for eight years, and she's already become known professionally by her maiden name.

John, when I got married, I didn't think of keeping my maiden name. I felt so proud when I became Mrs. "Smith" (not my real name). We named our son after my father, but our surname showed that we three were a family.

I've read several articles about this trend, and now I can understand her decision to use her maiden name professionally. But I've been worried about her using it socially. Why isn't she proud to show she's married to my son? Has she really made a commitment to this marriage? And what last name will their children use?

My husband and I have been trying to hide our hurt feelings, but it's getting harder. I want to tell her and my son what I think, but my husband says it's none of our business.

My son hasn't said anything, so we don't know how he feels. Have I made the right choice by keeping quiet?

HASN'T SAID A WORD YET

Dear HASN'T:

Yes, you have. Since your son hasn't indicated his own feelings, you must assume he approves. Your husband is right: It's none of your business. The couple has a right to make this decision for themselves.

Don't take your daughter-in-law's decision personally. She hasn't rejected your family by keeping her own last name. The recent trend has been for women to keep their birth names after marriage—both socially and professionally. According to studies, families haven't suffered because of this trend—love, not a surname, is the glue that keeps a family together.

As for the children's last names, couples have been finding their own solutions. Many parents have been using hyphenated surnames composed of the mother's and father's last name. (Readers: Has anyone figured out what to do when Roger Smythe-Sanders marries Julia Bernstein-Burke?) One couple I know chose the father's last name when their son was born. They gave the mother's last name to their daughter.

Social customs with regard to naming have been changing quickly, and right now almost anything goes. You and your husband showed a lot of self-control when you decided not to voice your opinion. Let the couple figure this one out themselves, and try to smile approvingly no matter what happens.

Exercise 11 (Student's Book, page 21). *Alison and Jason have been planning a trip. Look at their To Do list and listen to their phone conversation. Then listen again and check the things that they've already done.*

Jason: Hi, honey. I'm calling from the passport office. You wouldn't believe the lines here. I've been waiting for forty minutes.

Alison: Well, that's what happens when you leave things till the last minute. What about the airplane tickets?

Jason: I picked them up on the way over here.

Alison: Well, is there anything you can do while you're waiting? What about that travel guide I gave you to read?

Jason: I've read it. It has some good ideas. I'll tell you about it later. That reminds me—have you made the hotel reservations?

Alison: I've been calling all morning, but I haven't gotten through. Oh—I went to the post office to arrange for our mail to be held. The lines were long there, too. I had to wait more than a half an hour.

Jason: Well, at least it's taken care of. Have you found a bathing suit?

Alison: I've been looking, but . . .

Jason: [interrupting] Oops, gotta go. It's almost my turn. Someone's been holding my place in line. See you later.

Alison: Love you.

Jason: Love you, too.

Exercise 16 (Student's Book, page 26). *Listen to these conversations that take place at a wedding reception. Then listen again and circle the letter of the pictures that illustrate the situations.*

Conversation 1:

A: The bride looks beautiful.

B: There's something different about her, though. Doesn't she usually wear glasses?

A: Uh-huh. I guess she's wearing contact lenses.

Conversation 2:

A: This is a great wedding, isn't it?

B: Yes. Everything is lovely. The bride, the food . . .

A: Have you tasted the cake? It's really good.

B: I know. I've eaten a piece. It's great.

Conversation 3:

A: What does the bridesmaid do?

B: Alicia? Oh, she's a writer.

A: You mean a novelist?

B: No. She only writes non-fiction.

A: Oh. What does she write about?

B: Different things. Uhm, let's see. . . . She wrote a book about Native Americans and one about Hollywood. And now she's been writing a baby-name book.

Conversation 4:

A: Oh, I saw you catch the bridal bouquet. That means you're getting married next!

B: I wonder what my boyfriend thought about it.

A: Well, when you caught it, he smiled.

Conversation 5:

B: Have you seen the bride and groom?

A: Yeah. I just saw them upstairs.

B: Oh. The party's not over. What are they doing there?

A: I don't know, but they were laughing when I walked into the room.

Conversation 6:

A: I didn't know that Al and Anita were such good dancers.

B: They weren't. They took lessons.

A: You mean in preparation for the wedding?

B: Uh-huh.

Conversation 7:

A: What are you drinking? I thought you usually drink coffee.

B: Yeah. But because it's so late, I'm having herbal tea instead. Caffeine makes it too hard for me to fall asleep.

UNIT 2

Introduction (Student's Book, page 32). *Read and listen to this selection about talk-show host and actress Oprah Winfrey.*

     Oprah Winfrey began speaking publicly in church at the age of two. By the time she was twelve, she had already decided what she wanted to do for a living. She wanted to be "paid to talk." In fact, it wasn't too long afterward that she got her first radio job. Although she hadn't had any previous experience, she was hired to report the news.

     When Winfrey got her own TV talk show in 1986, she had already been a TV news reporter and had made her acting debut in a major Hollywood movie, *The Color Purple*. Oprah's warm personality made her TV guests comfortable, and her human-interest stories on topics such as child abuse—Oprah, herself, had been a victim—touched the hearts of her viewing audience. "The Oprah Winfrey Show" quickly became one of the most popular shows in the United States, and by the late 1980s, "Oprah Winfrey" had become a household word. When asked about her future, Winfrey says, ". . . it's so bright it burns my eyes."

Exercise 6 (Student's Book, page 39). *A talk-show host is interviewing a successful newspaper reporter. Listen to the reporter talk about some events in her life. Then read the list. Listen again and put the events in the correct chronological order.*

Molly: I moved to Chicago a year after Andrew and I got married. You know, I'm from a small town, and I'd always wanted to live in a big city. But, believe me, it wasn't easy at first. We didn't know *anyone* in Chicago, so we lived in this awful hotel for about a month. It was *terrible*—the room was tiny, and the place was noisy all the time. It was very hard for me to work there. Remember, we'd always lived in a quiet country town before. We looked for our own place every week, but cheap apartments were hard to find. And I hadn't found a job yet, so we didn't have a lot of money. Well, anyhow, finally our luck changed. We found a nice apartment, and we could actually afford it! And we'd only lived there a week before a magazine bought one of my articles. (I'd written several articles about runaway children, but this was the first one I sold.) It was right after that that I got this really great job as a newspaper reporter. Well, we'd been discouraged about moving here—I admit it. But after we moved into our apartment and I started working, that changed. Now we love Chicago.

UNIT 3

Introduction (Student's Book, page 41). *Read and listen to this part of a newspaper sports column.*

A Dream Finally Comes True
By A. L. Sotomayor

     Yesterday, along with an estimated 2 million other spectators, I attended New York City's 23rd annual marathon. It was a beautiful fall day. It had been raining hard the night before, but that morning the weather was clear and cool—perfect for the 26.2-mile run.

     I found my usual spot in Central Park, three miles before the finish line. This is where experienced runners give their best effort, and exciting things have often happened here. I wasn't disappointed. As I watched, 28-year-old Willie Mtolo from South Africa overtook front-runner Andrés Espinosa of Mexico. By the time he passed Espinosa, Mtolo had been running for almost two hours, but he still looked fresh and confident. With just a short distance more to run, Mtolo was sure the race was his. The crowd had been gathering at this spot for hours, and as Mtolo came through the tunnel of spectators, the cheers were deafening.

     Mtolo finished first out of 26,000 runners representing more than 90 different countries. He finished the race in just 2 hours, 9 minutes, and 29 seconds.

     Yesterday's race fulfilled a lifelong dream for Willie Mtolo of South Africa. Because of its policy of apartheid, his country had been banned from international races for 21 years. Several of Mtolo's well-known compatriots had emigrated to the United States and the United Kingdom because they wanted to continue their athletic careers, but Mtolo had stayed in South Africa and had worked to improve conditions there. For years before this event, he had been waiting for this chance to compete internationally. The ban was lifted this year, and yesterday Mtolo found himself running in—and winning—the world's largest marathon.

Exercise 5 (Student's Book, page 47). *Two friends had been at a post-marathon party the night before. Listen to their conversation the next day. Then read the sentences. Listen to the conversation again and mark each sentence true* (T) *or false* (F).

A: Did you see Alice at the party last night? She looked like she'd been crying for hours.

B: I know. I also noticed that her husband came late. And it looked like he'd been walking in the rain.

A: Yeah. I wonder what was going on.

B: I don't know. Maybe they'd been arguing.

A: Could be. I just don't think they've been very happy since they left California.

UNIT 4

Introduction (Student's Book, page 55). *Read and listen to this magazine article about what the new millennium will bring.*

Presenting—The Future!

A new millennium is dawning and with it the powerful feeling that a new era has begun. Where will we be working in this new era? How will we be traveling? What will we be wearing? Here's what futurists predict.

WORK. Futurists see a breakdown in the division between home and office. In the twenty-first century, more and more people will be telecommuting—working at home with telephones, faxes, and computers. They'll be spending much less time in offices. This development will allow people to spend more time with their families as well as cut down on pollution from automobiles.

HOME. Who'll be cleaning house while Mom and Dad are sending faxes? Robots—tiny, insectlike ones that hang around in corners and eat the dust. One Massachusetts Institute of Technology designer predicts that in just a few years, small, intelligent robots are going to be doing all the household chores.

TRANSPORTATION. You'll still be driving the family car to the grocery store—at least for a while. However, for middle-distance travel, high-speed mass transit like Japan's Bullet Train will probably replace individual cars.

CLOTHING. Like a *Star Trek* officer, the well-dressed millenarian will be wearing a body suit. Made of high-tech materials, the suit will be cool in summer and warm in winter. Most likely, we're going to be wearing our technology as well—wrist video phones and sunglasses with computer screens etched onto the lenses.

ENTERTAINMENT. Before the end of the new century, people will be watching life-size images on TV—ones that they can see, hear, feel, and smell. Called "virtual reality," this technology creates powerful images that audiences experience as real. The new entertainment will also be interactive. Viewers won't be sitting 106passively watching the explorer shoot the rapids; they will be guiding the raft themselves.

EDUCATION. Virtual-reality technology will transform instruction as well as entertainment. On a typical school day, the geography class will be experiencing life in a rain forest, while the history class next door shudders at the sights, sounds, and smells of the Battle of Waterloo.

The line between education and employment will blur. Our grandchildren will probably be dividing their time between the classroom and an apprenticeship. However, job skills will quickly become obsolete in the new era, so they'll also be updating their skills and knowledge continually throughout their lives.

THE NEW SUBURBS. In 1992, radio antennas in California and Puerto Rico began a systematic search for signs of life in the universe. For the next several years, astronomers will be scanning the heavens for other civilizations. Meanwhile, the Mars Underground, a group of visionary scientists, has already planned the first real-estate development project on Mars. The shuttles will be leaving as soon as they iron out a few transportation problems.

Many of these changes have already begun, and we'll be seeing others, such as changes in school systems, very soon. The future will be arriving any minute. Are you ready for it?

Exercise 5 (Student's Book, page 62). *Four members of the Mars Underground are trying to arrange a conference on Venus. Listen to their conversation. Then listen again. Mark the chart below to help you figure out when they are all available.*

Lorna: You know, interest is really growing in real-estate development on Venus. We should try to organize a convention there this summer.

Jennifer: Good idea. But I don't think it's going to be possible for us to find a time we're all available. We're all so busy.

Brian: Well, we won't know unless we try. Jennifer, what are your summer plans?

Jennifer: I don't know exactly, Brian. I do know that I'll be taking a vacation with my family the last two weeks of August. What about you, Brian?

Brian: Well, I don't have any vacation plans yet. But I'll be going on a business trip to Mars in the second and third weeks of July. Lorna, what are your plans?

Lorna: Well, it's already the end of June, and I need at least two weeks' advance notice for work.

Brian: Hmmmm. So, let's see. That means the earliest you could go would be the third week of July. Tranh, what about you? Any plans?

Tranh: I hate this planet in the summer. Too many intergalactic tourists. I'll be getting away from Earth as much as I can.

Lorna: Really? Where will you be going?

Tranh: Well, I'll be flying to Mars to visit my sister every other weekend, starting the second week in July.

Brian: Hmmm. Every other weekend, starting the second week in July . . . The convention has to run through the weekend, so that rules out the second and fourth weeks of July.

Lorna: And the second and fourth weeks of August, too. What about the rest of the time, Tranh?

Tranh: Well, I'll be doing underground research the third week in July, and with a little luck, I'll be traveling to Jupiter with my new girlfriend the third week in August.

Brian: Well, according to my calculations, that leaves only one week that we all have free . . .

UNIT 5

Introduction (Student's Book, page 64). *Read and listen to this newsletter about saving money.*

The Penny-Pinching Times   *Volume 5, Number 1*   *January*

From the Editor's Desk:

In our New Year's issue, we traditionally talk about savings goals for the coming year. But is it possible to save money in these hard times? This question has been on the minds of many of our subscribers. Let's turn to one of our readers for the answer.

Janice Bedford's goal is to buy a car by the end of the year. Janice works as a word processor and takes home about $20,000 a year. About $15,000 of that goes to pay essential costs—food, clothing, rent. Another $5,000 goes for optional expenses such as books, movies, and gifts. Janice has figured out that if she saves just $15.00 a week, by the end of the year, she will have met her savings goal of $780—enough for the down payment on a good used car.

How will she do it? Well, to begin with, Janice, an avid reader who usually buys three paperback books a month, will become reacquainted with her local library. By borrowing instead of buying, Janice will have saved about $200 by the end of the year. And with no sacrifice—she'll still have been keeping up with all those best sellers while she saves. If she continues her new habit, by the year 2001, Janice will have put away an impressive $1,200. And that's just one of many painless ways that Janice, and you, can save money for the things you want and need. Read on for more . . .

Happy penny pinching!

Mary Dobbs, Editor

Sayings worth saving . . .

The safest way to double your money is to fold it over once and put it into your pocket.
(Frank McKinney Hubbard, 1868–1930)

A Penny Saved . . .

Tips from our Readers

- A year ago, Anne Marie DuPont wanted her daughter Jennifer to start studying piano, but she just couldn't afford the lessons. By packing four inexpensive lunches a week for Jennifer and herself, Anne Marie saved the $60 a month she needed for private lessons. On the fifteenth of this month, Jennifer will have been studying piano for six months, and Anne Marie will have the pleasure of attending her daughter's first recital. Happy New Year, Anne Marie!

- Don Caputo wants to pay off a costly credit-card debt. By writing letters to his relatives instead of making expensive long-distance phone calls, he can pay an additional $50 a month on his card. By June, Don figures, he'll have cut the debt in half—just by putting pen to paper. By a year from June, he'll have paid off the whole thing. This seems like a long haul, but remember that all along, Don will also have been saving on the costly 20 percent that the credit-card company charges for the unpaid balance.

- Tom Lu has wanted a CD player for a long time. A student with very little disposable income, Tom had to look hard for places to save. Recently, Tom has started hanging his clothes up to dry instead of putting them in the dryer at his local laundromat. Considering that it costs him $1.50 a machine, and he needs to do two loads a week, Tom will have accumulated an extra $156 by the time the holidays are here again. That's enough to buy himself the present he wants—a used CD player.

Write to us with your own penny-pinching tips. If we publish yours, you'll receive a FREE copy of our popular booklet, More Bang for the Buck—AND you'll have helped others pinch a penny.

Here's this month's Penny-Pincher Problem: A ten-ounce box of Boast Cereal costs $1.59. The same brand costs $2.29 for eighteen ounces. Which is the better buy? If you buy two boxes a month of the better buy, how much will you have saved by the end of twelve months?

Answer: The eighteen-ounce box at 13 cents an ounce is a better buy than the ten-ounce box at 16 cents an ounce. By buying the eighteen-ounce box, you'll have saved $12.96 by next January.

Exercise 5 (Student's Book, page 72). *Don and Thea Caputo want to save for a summer vacation with their two children. Listen to their conversation about how to cut back on their spending. Then listen again and write the amount they will have saved in each category by next summer.*

Thea: [Long sigh . . .] The kids' summer vacation will be over in a week, and we haven't even left Seattle. Next year I want to *go* somewhere during the summer.

Don: Well, we'd better start planning right now if we want to save enough for next year.

Thea: OK. Let's get out the budget and calculator. . . . Hmmm . . . You know, our food budget seems awfully high. Why don't you try packing a lunch?

Don: Do you really think it's worth it?

Thea: Well . . . let's figure it out. How much do you spend on lunch every day?

Don: Erhh . . . about $4.00 . . . five days a week uhmm . . . that's $20 a week.

Thea: Well, it only costs me $2.00 a day at the most to pack my lunch, so I only spend about $10.00 a week . . . Hmm . . . That means you can save $10.00 a week on lunch.

Don: OK—so figure fifty weeks of work. That means by the end of the year I'll have saved . . . uhmmmm $500. Good grief. That's a lot of money!

Thea: Uh-huh. It adds up, doesn't it?

Don: Now, you're going to need some new clothes for work this year. How much do you want to budget for that?

Thea: Actually, I think I'll only need about $250. That's only half of what I spent last year. I can just buy some new scarves and earrings to make my suits look new.

Don: OK, if you're sure you don't mind. And if Ned and Valerie will wear some things from the thrift shop, we can save another $300 on their clothes.

Thea: I think they will. They know they'll be saving for a special vacation.

Don: Great. So by next August, we'll have saved $550 on clothes.

Thea: That's terrific. Now, let's look at transportation. You know, I've been thinking that we could save some money taking the commuter shuttle. Two weekly shuttle tickets cost $15.00.

Don: Well, right now we're spending about $35 a week on gas, tolls, and parking downtown.

Thea: OK. Let's try the commuter shuttle, then. We'll save $20 a week. So, how much will we have saved by next summer?

Don: Let's see. . . . That's fifty weeks from now. Fifty times twenty . . . in fifty weeks, we'll have saved $1,000. Wow! Why didn't we think of this sooner?

Thea: Can we cut back on entertainment?

Don: I think so. We could rent videos instead of going to the movies. By next summer we'll have saved $420 just by watching movies at home.

Thea: How did you figure that?

Don: Look—we go out for pizza and a movie about once a month, and we spend $40 every time. Videos cost $5.00 each to rent. We save $35 a month, times twelve months.

Thea: This is going to be a nice vacation. What's our total so far?

Don: Well, so far I figure we'll have saved . . .

UNIT 6

Introduction (Student's Book, page 78). *Read and listen to these on-the-street interviews reported in a popular magazine.*

Around Town

It's a Nice Place to Live, Isn't It?

La Costa: Excuse me. I'm conducting a survey to find out how people feel about living in L.A. Would you mind answering a few questions?

Moffet: Hey, you're Jackie La Costa from Channel 7, aren't you?

La Costa: That's right.

Moffet: I watch you all the time!

La Costa: Thanks. You're not originally from California, are you?

Moffet: No. I moved here two years ago from New York. You could tell by my accent, couldn't you?

La Costa: So, how do you like it here?

Moffet: Well, I'm a screenplay writer, and so Hollywood's the place to be.

La Costa: But it's gotten harder to sell scripts, hasn't it?

Moffet: Uh-huh. It's not like a few years ago when . . . I'm sorry. Will you excuse me? I think I see my agent over there . . . .

La Costa: No problem. Thanks.

* * * *

La Costa: Excuse me, ma'am. Can I ask a few questions?

Aguirre: Sure.

La Costa: Are you from L.A.?

Aguirre: No. I'm from New York.

La Costa: Oh. How long have you been in L.A.?

Aguirre: Almost twenty years.

La Costa: That's a pretty long time, isn't it? Why did you move here?

Aguirre: The weather. Two hundred and fifty-eight days of sunshine a year. You can't beat that, can you?

La Costa: Not if you don't mind the smog!

Aguirre: Well, New York has its problems with air pollution, too.

La Costa: That's true.

* * * *

La Costa: So, why did you move to L.A.?

Kato: I work in the computer industry. My company does a lot of business in Asia, and I have to fly to Japan at least once a month.

La Costa: L.A. *is* a lot closer to Japan, isn't it?

Kato: Yes, it is. I save a lot of time traveling. And our customers come here, too.

La Costa: L.A. has really become an international center, hasn't it?

Kato: It really has.

* * * *

La Costa: Excuse me, ma'am. You're not from L.A., by any chance, are you?

Wilson: I'm from L.A.

La Costa: Oh, I was beginning to think that no one was born here! I'm trying to find out how people feel about living here.

Wilson: That's funny.

La Costa: Funny?

Wilson: Yes. I've lived here all my life, but I'm moving next month. I just got laid off, so I'm moving east. I got a job in New York.

La Costa: It seems like everyone I speak to is either going to or coming from New York.

Wilson: Small world, isn't it?

La Costa: Well, how *did* you like living in L.A.?

Wilson: Except for the traffic on the freeway, I liked it a lot. I'm not even going to have a car in New York.

La Costa: Will you miss L.A.?

Wilson: Sure. It's a nice city to live in, isn't it?

Exercise 5 (Student's Book, page 85). *Listen to these people ask questions. Notice if their voices rise or fall at the end of each question. Listen again and decide in each case if they are really asking a question (and expect an answer) or if they are just making a comment (and don't expect an answer). Check the correct column.*

1. Hi, Ken. It's a nice day, isn't it? (falling intonation)
2. You're Professor Smith, aren't you? (rising intonation)
3. You're not moving, are you? (rising intonation)
4. The sun is shining. We really don't need to take our umbrellas, do we? (falling intonation)
5. Your wife's from New York, isn't she? (falling intonation)
6. Los Angeles is the capital of California, isn't it? (rising intonation)
7. You're not very happy about the move, are you? (falling intonation)
8. Mary's writing a new screenplay, isn't she? (falling intonation)

UNIT 7

Introduction (Student's Book, page 88). *Read and listen to this magazine article about identical twins.*

The Twin Question: Nature or Nurture?

Mark and Gerald are identical twins. Mirror images of each other, they also share many similarities in lifestyle. Mark hasn't ever been married, and Gerald hasn't either. Mark is a firefighter, and so is Gerald. Mark likes hunting, fishing, going to the beach, eating Chinese food, and watching John Wayne movies. Gerald does too.

These similarities might not be unusual in identical twins, except for one fact: Mark and Gerald were separated when they were five days old and grew up in different states with different families. Neither Mark nor Gerald knew that he had a twin. The two men found each other accidentally when they were thirty-one, and they discovered their almost identical lifestyles at that time.

Average people are fascinated by twins like Mark and Gerald. So are serious researchers. Identical twins share the same genes. Therefore, they offer researchers the chance to study the effect of genetic inheritance on disease, length of life, and personality.

However, identical twins who grow up together also experience the same influences from their environment. How can researchers separate environmental factors from genetic factors? Identical twins who are separated at birth and grow up in different environments offer researchers a way to investigate the age-old question: Which has more effect on our lives, heredity (the genes we receive from our parents) or environment (the social influences in our childhood)?

Some startling coincidences have turned up in recent studies of identical twins separated at birth. Perhaps the most astonishing twins of all are the Springer and Lewis brothers, who were adopted by different families soon after they were born. The Springer family named their adopted son Jim. So did the Lewis family. When the two Jims met for the first time as forty-year-old adults, they discovered that their similarities went way beyond their identical names and looks. Jim Lewis had worked as a gas station attendant and a law enforcement agent. So had Jim Springer. Lewis chewed his fingernails when he was nervous, and Springer did too. Both men had had dogs. Lewis had named his Toy; so had Springer. And believe it or not, Lewis had married a woman named Linda, divorced her, and later married a woman named Betty. So had Springer.

Do our genes really determine our names, the people we marry, the jobs we choose, even the pets we adopt? The lives of other twins indicate that the question of nature or nurture is more complicated than that.

Identical twins Andrea and Barbara, for example, were born in Germany and separated shortly after birth. Andrea stayed in Germany, but Barbara didn't. She moved to the United States with her adoptive American family. The twins grew up in different cultures, speaking different languages. Barbara didn't know she had a twin, but Andrea did, and she searched for her sister until she found her. When they met they discovered some amazing similarities. Each had a scar on her lip from an accident. Each had had a tonsillectomy—on the same day!

Nevertheless, their personalities and life histories were quite different. Andrea is outgoing and expressive, but Barbara isn't, despite her identical genetic heritage. Both sisters got married and had two children. Andrea stayed married to the same man, but Barbara didn't. In fact, Barbara married and divorced several times.

Clearly, heredity isn't the only force that governs our lives, and neither is environment. The lives of twins separated at birth suggest that we have a lot to learn about the complex role these two powerful forces play in our lives.

Exercise 5 (Student's Book, page 96). *A couple is out on a first date. Listen to their conversation. Then listen again and complete the chart.*

A: This is a great restaurant. I really love Italian food.

B: So do I. Do you cook?

A: Not really.

B: I do. I love trying out new recipes.

A: I eat out a lot.

B: Oh, so do I.

A: Or I buy some take-out food after work and rent a video. I love old movies.

B: I do too. [awkward silence] Er . . . do you like to read?

A: Uh-hum. Especially biographies.

B: So do I! What about novels?

A: I don't read much fiction.

B: I don't either. [pause] What about sports?

A: I don't really play any sports. What about you?

B: I do. I play tennis and volleyball every week. But I never watch sports on TV.

A: Me neither. I watch a lot of news programs, though.

B: So do I. In fact, there's an interesting documentary about world hunger tonight at eight.

A: Hhhhm. It's seven o'clock now. If we leave now, we can watch it.

B: I think that sounds good.

A: So do I.

UNIT 8

Introduction (Student's Book, page 104). *Read and listen to this editorial about gun control from a U.S. magazine.*

* * * Viewpoint * * *

STOP LIVING IN FEAR

Gerard Taylor

Some shocking statistics: In the United States, the rate of murders per 100,000 people is six times higher than in Europe and seven times higher than in Japan. The weapon of choice: guns. There are ninety-three gunshot deaths a day, more that 34,000 every year. And for every death, four to ten people are wounded by guns, many of them seriously.

Americans have long had an international reputation for being in love with their guns. But it seems like they are finally getting fed up with becoming victims of a growing epidemic of gun violence. In fact, according to recent opinion polls, a majority of voters are now in favor of Congress's passing more laws to control handguns, the most frequently used firearms.

The Brady law, passed in 1994 after years of debate, seemed like a victory for gun control at the time. This law requires would-be gun owners to wait five days before purchasing a handgun. The purpose of the waiting period is to give police time to check that the prospective customer does not have a criminal record. It also prevents people from committing impulse crimes. (The waiting period gives people time to stop to think things through before acting rashly.) Now some critics realize that the law doesn't go far enough in curbing gun violence. For one thing, criminals easily succeed in getting hold of the more than 200 million firearms already out there.

What else can be done besides imposing waiting periods on the purchase of guns? One senator has suggested "bullet control." Banning certain kinds of ammunition would make it harder to stand on top of buildings and spray bullets at crowds of people below. The same senator has also proposed taxing ammunition at a rate of 10,000 percent. Others suggest making it more difficult to get a license to sell guns. One social critic points out that it is much harder to get a California driver's license than it is to obtain a license that enables you to acquire a whole arsenal of weapons and to have them shipped right to your home.

The biggest opponent of gun control is, of course, the National Rifle Association. Its 2.5 million members have succeeded in defeating national gun-control legislation for years. Their position: "Guns don't kill people. People kill people."

A recent study, however, of two cities now goes far in providing an answer to the NRA. Seattle in the United States and Vancouver in Canada are similar economically, ethnically, socially, and culturally. Their crime statistics are also similar except for one: You are eight times more likely to get shot in Seattle than in Vancouver. The only factor that explains the large difference in their murder rates is the widespread availability of guns in the United States compared to Canada, which practices strict gun control. Clearly, people with guns kill people much more frequently than people without guns.

People around the world think our gun culture is crazy, and they are right. We must stop thinking of ourselves as noble frontierspeople who need weapons to survive—or the already shocking statistics will get worse. According to a recent Harvard School of Public Health Survey, 59 percent of children in the sixth to twelfth grade said it was easy for them to get handguns. Gun control may not be the entire answer, but it is a start.

What about our constitutional right to bear arms, ask members of the National Rifle Association. This "right" is undermining the very freedom our Constitution meant to protect: freedom from fear. Locking oneself behind closed doors and staying off the streets out of fear of being shot at does not constitute freedom. Do we want to stop living in fear? If so, restricting guns is a small price to pay.

Exercise 6 (Student's Book, page 113). *Listen to a radio talk-show debate on gun control. Then listen again and check the issues the debaters are in favor of.*

Smith: Good morning, and welcome to On The Line. I'm your host, Alice Smith, and this is KRVD talk radio. Today's topic: Gun Control. Joining us in our studio are two U.S. Senators, Senator Lois Blake of Colorado and Senator Tom Wilson of New Jersey. Welcome, Senators.

Blake: Thank you, Alice.

Wilson: Good morning, Alice.

Smith: Everyone is aware of the nation's growing concern with gun violence. The statistics are staggering. This year alone there have been more than 37,000 gunshot deaths. Thirteen thousand of those were handgun homicides. People are becoming afraid to leave their homes. What can we do about it? Senator Wilson?

Wilson: Well, banning weapons is the only way to stop this wave of violence.

Smith: Banning *all* weapons?

Wilson: Yes. Except for the police, security guards, and soldiers, no one really needs to carry firearms. No handguns, no rifles, no assault weapons.

Smith: The NRA won't be happy to hear you say this. What's your position, Senator Blake?

Blake: I support banning assault weapons. But I'm *not* in favor of keeping civilians from owning licensed handguns. First of all, our Constitution guarantees us the right to bear arms. Second of all, many noncriminals enjoy sports such as hunting, and they should be able to continue to do this.

Wilson: Yes, but at what price? People are living in fear.

Smith: Senator Blake brought up hunting, and of course many members of the National Rifle Association are hunters. What do you propose doing about hunting?

Wilson: I'm in favor of completely banning it. Not only are there a lot of hunting-related accidents, but I think it's cruel to shoot animals just for sport.

Smith: OK. Let's assume that all guns *won't* be banned in the near future . . .

Wilson: Unfortunately that's a pretty safe assumption.

Smith: Yes, well, what about placing limits on the number of guns an individual may purchase during a certain time period? Do you support that, Senator Blake?

Blake: Absolutely. There's no reason for anyone to buy more than a gun a month.

Wilson: A gun a month! Why does anyone need a gun a month! I support limiting the purchase of guns to just one per person—of course, I'd still prefer to see *all* guns banned.

Smith: What else would you like to see happen, Senator Wilson?

Wilson: Well, some people think this is extreme, but, you know, kids are carrying toy guns that look like real guns. And more and more kids are being shot because a frightened police officer mistakes a toy for the real thing. So, I'm in favor of banning the production of real-looking toy guns.

Smith: Would *you* go along with banning toy guns, Senator Blake?

Blake: No, [laughs] I wouldn't go along with banning toy guns. Again, I see that as limiting our freedom. It should be left up to the parents what their kids can or cannot play with. But, parents *do* have to be more aware of where their kids are and what they are doing.

Smith: That brings me to my next question. What do you think about holding parents responsible if their children find a real gun at home and use it?

Blake: I'm for holding parents responsible for that type of irresponsibility. If parents leave guns lying around, they must be held accountable.

Smith: And you, Senator Wilson, I suppose would agree with that.

Wilson: Absolutely.

Smith: Some senators have recently called for the death penalty for people using guns in committing a crime. Do you support this?

Wilson: No. I'm opposed to capital punishment in general. I don't think the death penalty stops people from committing crimes.

Smith: What about you, Senator Blake?

Blake: I agree with Senator Wilson. I think that all *current* laws should be strictly enforced, but I am not in favor of applying the death penalty to all criminals who carry guns in the commission of a crime.

Smith: Interesting. The two of you agree on several issues. We will be pausing now for these words. When we return, our listeners will be able to call in and ask Senators Blake and Wilson questions about gun control. Don't go away.

UNIT 9

Introduction (Student's Book, page 115). *Read and listen to part of an article on teaching.*

Two Teaching Styles

All teachers want to help their students learn. There are, however, different teaching approaches. Currently, student-centered teaching has become more popular. Teachers who use this approach believe you should let students choose their own curriculum. In other words, allow students to decide what they want to learn. In the student-centered classroom, the teacher is viewed as a facilitator who assists students in reaching their educational goals.

If you have only experienced teacher-centered learning, you would be surprised if you walked into the student-centered classroom of Sandra Jacobson, who teaches writing at a community college. For one thing, her classroom is noisy. Ms. Jacobson usually has her students work in groups or pairs, and often they are all talking at once. For another, it's hard to find the teacher. Ms. Jacobson often sits in on the groups, and she looks like a student herself.

Ms. Jacobson's methods also differ from those of the traditional teacher-centered course. Ms. Jacobson doesn't assign topics or cover the students' papers with red ink. Instead, she has her students keep journals, and she gets her students to select their own topics from interests that emerge in their journal writing. She also uses cooperative-learning techniques such as peer tutoring and group discussion. Her class publishes a newsletter with student writing, and a committee of students selects the writing to be published. The committee (not the teacher) makes the writers revise their writing several times, and a lot of peer tutoring occurs naturally as students do their revisions.

Although Ms. Jacobson's student-centered teaching is quite popular for some courses, many teachers still pursue a teacher-centered approach quite successfully. In this approach, the teacher controls what is taught and how it is taught. The students usually work from a textbook that has been assigned by the teacher.

Right down the hall from Ms. Jacobson is Mrs. Quintana's writing class. When you walk into this classroom, there is no mistaking who Mrs. Quintana is. At 8:05 she is standing in front of her class. The students are all at their desks. Everyone is quiet, eyes directed toward their teacher. Mrs. Quintana has everyone turn to page 51, an introduction to paragraph development. She has students read passages aloud from the book. She makes them stop several times while she explains points or corrects a mispronounced word. When she finishes the presentation, she asks questions. One student can't answer, so she has him go back and find the answer in the material they have just read. Mrs. Quintana is well prepared, and her students are attentive. At the end of the class, she assigns the rest of the chapter for homework and announces a test for the next Wednesday. Both homework and test papers will be corrected (in red) before they are returned.

Both of these teaching approaches have many followers, but it is unclear which approach makes students learn more effectively. Ms. Jacobson's student-centered approach seems more exciting, but how will students learn if the teacher doesn't make them correct their mistakes immediately? Do students really know enough about the subject matter to decide what they want to learn? Mrs. Quintana seems in complete control of her class, but can students learn to write just by reading about it and taking tests? By choosing topics, is she making them write about things that don't interest them?

Of course, such pure examples of each philosophy are not usually found. Rarely is a class totally student-centered or totally teacher-centered. Many traditional teachers have students work in groups. Many student-centered teachers structure their courses with a textbook, though they may use it less often than Mrs. Quintana. Most experienced teachers realize that students and situations differ, and they wisely choose the appropriate mixture of philosophies and techniques for each class.

Exercise 5 (Student's Book, page 122). *You are going to hear a conversation about school between a mother and her son. Before you listen, read the statements. Then listen again and write true (T) or false (F) next to each statement.*

Mother: So, how was school today?

Son: OK. Ms. Kirby let us choose a play to perform for the rest of the school.

Mother: That's great. What did you choose?

Son: A play called *Let Them Eat Cake.* She's even letting us make our own costumes.

Mother: Sounds like fun. Oh, look at the time. It's almost six o'clock.

Son: What's for dinner?

Mother: I made your favorite!

Son: Mmm, pot roast. But I have to eat quickly. Ms. Kirby's making us learn the whole first act for tomorrow.

Mother: Slow down. I'm going to make *you* eat pot roast before *you* get to *Let Them Eat Cake!*

UNIT 10

Introduction (Student's Book, page 131). *Read and listen to this advertisement for "the world's most widely read magazine."*

  Reader's Digest was founded in 1922. Today it is read by people in every country in the world. It is published in eighteen languages and forty-six editions. Each foreign-language edition is especially tailored to fit the needs and interests of its international audience. Last year *Reader's Digest* was read by 100 million people. Shouldn't you be one of them? Subscribe today.

Exercise 7 (Student's Book, page 140). *Listen to the conversations between editors at* Modern Reader. *Then listen again and circle the letter of the sentence you hear from each pair.*

Conversation 1:

How long has Jill worked here?

Jill? Let's see. I think it's been about fifteen years.

Fifteen years? Was that before or after Bob started working here?

After. Jill was hired by Bob.

Oh.

Conversation 2:

How did you learn to use all these new computer programs? Did you take classes?

Yeah. I took some classes at the college. The company sent me.

Minna really knows a lot, too. Did she take classes with you?

No. I trained Minna.

Conversation 3:

Have things changed a lot since you've been here?

They sure have. When I started, we were just a small company. There were just ten employees.

What about the magazine itself?

First of all, it was just about half the size it is now, and it was published just six times a year.

Wow.

Conversation 4:

I haven't seen Jill lately. Is she on vacation?

No. Haven't you heard what happened?

No. What happened?

Tony fired Jill.

You're kidding! How come?

Well, you know, she really made a lot of mistakes on that Bolivia article.

That's terrible.

Conversation 5:

Are they going to replace Jill?

They have to. They need another writer.

Are they interviewing for the position?

Uh-huh. They started interviewing last week. They're trying to fill the position with someone from within the company.

Really?

Yes. In fact, Diana is applying for the position.

That's interesting. Did her own boss interview her?

No. She was interviewed by Jay.

Conversation 6:

Do you know John Delgado?

The name sounds familiar. Who is he?

A sports writer.

Oh, right. I think I know who you mean. He was laid off.

Yes, he was.

UNIT 11

Introduction (Student's Book, page 144). *Read and listen to this article about an international space project.*

Close Quarters

Japanese astronauts fear that decisions will be made too fast, while Americans worry that in an emergency, they might not be made quickly enough. The French and Dutch worry that dinner won't be taken seriously, and Italians suspect that their privacy may not be respected.

The focus of all this apprehension is the space station *Freedom*, a major international project that will be launched from the Space Shuttle in the very near future. By the end of the century, *Freedom* will be operated by a crew of astronauts from Europe, Japan, Canada, and the United States. At first, the crew will be replaced every ninety days, but the stay could be lengthened to prepare for a two-year trip to Mars.

How can an international group of astronauts be expected to get along during long periods in this "trapped environment"? To find out, anthropologist Mary Lozano and engineer Clifford Wong have begun to ask astronauts from around the world about their concerns. The two scientists hope that many cross-cultural problems can be avoided by what they learn.

Besides the concerns already mentioned, all the astronauts worry about language. English will be the official language of the station, and, of course, a great deal of technical language must be mastered by everyone. However, on a social level, some partners fear that they might be treated like outsiders because they won't know American slang. Another concern is food. What time should meals be served? How should preparation and cleanup be handled? Can religious dietary restrictions be observed on board?

To deal with cross-cultural differences like these, Lozano and Wong feel strongly that astronauts should be taught interpersonal skills as well as given technical and survival know-how. They have interviewed participants in each country, and they hope that what they learn from them will be applied in training. Ultimately, they believe, cross-cultural training will save money and reduce errors caused by misunderstanding, ranging from misreading a facial expression to incorrectly interpreting data.

Often qualities like sensitivity and tolerance can't be taught from a textbook; they must be observed and experienced. Lozano and Wong say that the necessary model for space station harmony can be found in the TV series *Star Trek*. The multicultural *Enterprise* crew has been getting along in space for eons now, and the scientists suggest that watching the show might be helpful for future astronauts. Since cross-cultural harmony could be imagined by the *Star Trek* creators, perhaps it can be achieved by the crew of *Freedom*.

Exercise 5 (Student's Book, page 151). *Some crew members aboard the Space Station are watching television. Listen and read the script below. Then listen again and circle the underlined words you hear.*

Picarro: Spaceship Endeavor calling Earth. . . . This is Captain Picarro speaking. We've been hit by a meteorite.

Earth: Is anyone hurt?

Picarro: No, everyone is safe.

Earth: You'd better start repairing the damage immediately.

Picarro: It can't be repaired out here.

* * * *

Picarro: We'll be approaching Planet CX5 of the Delta solar system in a few hours. Is their language on our computer, Dr. Sock?

Sock: I'm checking now. . . . We don't have a language for CX5 on the computer, but we have one for CX4. Shall we try it?

Picarro: We'd better be very careful. Our messages could be misunderstood.

* * * *

Lon: OK. I'm ready. Let's go.

Ray: What about oxygen?

Lon: Isn't the atmosphere on CX5 just like Earth's?

Ray: I think you've been in space too long. Read your manual. Oxygen must be used on all other planets.

* * * *

Picarro: I've lost contact with Lon and Ray. I hope their electronic equipment works on CX5.

Sock: Don't worry. They'll be picked up by the radar pretty soon.

* * * *

Lon: Look at those plants. I want to take some back to the ship.

Ray: But they're huge!

Lon: Well, let's try. I bet they can be grown on board.

* * * *

CX5 Leader: What do you want to ask us, Earthlings?

Ray: Our vehicle was hit by a meteorite. We have to get it ready to return to Earth.

CX5 Leader: What do you want of us?

Ray: It must be repaired on the ground. May we have permission to land on your planet?

UNIT 12

Introduction (Student's Book, page 154). *Read and listen to this TV news report.*

Anchor: Your time is running out. If you haven't yet mailed your tax return, you have just a little more than half an hour to have it postmarked by midnight tonight. We turn now to Ken Watanabe, reporting live from Manhattan. Ken, what's happening?

Reporter: I'm standing in Manhattan's Main Post Office on West 33rd Street and Eighth Avenue. It's 11:25 P.M. on April 15, the deadline for mailing in federal income tax returns. As you can see, the place is mobbed— there's a carnival atmosphere here. People are selling t-shirts, food, and drinks. You can even get your back rubbed while you wait on line.

Let's go find out why some of these people are mailing their returns in at the eleventh hour.

Excuse me. Is that your Federal Income tax you're filing?

Woman: Yes, it is.

Reporter: Do you always file at the last minute like this?

Woman: Oh, no. I've always had my taxes prepared by an accountant, but this year I decided to do them myself. It took a lot longer than I thought it would. Right up until about an hour ago, as a matter of fact.

Reporter: Why are *you* here at the eleventh hour?

Man: Well, I got my taxes done by R. H. Brock a couple of weeks ago. Then I lost them.

Reporter: You *lost* your taxes?

Man: Yeah. I was having my apartment painted at about that time, and I was moving stuff around a lot. I guess I just slipped them into the wrong folder.

Reporter: But you did find them in time.

Man: Right. Just in time.

Reporter: And you, sir? What's your excuse?

Man: The dog ate my W-2 form.

Reporter: Oh, come on. You can do a lot better than that!

Man: No, it really happened.

Reporter: What did you do when you found out?

Man: Well, I had moved, and this employer was in another state, so I called and got another W-2 sent. That took about a week.

Reporter: So you waited until last week.

Man: Yeah.

Reporter: What do you plan to do next year?

Man: First, I think I'll get my dog trained.

Reporter: Sounds like a good idea.

Well, there's probably a story behind every tax return here tonight. These folks may be filing at the last minute, but the bottom line is, they got it done.

Reporting live from Midtown, I'm Ken Watanabe, Channel 7 News.

Exercise 4 (Student's Book, page 160). *It's a year later, and Art is having his taxes done. Listen to the conversation between Art and his new accountant. Then listen again and check the correct column.*

Accountant: So, you moved to California and set up your own carpentry business.

Art: That's right.

Accountant: Well, that means you'll be able to deduct some of your expenses.

Art: Great.

Accountant: You work right out of your own home, right?

Art: Yes. The house came with a two-car garage, so I had part of the garage converted into a workshop.

Accountant: You have receipts, I hope.

Art: I kept receipts for everything.

Accountant: Great. Did you have the workshop painted?

Art: No. I painted it myself. Can I still claim a deduction?

Accountant: Well, you can deduct the materials but not the labor.

Art: Oh, well.

Accountant: What else did you do in connection with setting up the workshop?

Art: Well, I had a second telephone line installed, and I had a computer system set up.

Accountant: Do you use the phone only for business?

Art: Yes.

Accountant: OK. What about the computer? Do you use the computer for anything personal?

Art: No. Just for keeping records.

Accountant: Good. Any other expenses? Uhm, did you purchase any new tools?

Art: No. But that reminds me—I had the entire garage rewired so I could use my power tools.

Accountant: Good. Anything else? Shelves? Workbenches?

Art: Oh, right. I built shelves in the garage.

Accountant: OK. Again, we can deduct the cost of materials for that. Anything else? How about office supplies?

Art: Let's see. Oh, yeah. I almost forgot. I had business cards printed.

UNIT 13

Introduction (Student's Book, page 166). *Read and listen to this article from a popular psychology magazine.*

Useless Regrets

For all sad words of tongue or pen
The saddest are these: "It might have been."
John Greenleaf Whittier

Not only the saddest, but perhaps the most destructive. According to recent ideas in psychology, our feelings are mainly the result of the way we *think* about reality, not reality itself. Take Paul, for example. Talented in school, he decided not to go on to college. Here's what Paul thinks about this decision now:

I ought to have applied to college.

I could have become a doctor.

My parents might have encouraged me more.

I shouldn't have missed that opportunity.

I could have been rich and famous by now.

According to Nathan S. Kline, M.D., it's not unusual to feel deep regret about things in the past that you think you should have done and did not do—or the opposite, about things you did do and feel you should not have done. In fact, we learn by thinking about past errors. However, dwelling too much on past mistakes and missed opportunities can create such bad feelings that people become paralyzed and can't move on with their lives. Arthur Freeman, Ph.D., and Rose DeWolf have labeled this process "woulda/coulda/shoulda thinking," and they have written an entire book about this type of disorder.

In *Woulda/Coulda/Shoulda: Overcoming Regrets, Mistakes, and Missed Opportunities* (New York: William Morrow, 1989), Freeman and DeWolf suggest challenging regrets with specifics. "Instead of saying, 'I should have done better,'" they suggest "write down an example of a way in which you might have done better. Exactly what should you have done to produce the desired result? Did you have the skills, money, experience, etc., at the time?"

When people examine their feelings of regret about the past, they often find that many of them are simply not based in fact. A mother regrets missing a football game in which her son's leg was injured. She blames herself and the officials. "I should have gone," she laments. "I could have prevented the injury. They might at least have telephoned me as soon as it happened." Did she really have the power to prevent her son's injury? Should the officials have called her before they had looked at the injury? Probably not.

Once people realize how unrealistic their feelings of regret are, they are more ready to let go of them. Cognitive psychologist David Burns, M.D., suggests specific strategies for dealing with useless feelings of regret and getting on with the present. One amusing technique is to spend ten minutes a day writing down all the things you regret. Then say them all aloud (better yet, record them), and listen to yourself. Here's a typical session:

I shouldn't have told that joke in the office. My career is ruined.

I ought to have cleaned the house instead of going out this weekend. My mother's right. I'm just lazy.

My boyfriend could have told me he was going out of town this weekend. He's an inconsiderate jerk. I should never have started going out with him.

Once you listen to your own "woulda/coulda/shoulda" thoughts, it's easier to see their illogic. For example, it's unlikely that your entire career is in ruins because of one joke. You're an adult and you can choose to go out instead of cleaning house. That doesn't make you a lazy person. Nor is your boyfriend a jerk for making a single mistake.

After you recognize how foolish most feelings of regret sound, the next step is to let go of them and to start dealing with life in the present. For some, this might be harder than sighing over past errors. An Italian proverb notes, "When the ship has sunk, everyone knows how she could have been saved." The message from cognitive psychology is similar. It's easy to speculate about the past; the real challenge is to solve the problems you face right now.

Exercise 5 (Student's Book, page 172). *Jennifer is taking some of Dr. David Burns's advice by recording all the things she regrets at the end of the day. Listen to her recording. Then listen again and check the things she did.*

(Sigh) What a day! I really messed up in a big way. For starters—I should've done my homework. Now I've got to get up early tomorrow morning, and it's already midnight. What a bummer! And I shouldn't have walked to work today. I was late again, and I could see that Doug was really annoyed. Then, I got a notice from my bank that one of my checks bounced! Now, I'm afraid I'm going to bounce another one. I really should've made that $100 deposit today. I'll never learn. Speaking of money, I shouldn't have bought a new coat. My old one's good enough, and I could use the extra money. I just don't have any self-control. Oh, and now Aunt Rose is furious with me. I didn't send her a card for her birthday. I might've at least called to wish her a happy birthday. I only think of myself. On the other hand, I shouldn't have called Ron. All he does is complain. He regrets this, he regrets that . . . it's so depressing, but I guess I asked for it! Let's see . . . what else? Oh, yeah. I ought to have gone to the supermarket before it closed. I never plan ahead. And now there's nothing in the house to eat. Oh. And I should've finished that David Burns book. Maybe then I'd know how to feel better. Oh well, there's always tomorrow.

UNIT 14

Introduction (Student's Book, page 175). *The great achievements of ancient cultures fascinate modern people. Read and listen to one writer's theories regarding these achievements.*

Close Encounters

In 1927, a Peruvian surveyor must have been astonished to see lines in the shapes of huge animals and geometric forms on the rocky ground below his airplane. Created by the ancient Nazca culture, these beautiful, clear-cut forms (over 13,000 of them) are too big to be recognized from the ground. However, seen from about 600 feet in the air, the giant forms take shape. Toribio Mexta Xesspe may have been the first human in almost a thousand years to have recognized the designs.

Since their rediscovery, many people have speculated about the Nazca lines. Without airplanes, how could an ancient culture have made these amazing pictures? What purpose can they have served?

One writer, Erich von Däniken, has a theory as amazing as the Nazca lines themselves. According to von Däniken, visitors from outer space brought their civilization to the Earth thousands of years ago. When these astronauts visited ancient cultures here on Earth, the people of those cultures must have believed that they were gods. Since the Nazcans could have built the lines according to instructions from an aircraft, von Däniken concludes that the drawings might have marked a landing strip for the spacecraft of the ancient astronauts. Von Däniken writes, "The builders of the geometrical figures may have had no idea what they were doing. But perhaps they knew perfectly well what the 'gods' needed in order to land."

In his book *Chariots of the Gods?* (New York: Bantam, 1972), von Däniken offers many other "proofs" that ancient cultures had contact with astronauts from advanced civilizations in outer space. Giant statues on Easter Island provide von Däniken with strong evidence of the astronauts' presence. Von Däniken estimates that the island could only have supported a very small population. After examining the tools that the islanders probably used, he concludes,

> Even 2,000 men, working day and night, would not be nearly enough to carve these colossal figures out of the steel-hard volcanic stone with rudimentary tools—and at least part of the population must have tilled the barren fields, gone fishing, woven cloth, and made ropes. No, 2,000 men alone could not have made the gigantic statues.

Von Däniken finds no resemblance between the statues and human beings, and he suggests that islanders may have modeled them after the space visitors.

In a later book, *In Search of Ancient Gods* (New York: Putnam, 1974), von Däniken points to creation myths to support his theory of contact from another solar system. He notes, "All the stories of creation assert, with variations, that man was created by gods from the cosmos, after they had come down to earth from heaven." These mythological gods must actually have been space creatures, according to von Däniken. He believes that ancient pictures of creatures with wings record the visits of these space beings. Arriving on Earth millennia ago, these beings brought amazing scientific and technological information to primitive cultures. The cultures couldn't have been able to understand or use this knowledge, but they preserved it in their art. Von Däniken sees rocket ships, robots, and wristwatches in the art of many different cultures.

Von Däniken also finds touching evidence of gifts from these wise astronauts in the map of a sixteenth-century Turkish admiral, Piri Reis. Dated 1513, the map (several copies of which exist) was compiled from a number of other charts. Von Däniken believes that in 1513 cartographers couldn't possibly have had the information shown in this map. He insists, "Whoever made it must have been able to fly and to take photographs." According to von Däniken, only one conclusion is possible:

> To me it is obvious that extraterrestrial spacemen made the maps from space stations in orbit. During one of their visits, they made our ancestors a present of the maps.

Obvious? Well, perhaps not to everyone. Scientists, among others, remain skeptical and prefer to look for answers closer to home. However, von Däniken's theories continue to fascinate millions of readers, both believers and nonbelievers. And even nonbelievers must admit that space visitors might have contributed to human culture. After all, no one can prove that they didn't. . . .

Exercise 5 (Student's Book, page 184). *Some archaeology students are discussing artifacts they have found at various sites. Look at the pictures. Then listen to the students speculate and draw conclusions about what each item is. Listen again and match the pictures with the appropriate conversation.*

Conversation A:

Wow! Look at that! It's got a blade. And this looks like a handle.

Yeah. It might've been used as some sort of cutting tool, like a sickle.

A sickle? What's that?

It's a kind of farming tool. Something used to cut down high grass.

You mean like wheat?

Yeah. They could've harvested wheat with this.

Conversation B:

That's a strange-looking design.

Yeah. They must've seen one of those astronauts that von Däniken writes about.

Right. What do you think they used it for?

Well, look at the hole. They may have worn it around their necks for good luck or something.

That's right. They could have.

Conversation C:

Look at this ring. What do you suppose they used it for?

Hmmm. It could've been part of a shoe.

Part of a shoe? What do you mean?

Like an eyelet. They could've pulled some kind of shoelace through the hole, and then tied the laces.

Oh. I see.

Conversation D:

That's beautiful. What do you think it came from?

Well, from the round shape and from the design, I'd say it must've been part of a vase.

Or it could've been a cooking or serving utensil.

Yeah, the design looks like some kind of border.

It could've been part of the base.

No, it's too narrow. It must've been part of the neck. They could've poured things out of it.

You're right.

Conversation E:

That looks like a pretty sophisticated instrument!

Is it a pump?

I don't think so. I remember reading about something like this in one of our books. I think they could've used this to make fire!

Really? How?

Well, they could've had a tinder inside the cylinder . . .

A tinder?

Uh-huh. Something that burns easily. Look—when you push this piece down into the cylinder, it quickly compresses the air. That makes the air hot, and the tinder could start to burn.

Incredible! They must've been really intelligent to have figured that out!

Yeah, really!

Conversation F:

What's that you've got there? It looks just like a rock.

I don't think it's a rock. Look at the shape. It's too clear. Someone must've made it.

You know, you're right. It couldn't have just formed like that naturally. Someone must've chipped away at it to produce all those different angles. What do you think it was used for?

I think it must've been used as some kind of tool.

Hmmm. They could've used it to cut hard material—like wood.

You mean like a hand axe?

Exactly. Like a hand axe.

UNIT 15

Introduction (Student's Book, page 192). *Read and listen to this informational brochure containing advice for travelers.*

Know Before You Go

High-speed air travel is usually fast and efficient. However, it has its special hassles, and these can cause delay and discomfort if you don't know how to avoid them. Know before you go and enjoy your journey more.

RECONFIRMING. If you are traveling internationally, you should reconfirm your flight 72 hours ahead of time. In spite of electronic reservation systems, many airlines rely on your telephone call to reserve your seat.

CHECKING IN. A good travel agent can often get you a boarding pass in advance. However, even with a previously issued boarding pass, you should still check in at the gate. You could be bumped from a flight if you don't.

MEALS. If you need a low-calorie, low-sodium, or low-cholesterol meal, order it in advance from the airline. You can also order vegetarian and kosher meals ahead of time. If you hate airplane food (and many people do), then it's a good idea to order one of these special meals anyway. It will be fresher and taste better than the standard meal.

COMFORT. One common cause of discomfort on a plane is dehydration, caused by traveling in a pressurized cabin. To avoid this problem, drink a glass of juice or water every hour you are on the plane. Sitting in one place for too long is another cause. If you move around the cabin every hour, you can avoid stiffness. We also suggest doing stretching exercises in your seat.

JET LAG. When you get to your destination, jet lag will catch up with you. There's no way to avoid it. If you travel across time zones at high speeds, your internal clock doesn't keep up with the time changes. That's why your body thinks it's midnight when it's really 9:00 A.M. To minimize the discomfort, reset your watch for the time zone of your destination before you leave home. Also, arrange to arrive late in the day. You are psychologically prepared to sleep at the right time if it's evening when you get to your destination.

WHEELCHAIR FLYERS. Airline wheelchairs are heavy, and someone must push you from behind. You have much more mobility if you store your own wheelchair in the cabin. Terry Winkler, a physician who is also a paraplegic, gives this advice: "If my wheelchair can't be stored on board, I insist that they bring it from the baggage compartment as soon as the plane lands." If you have a disability, be aware of your rights as a passenger. Most airlines cannot bar you except under very special circumstances. If you do not require special equipment, you do not even have to notify the airline of your disability in advance.

FLYING WITH CHILDREN. If you are traveling with children, your big challenge is to stay together on the plane. Ask for seats as early as possible (30 days before your flight). If you get scattered seats, preboard and ask the flight attendant to help you. He or she may be able to reassemble the family before the flight. Always try to get a direct flight. If you must make a connecting flight, you might be able to arrange for an electric car to drive you from one gate to the next. Ask your flight attendant to radio ahead for one.

Exercise 5 (Student's Book, page 200). *You and your nephew, Pietro, are flying to Hong Kong by way of Los Angeles. Listen to the announcements. Then read each situation. Listen to the announcements again and check the appropriate box.*

Number 1

Flight 104 to Los Angeles, continuing on to San Francisco, will be ready to board at Gate 8 in just a few minutes. Please have your boarding passes ready. If you have more than two pieces of carry-on luggage, you must check them at the gate. We will begin boarding in about five minutes.

Number 2

Flight 104 to Los Angeles, continuing on to San Francisco, is now ready for boarding. If you are traveling with a small child, or if you need extra time, please go to the gate now. If you are flying standby, please wait until all other passengers have boarded. If you are sitting in rows 17 to 24, please proceed to the gate for boarding. All other passengers, please wait until your row is called.

Number 3

Flight 104 is now continuing boarding. If you are sitting in rows 7 to 16, please proceed to the gate for boarding. Please have your boarding pass ready. If you are traveling standby, please continue to wait until all other passengers have boarded.

Number 4

Welcome to Flight 104 en route to Los Angeles with connecting flights to Tokyo and Hong Kong. Please pay careful attention while the flight attendants review some important safety procedures. In the unlikely event that the cabin loses pressure, oxygen masks will automatically descend from the overhead panels. If you are traveling with a child, put your own mask on first. Then assist the child. This cabin is equipped with six emergency exits. Please take the time to locate the one nearest to you.

Number 5

Good afternoon. This is Captain Richard Jackson speaking. We hope you're enjoying the flight. We are flying at an altitude of 35,000 feet, and we have clear skies with excellent visibility. For passengers sitting on the left—if you look out your window, you can see the Great Salt Lake. We're expecting to arrive on schedule, and the weather in Los Angeles should be good.

Number 6

We're beginning our initial descent into the Los Angeles area. The temperature is a balmy 72° and the skies are pretty clear. If you need information about a connecting flight, be sure to check the overhead monitors in the airport terminal. If you are continuing on to San Francisco, you can stay on the plane. Please put your seats and tray tables in an upright and locked position and make sure all carry-on luggage is safely stowed under the seat in front of you or in the overhead compartments. We should be landing in Los Angeles in approximately ten minutes. We thank you for flying UPAir and hope you have had a pleasant trip.

UNIT 16

Introduction (Student's Book, page 204). *Two candidates are running for mayor of a large city. Read and listen to their statements from a voter's guide.*

Four years ago, I promised to create a government that you could count on. Today, after four years as mayor of this great city, I am proud to say that we have come a long way. But the job is not finished. If I am reelected, together we will finish the work we started four years ago.

The backbone of our effort must be education. In the next ten years, there will be 16 million new jobs in the United States. A lot of those jobs will be filled by citizens of our city if we prepare them. But they won't be ready unless we improve our school system now.

My second priority is housing. It won't do any good to provide jobs if people continue to live in bad conditions. We must continue to rebuild housing in our city neighborhoods. My opponent talks about waging a war on crime and drugs. I agree that violent crime is a problem. But we're not going to solve the social problems in this city unless we house people better.

If our city offers an educated work force, business will thrive here. And as business thrives, we will have more money to rebuild housing. If our citizens have decent homes, then our neighborhoods will become healthy again. I'm not going to pretend that these problems will go away quickly. But if we work together, we will solve them.

I urge everyone to get out and vote on election day. Unless you vote, you will not have a say in the future of our great city.

*   *   *   *

Our streets are plagued by crime, and many people are afraid to go out of their homes. If I am elected, my highest priority will be to give the neighborhoods back to the citizens. A lot of this violence is being committed by very young offenders. My administration will say to these young people: If you want to stay out of trouble, we will help you do that. But if you do the crime, you'll do the time. If you commit a violent crime, you will go to jail, and you will serve your full sentence.

If I become mayor, I will help citizens protect their neighborhoods. I will put more police on the streets, demand mandatory prison sentences for drug dealers, and set up a cooperative program between police and communities. If I am elected, I will help you fight for every street, for every house. Together we will win.

But our young people won't have a reason to avoid crime unless they have some hope for their futures. That's why my second priority as mayor will be to bring businesses back to our city. My opponent raised taxes as soon as he took office four years ago. As a result, businesses left in droves—we have lost over 100,000 jobs in the last four years. If we lower taxes, businesses will return. If businesses return, our youth will have jobs to look forward to and some reason to hope. And if they have hope, they will not turn to a life of crime.

I urge you to vote for me next Tuesday. If I am elected, we'll hang out a sign: "Open for business again."

Exercise 6 (Student's Book, page 209). *Gabriela Ibarguen is talking about her political platform. Listen to the interview. Then read the list of issues. Listen again and check the things that Ibarguen promises to do if she is elected.*

Interviewer: Welcome to Meet the Candidates. Tonight we are talking to Gabriela Ibarguen, who, as most of you know, is running for mayor. Welcome, Ms. Ibarguen.

Ibarguen: Thanks, Kathleen. It's a pleasure to be here.

Interviewer: Ms. Ibarguen, what will you do first if you do become our city's mayor?

Ibarguen: If I'm elected, I'm going to hold neighborhood meetings throughout the city. I want people to come and talk about their concerns and present their ideas. That will be my first step. We have a lot to do after that. The biggest problems will be crime, health care, and education.

Interviewer: Tell us specifically what you have in mind.

Ibarguen: Again, I want to start in the neighborhoods, Kathleen. If I become our city's new mayor, I will open neighborhood recreation centers. We need places in the community for kids to play sports and take part in other activities like Scouting. I'm also going to extend the hours of local health centers. Right now, these centers close at six o'clock, and working parents can't use them. If I'm elected, I will keep neighborhood health centers open until 9 P.M. and on weekends.

Interviewer: What about education?

Ibarguen: I want to attract talented teachers to our city. I also want to keep skilled people in our school system. If I become your mayor, I will raise teachers' salaries so that good teachers will want to work here.

Interviewer: All these proposals are going to cost money. Are you planning to raise taxes?

Ibarguen: Unless we keep taxes low, businesses will continue to leave the city. And we need those businesses for jobs. If I am mayor, I won't raise taxes. In fact, I want to lower them.

Interviewer: What else will you do to keep business here?

Ibarguen: There's a lot we can do. If I have enough support, I'm going to improve our public transportation system. We can't attract business unless we have a good bus and subway system.

Interviewer: Thanks, Ms. Ibarguen. Our time is up. Good luck at the polls tomorrow.

UNIT 17

Introduction (Student's Book, page 211). *Read and listen to this version of a famous fairy tale.*

The Fisherman and His Wife

Once upon a time there was a poor fisherman and his wife who lived in a pigsty near the sea. Every day the man went to fish. One day, after waiting a very long time, he caught a very big fish. The fish said, "Please let me live. I'm not a regular fish—I'm an enchanted prince. It wouldn't do you any good if you killed me. If you ate me, I wouldn't even taste right." The fisherman agreed, threw the fish back into the clear water, and went home to his wife.

"Husband," said the wife, "didn't you catch anything today?"

"I caught a fish, but it said it was an enchanted prince, so I let it go."

"You mean you didn't wish for anything?" asked the wife.

"No," said the fisherman. "What do I need to wish for?"

"Just look around you," said the wife. "We live in a pigsty. I wish we had a nice little cottage. If we had a cottage, I would be a lot happier. You saved the prince's life. Go back and ask him for it."

The fisherman didn't want to go, but he did. He was afraid that if he asked for a cottage, the fish would be angry. But he was also afraid that if he didn't ask, his wife would be even angrier.

When he got to the sea, it was all green and yellow.

"My wife wishes we had a cottage," said the fisherman.

"Just go on back," said the fish. "She already has it."

When he returned home, the fisherman found his wife sitting outside a lovely little cottage. The kitchen was filled with food and all types of cooking utensils. Outside was a little garden with vegetables, fruit trees, hens, and ducks.

Things were fine for a week or two. Then the wife said, "This cottage is much too crowded. I wish we lived in a bigger house. If we lived in a big stone castle, I would be much happier. Go and ask the fish for it."

The fisherman didn't want to go, but he did. When he got to the sea, it was dark blue and gray.

"My wife wishes we lived in a big stone castle," he said to the fish.

"Just go on back. She's standing in front of the door," said the fish.

When he returned home, the fisherman found his wife on the steps of a great big stone castle. The inside was filled with beautiful gold furniture, chandeliers, and carpets, and there were servants everywhere.

The next morning the wife woke up and said, "I wish I were King of all this land."

"What would you do if you were King?" asked her husband.

"If I were King, I would own all this land. Go on back and ask the fish for it."

This time, the sea was all blackish gray, and the water was rough and smelled terrible.

"What does she want now?" asked the fish.

"She wants to be King," said the embarrassed fisherman.

"Just go on back. She already is."

When the fisherman returned home, he found an enormous palace. Everything inside was made of marble and pure gold, and it was surrounded by soldiers with drums and trumpets. His wife was seated on a throne, and he said to her, "How nice for you that you are King. Now we won't need to wish for anything else."

But his wife was not satisfied, "If I were Emperor, I would be much happier," she said. "I am King and I command you to go back and ask the fish to make me Emperor."

Reluctantly, the fisherman went back to the fish, and again the wish was granted. Next, his wife wanted to be Pope, and that wish, too, was granted. "Wife, now be satisfied," said the fisherman. "You're Pope. You can't be anything more."

The wife, however, wasn't convinced. She kept thinking and thinking about what more she could be.

"I wish I were like the Lord of the universe," she finally said. "If I were like the Lord, I could make the sun rise and set. Then I would be much happier. Go right now and tell the fish that I want to be like the Lord."

"Oh, no," said the fisherman. "The fish can't do that. If I were you, I wouldn't ask for anything else." But his wife got so furious that the poor fisherman ran back to the fish. There was a terrible storm, and the sea was pitch black with waves as high as mountains.

"Well, what does she want now?" asked the fish.

"She wishes she were like the Lord of the universe," said the fisherman.

"Just go on back. She's sitting in the pigsty again."

And they are still sitting there today.

Exercise 7 (Student's Book, page 220). *You are going to listen to a modern fairy tale about Cindy, a clever young girl, and a toad. Before you listen, read the statements. Then listen again and mark each statement true* (T) *or false* (F).

Once there was a young girl named Cindy who was very good at math, sports, and languages. She wanted to be a scientist when she grew up so that she could help many people. One day, while Cindy was playing soccer in the park with her friends, the ball flew into the woods. She looked and looked for the ball, but she couldn't see it anywhere.

"I wish I could find that soccer ball," Cindy muttered angrily. At that she heard a strange sound.

"Ree-beep. Over here! Your ball is over here."

She looked in the direction of the sound, and she saw the soccer ball in the middle of some bushes. Next to the ball was a large toad.

"Thanks for finding the ball," she told the toad.

"You're welcome," said the toad. "But before I give it to you, you have to grant me one wish."

Cindy started to run toward the ball, but she couldn't get through the bushes. There was some sort of magic spell around them. "What's your wish?" she asked the toad. "Please hurry up. We want to finish our game."

"I wish that you would marry me."

"Yecch!" screamed Cindy. "You're a toad. I'm a girl. I can't marry you."

"I'm not really a toad," he replied. "I'm under a spell. If you married me, you would break the spell. I would become a handsome prince. And if I were a prince, you would be my princess."

Cindy thought about the princesses she had read about in magazines. "I don't think so, Toad," Cindy told him. "You see, I plan to become a scientist and help a lot of people when I grow up. If I were your princess, I'd have to spend a lot of time having my photograph taken and going to ceremonies. If I did that, I'd be too busy to study science. But thanks anyway." Cindy turned to leave the woods.

"Wait!" shouted the toad. "If you really wanted to help people, you wouldn't leave me here in these bushes."

Cindy stopped. "If you give me back the soccer ball, I'll try to help you. But no weddings."

The toad agreed, and Cindy picked up the ball.

"So, who put you under the spell?" she asked.

"A magician turned me into a toad. He also gave me some magic powers. He keeps telling me that if I used my powers properly, I'd find a way to become a prince again. But so far, nothing has worked."

"Can you grant wishes?" asked Cindy.

"Just one," replied the toad.

"Then I wish you would turn me into a scientist right now. If I were a scientist, I would find a way to turn you back into a prince."

In a flash, Cindy and the toad found themselves in a large, modern laboratory. Cindy thought hard and worked long hours. At last she succeeded in turning the toad back into a prince. The prince became a good king, and Cindy worked hard in her laboratory. Her discoveries helped many people.

UNIT 18

Introduction (Student's Book, page 222). *Read and listen to this video review from the entertainment section of a newspaper.*

Best Bets for Holiday Viewing

It's a Wonderful Life (1946)**** What would have happened if you had never been born? George Bailey (played by Jimmy Stewart) learns the answer in Frank Capra's movie classic.

When the film opens, George Bailey, the president of a small-town building-and-loan association, is in desperate trouble with his business. Unable to see a way out, he is about to commit suicide by jumping off a bridge. In a long flashback, we see George as a boy, playing on a frozen pond with his brother and friends. Suddenly his brother falls through the ice. Without thinking of his own safety, George pulls him out of the water. If George hadn't been there, his brother Harry would have drowned. We later learn that Harry went on to become a war hero. If he had died that day, he wouldn't have saved hundreds of other lives in battle.

The scene is typical of George's life. As the flashback continues, we see George as a young man, bursting to do great things in the world outside his home town of Bedford Falls. However, each time he starts to fulfill his own dreams, someone needs him at home. George always stays, even though he feels frustrated and somewhat bitter. He wishes he could have gone to college, like his brother. He wishes he had traveled around the world and built great buildings. But George can't refuse the people who need him.

Now, with his business in ruin and facing a possible jail sentence because of misplaced money, George needs a miracle to save him from suicide. The miracle appears in the form of Clarence, a pudgy, middle-aged "second-class angel" sent down from heaven to rescue George.

"I suppose it would have been better if I had never been born at all," George bitterly tells his genial rescuer.

Clarence then teaches George a hard lesson. In a series of painful episodes, he shows him what life would have been like in Bedford Falls without George Bailey. George goes back to the site of his mother's home. He finds, instead, a depressing boardinghouse. If George had not supported his mother after his father's death, she would have become an embittered, overworked boardinghouse owner. George's own home is a ruin, and his wife, Mary, is living a sad life of isolation. If she had not married George, she would not have had a happy family life. She wouldn't have converted the crumbling old mansion into a beautiful home. Each vignette is more disturbing than the last, until finally we see the graves of hundreds of soldiers who died because George's brother had not been there to save them.

At that point, George is desperate to return to his own life, no matter how different it is from his boyhood fantasies. He returns home and joyfully announces that he is going to jail. However, the real ending brings a heartwarming holiday message. "It's a Wonderful Life" shows us the importance of each person's life and how each of our lives touches those of others. We see through George's eyes how the lives of those around him would have been different if George hadn't known them. If I had only one movie to watch this holiday season, I would choose this movie. Highly recommended.

Exercise 5 (Student's Book, page 228). *Some friends are discussing a party. Listen to their short conversations. Then listen again and circle the letter of the sentence you heard.*

Conversation 1:

I haven't seen Stephanie lately. Have you?

No. Why wasn't she at David's party last weekend?

Er, I don't know.

Hhmm. If I'd had her number, I would've called her.

Oh. Isn't it in the phone book?

I looked, but I couldn't find it.

Conversation 2:

You know, I didn't see Jean-Claude at the party. I thought the two of you were good friends. What happened?

I would've invited him, if he'd been in town.

He was out of town? Where was he?

Chicago.

Conversation 3:

Brian seemed kind of depressed.

He was. He's unhappy with his job. Remember that job offer he had? He turned it down.

Oh, how come?

If he'd changed jobs, he wouldn't have gotten the same benefits.

Oh, I see why he didn't do it, then.

Conversation 4:

After the party, we all watched *It's a Wonderful Life* on TV. Have you ever seen it?

Many times. It's on TV every year around the holidays. What did you think of it?

I would've liked it better on a big screen.

Yeah. Sometimes screen size really makes a big difference.

Conversation 5:

How do you know Tania?

She was in my class last year. How do *you* know her?

She's a friend of my sister's.

I wish David had invited her.

Me too.

Conversation 6:

That woman Rosario seemed really nice.

Oh. Did you ask for her phone number?

No. Do you think I should have?

I would have.

Well, maybe I can get it from John.

Good idea.

Conversation 7:

Was Holly at the party?

Yeah. Holly was there.

What about Greg?

He was there, too. Holly was avoiding him all night.

Oh. That must've really been hard for both of them.

I know. If I'd invited Holly, I wouldn't have invited Greg.

Me neither.

Conversation 8:

Where were Tony and Rosa? I don't remember seeing them at the party.

They weren't able to come.

Oh, that's too bad.

If the party hadn't been on a Saturday, they could've come.

Oh. Is Tony still working on weekends?

Yeah. That's why he couldn't make it. And Rosa didn't want to go without him.

UNIT 19

Introduction (Student's Book, page 239). *Read and listen to the article about friendship.*

A Word with Many Meanings

Almost everyone has at least one. Most people have several. But definitions of *friend* vary from person to person. For some, a friend is someone who plays cards with you every Friday night. For others, a friend is someone who has known you all your life. Someone whose family knows you, too. Others reserve the term for someone who knows your innermost secrets. What one person defines as a friend, another calls an acquaintance, and vice versa.

If definitions of friendship can vary so much within a single culture, imagine the differences between cultures. But interestingly, there have been very few cross-cultural studies on the topic. Writing in 1970, anthropologist Margaret Mead compared notions of friendship in the United States, France, Germany, and Great Britain. She says:

For the French, friendship is a one-to-one relationship that demands a keen awareness of the other person's intellect, temperament and particular interests. A friend is someone who draws out your own best qualities. . . . Your political philosophy assumes more depth, appreciation of a play becomes sharper, taste in food is accentuated. . . , enjoyment of a sport is intensified.

In contrast to the French, says Mead, friendship in Germany has more to do with feelings. Young Germans form bonds early, and usually incorporate their friends into their family life. According to Mead,

Between French friends, who have chosen each other for the congeniality of their point of view, lively disagreement and sharpness of argument are the breath of life. But for Germans, whose friendships are based on mutuality of feeling, deep disagreement on any subject that matters to both is regarded as a tragedy.

As a result of their expectations of friendship, young Germans who come to the United States often have difficulty making friends with Americans, "who view friendship more tentatively . . . ," reports Mead. These friendships are subject to changes in intensity as people move, change their jobs, marry, or discover new interests.

The British follow another pattern. According to Mead, the basis for friendship among the British is shared activity. Unlike German relationships, British friendships usually remain outside the family. Mead compares this type of friendship to a dance whose partners must stay in step with each other.

Americans who have made English friends comment that, even years later, "you can take up just where you left off." Meeting after a long interval, friends are like a couple who begin to dance again when the orchestra strikes up after a pause.

Studies of American friendships indicate that, like the French and British, people in the United States often form friendships around interests. They have friends who enjoy sports, friends who go shopping with them, friends who share a hobby. However, like the Germans, they also form long-lasting friendships which are based on feelings. In fact, the variety of relationships that Americans call friendships can confuse people from other cultures, especially when Americans say things like, "I just made a new friend yesterday." However, the term does not seem to confuse Americans, who know very well the difference between friends and acquaintances. According to a 1970 survey in a U.S. magazine, *Psychology Today,* those who answered the survey "find it easy to distinguish between close and casual friends and reported they have more close friends than casual ones."

Although different people and cultures emphasize different aspects of friendship, there is one element which is always present, and that is the element of choice. We may not be able to select our families, our co-workers, or even the people that ride the bus with us, but we can pick our friends. As Mead puts it, "A friend is someone who chooses and is chosen." It is exactly this freedom of choice, without the legal ties of marriage, that makes friendship such a special and unique relationship.

Exercise 6 (Student's Book, page 249). *Some friends are at a high school reunion. They haven't seen one another for twenty-five years. Listen to the friends talk about the people at the table below. Then listen again and label the people with their correct names.*

A: Wow, people have really changed!

B: You're not kidding! Can you recognize anyone at that table over there?

A: Uhm. Let's see. Isn't that Bob Gramer?

B: Which one?

A: The man who has the beard and moustache.

B: You know, I think you're right! He actually looks even better than he used to!

A: And isn't that Ann Richardson over there?

B: Where? The woman sitting next to Bob?

A: No. The one who's wearing glasses.

B: You're right! That is Ann! And that's John Smith!

A: Where?

B: The man who's talking to Ann.

A: So, who's the woman sitting next to Bob?

B: You know, that must be Pat. Remember Pat Wayne? She and Bob used to go out together.

A: Do you think they got married?

B: I don't know. Maybe. Who's the woman whose back is toward us? I can't see her face . . .

A: You mean the one who's wearing the big hat?

B: Uh-huh. Do you think that could be Sue what's-her-name?

A: Sue Rogers?

B: Yeah, that's the one. Didn't she always use to wear hats, even inside?

A: Yep! You're right! Some things never change! That's Sue all right.

B: She got married to Al Baker, didn't she?

A: Yeah. But that's not Al who's sitting next to her.

B: No. It looks more like Pete Rizzo.

A: Pete Rizzo? Who's he? The name sounds familiar.

B: Oh, you remember Pete. He was the guy who ran for class president in our senior year.

A: The man who's sitting next to Sue?

B: Uh-huh. He's changed a lot, but I'm sure it's Pete.

A: Why don't we go over and find out?

B: Good idea. Then we can find out who the couple is that's sitting between John and Pat.

A: Yeah, I don't have a clue who they are!

UNIT 20

Introduction (Student's Book, page 253). *Read and listen to a review of two autobiographies.*

Torn between Two Worlds

I'm filled to the brim with what I'm about to lose—images of Cracow, which I loved as one loves a person, of the sun-baked villages where we had taken summer vacations, of the hours I spent poring over passages of music with my music teacher, of conversations and escapades with friends.

So writes Eva Hoffman, author of *Lost in Translation, A Life in a New Language* (New York: Penguin, 1989). Hoffman, whose early childhood was spent in Cracow, moved with her family to Vancouver, Canada, when she was thirteen. Her autobiography relates her experiences as she is uprooted from her beloved Cracow and as she struggles to understand her surroundings and herself in a new language.

In spite of poverty, a cramped apartment, and her parents' wartime memories, home to Ewa Wydra (Hoffman's Polish name) had seemed a paradise. Cracow was a city of "shimmering light and shadow," a place where life was lived intensely. As a child, she had visited its cafes with her father, who she watched in lively conversations with his friends. Her mother, she recalls, also took her to cafes where they ate ice cream from tall, elegant glasses. Hoffman remembers neighbors, "people between whose apartments there's constant movement with kids, sugar, eggs, and teatime visits." By the age of seven, Ewa was able to travel to some places alone. Her friendship with Marek, whose apartment she visited almost daily, deepened, and the two grew up assuming that they would be married.

At eight, Ewa and Marek began piano lessons together, and Ewa's musical talent became apparent to her teachers and her family. When she was twelve, a new teacher was found for her, one with whom some well-known young pianists had studied. At music school, Ewa developed her other deep friendship, with Basia, another music student. Pani Witeszczak, Ewa's teacher, was the last person Ewa said good-bye to before she left Poland. "What do you think you'll miss most?" her teacher asked.

"Everything. Cracow. The School. Basia. You. Everything . . . " It turns out that this is the person and the room I can least bear to leave: after all, it's here that I've felt most intimately understood; it's here that I've felt most intensely all my hopes for the future . . .

At her new school in Vancouver, Ewa is given her English name, Eva, which her teachers find easier to pronounce. Eva, however, feels no connection to the name, or to the English name of anything that she feels is important. All her memories and feelings are still in her first language, Polish. The story of Eva as she grows up and comes to terms with her new identity and language is fascinating and moving. *Lost in Translation* is highly recommended reading.

Also recommended is *The Rice Room* by Ben Fong-Torres (New York: Hyperion, 1994). Unlike Hoffman, a first-generation immigrant, Fong-Torres was born in the United States of parents who had emigrated from China. Many of the problems that he faces, however, are similar to Hoffman's. Fong-Torres must try to reconcile his family's culture with his new culture. To do this, he must grapple with a language barrier. A successful radio announcer and journalist, Fong-Torres describes the frustration of trying to communicate with his parents, for whom English is still a foreign language.

Over the years, I've talked with my parents many times, but we've never really communicated. . . . When we talk, it sounds like baby talk—at least my half of it. . . . I don't know half the words I need; I either never learned them, or I heard but forgot them. The Chinese language is stuck in its own place and time. When we were growing up, we learned to say *police* in Chinese: *look yee*. That means "green clothes," which referred, we'd learn years later, to the uniforms worn by the police in Canton. There are no Chinese words for: "computer," "laser," "Watergate," "annuity," "AIDS," or "recession." When the telephone was invented, the Chinese, who concocted so many things that the rest of the world has to find words for, simply called it "electric line."

. . . What we have here is a language barrier as formidable, to my mind, as the Great Wall of China.

The barrier has stood . . . through countless moments when we needed to talk with each other, about the things parents and children usually discuss: jobs and careers; marriage and divorce; health and finances; history, the present, and the future.

This is one of the great sadnesses of my life. How ironic, I would think. . . . I'm a journalist and a broadcaster—my job is to communicate—and I can't with the two people with whom I want to most.

First- or second-generation immigrant—the issues persist. These two books eloquently describe the lives of people trying to bridge the gap between the worlds that were left behind and the worlds that they now call home.

Exercise 5 (Student's Book, page 262). *Listen to a woman describe the room of her childhood. Then listen again and choose the correct picture.*

I remember my childhood bedroom very well. It was a small room, which I shared with my older sister, Katie. There were two beds. The one which I slept in was in a corner. My sister's bed, under which was a large beautiful old rug, was in the middle of the room against the wall. To the left of my bed was a window through which we could see a tree. There was also a big wall mirror in which we both enjoyed looking at our own reflections. That was in the corner that was nearest my sister's bed. Across from my bed was a desk at which we both did our homework after dinner, which we always ate in the kitchen with the rest of the family. My sister, whose greatest passion in life those days was music, kept her guitar on her bed, where she would practice for hours after our homework was done. I remember those as happy times, when we were both young and full of hope and excitement.

UNIT 21

Introduction (Student's Book, page 269). *Read and listen to this excerpt from an article about lying.*

The Truth about Lying

At 9:00 Dick Spivak's bank telephoned and said his credit card payment was late. "The check is in the mail," Dick replied quickly. At 11:45 Dick left for a 12:00 meeting across town. Arriving late, he told his client that traffic had been bad. That evening, Dick's fiancée wore a new dress. Dick hated it. "It looks just great on you," he said.

Three lies in one day! Yet Dick Spivak is just an ordinary guy. Each time, he told himself that sometimes the truth causes too many problems. Most of us tell similar white lies, harmless untruths that help us avoid trouble. In fact, everyone probably recognizes these four most frequent reasons people tell lies:

1. To get something more quickly or to avoid unpleasant situations: "I have to have that report by 5:00 today," or "I tried to call you, but your line was busy."

2. To appear more acceptable to a new friend or to feel better about yourself: "I run a mile every day," or "I'm looking better these days."

3. To make a polite excuse: "I'd love to go to your party, but I have to work this evening."

4. To protect someone else's feelings: "That tie looks great on you."

Like Dick, almost everyone lies sometimes. How often depends in part on our age, education, gender, and even where we live. According to one U.S. survey, young, college-educated men from New England lie the most, while elderly, high-school-educated women from the South are the most truthful. In general, women are more truthful than men (57 percent report that they always tell the truth), and honesty increases as we get older.

While most people use little white lies to make life easier, the majority of Americans are concerned about honesty in both public and personal life. In a recent survey, seven out of ten people said that they were dissatisfied with current standards of honesty. The majority told interviewers that people today are less honest than they were ten years ago. However, in spite of our belief that things are getting worse, lying seems to be an age-old human problem. The French philosopher Vauvenargues, writing in the eighteenth century, touched on the truth when he wrote, "All men are born truthful and die liars."

Exercise 5 (Student's Book, page 277). *Read Lisa's weekly planner. Then listen to the conversations. Lisa wasn't always honest. Listen again and note the differences between what Lisa said and the truth.*

Conversation 1:

Alex: Hi, Lisa. This is Alex. Let's have dinner together Saturday night. I know you don't like to eat meat, but I found this great new vegetarian restaurant on the West Side.

Lisa: I'd really love to, Alex, but my parents are in town for the weekend. I want to spend time with them on Saturday night. Let's do it another weekend, OK?

Alex: Sure.

Conversation 2:

Lisa: So, what do you do in your spare time, Ben?

Ben: I like to go to the gym when I get a chance. I usually work out about three times a week.

Lisa: Oh really? So do I. I'm even taking aerobics on Sunday, and I love it. I never miss a class.

Conversation 3:

Lisa: Hi, Mark. This is Lisa. How's the report coming?

Mark: Pretty well. Let's see. . . .Today's Monday. I'll have it ready for you tomorrow morning.

Lisa: Gee, Mark. I really need to have it today.

Mark: Oh? What's the rush?

Lisa: Our weekly staff meeting is Monday afternoon. I need to have the report before the meeting.

Mark: OK. I'll do my best.

Conversation 4:

Lisa: Dinner looks absolutely wonderful, Chris.

Chris: Try the meat sauce. I want to know what you think.

Lisa: Mmmmmm. I love it. It's just delicious. How did you make it?

Chris: Oh, it's an old family recipe. But I can give it to you if you like.

Lisa: Yes, please do. I'd love to make this sauce.

UNIT 22

Introduction (Student's Book, page 280). *Read and listen to this excerpt from an article about Hurricane Andrew.*

Force Five

In late August, 1992, meteorologists from the National Hurricane Center in Florida noticed a small tropical storm over West Africa. When the storm grew stronger and moved west, they named it Andrew. A few days after that, Lixion Avila of the National Hurricane Center, who had been tracking Andrew all night, called his boss at 3:00 A.M. and told him that they had a hurricane. Andrew quickly grew to a force four, and the National Hurricane Center went on the air to warn Florida residents that a giant storm was coming. They said Andrew might even be a force five—the most powerful class of hurricanes.

Government workers told people that they had to leave homes near the coast, and television reporters announced that everyone should buy extra food and water. As Floridians prepared for Hurricane Andrew, stores and gas stations reported that they could not keep up with demands for gasoline, canned food, and bottled water.

In spite of their preparation, Andrew's 170-mile-an-hour winds caused terrible damage. After the storm, officials at the National Hurricane Center reported that the electricity had gone out and the radar had been torn off the roof of the twelve-story Center.

Those in private homes and trailer parks suffered most. One family said they had run from room to room with windows exploding around them. Jim Jenkins, who had just moved to Florida in June, told a reporter that if he had known what a force-five hurricane was like, he would have left immediately. He said that he and his family had spent a terrifying night in a closet after a trailer had blown through the house. Jim said, "I'm from New Jersey, and I've seen hurricanes. But there are no words to describe this storm."

After the terror came the realization of loss. In one trailer park, a young woman held her baby as she sifted through the scraps of metal that had been their home. Her husband, still dazed, told us he had lost his home, his job, and his dog in just two hours. While the government struggled to provide emergency services for the victims, officials predicted it would cost at least $20 billion to rebuild after Andrew.

Exercise 5 (Student's Book, page 289). *Work in groups of four. Listen to the weather advisory. Listen again and check the correct information. It's all right to leave something blank. You're not expected to answer every question. After you listen, you will pool your information.*

The weather service has issued a winter storm warning. About a foot of snow has fallen in our area since early this morning, and more snow is expected during the day. All schools closed by 10:00. We advise students, teachers, and other employees to return home immediately. Schools may remain closed tomorrow, so keep listening for further reports.

Snow and high winds are causing dangerous conditions on the roads. Drivers must drive slowly and with a great deal of caution to avoid accidents. If possible, everyone should avoid driving until conditions improve. If you must drive, you should take along extra clothing and blankets. You should also make certain you have plenty of gas.

Many government offices will close today. Libraries are closing at 1 P.M. However, post offices will stay open until 5:00. All government offices will be closed tomorrow.

Many businesses in the area are also closing early because of the storm. Banks are closing at noon to allow employees time to get home safely. Most supermarkets and gas stations will remain open until this evening. You are advised to stock up on food and other necessities since driving conditions could be difficult for several days.

UNIT 23

Introduction (Student's Book, page 291). *Read and listen to a radio interview with the director of a sleep clinic.*

Connie: Good morning! This is Connie Sung, bringing you "Here's to Your Health!," a program about modern health issues. Today we've invited Dr. Ray Thorpe to talk to us about insomnia. Dr. Thorpe is the director of the U.S. Sleep Disorders Clinic and he has just written a book, *Night Shift*, which will be coming out shortly. Dr. Thorpe, welcome to "Here's to Your Health!"

Dr. Thorpe: Thanks, Connie. It's great to be here.

Connie: In your book, you tell people to pay more attention to sleep disorders. What's the big deal about losing a little sleep?

Dr. Thorpe: Whenever people ask me that, Connie, I tell them to think of the biggest industrial disaster they've ever heard about. It usually turns out that it was caused at least in part by sleep deprivation. On a personal level, think about what can happen if you drive when you're tired. Did you know that every year, up to 200,000 automobile accidents are caused by drowsy drivers?

Connie: Wow. That *is* a big problem.

Dr. Thorpe: Yes, and it adds up. Besides the price in human misery, we figure that fatigue costs U.S. businesses about $70 billion a year.

Connie: Now I see why we should be paying more attention to sleep. . . . But let's bring this back to the personal level. Say that I'm suffering from insomnia. I come to your clinic. What advice would you give me?

Dr. Thorpe: First, I would find out about some of your habits. If you smoked or drank alcohol, I would tell you to stop.

Connie: Really? A lot of people have a drink to relax.

Dr. Thorpe: Bad idea. Both habits are not only bad for your general health, but they interfere with sleep.

Connie: What about the old-fashioned remedies like warm milk? Are those mistakes too?

Dr. Thorpe: Actually, a lot of home remedies do make sense. We tell patients to have a high-carbohydrate snack like a banana before they retire for the night. Warm milk works too. But I'd advise you not to eat a heavy meal before bed.

Connie: Does exercise help?

Dr. Thorpe: Yes, if you exercise regularly, you'll sleep better. But we always ask patients not to exercise within three hours of bedtime.

Connie: My mother always said to get up and scrub the floor when I couldn't sleep.

Dr. Thorpe: That works. I advised one patient to balance his checkbook. He went right to sleep, just to escape from the task.

Connie: Besides insomnia, what other problems do you treat?

Dr. Thorpe: Many people say that they get to sleep with no trouble, but that they wake up feeling exhausted.

Connie: You know, that happens to me. What's that all about?

Dr. Thorpe: You sleep in cycles of light sleep and deep slumber. If you feel tired after a night's sleep, you could have a problem with the sleep cycles. We often ask patients with this problem to spend a night at our sleep clinic.

Connie: What happens there?

Dr. Thorpe: We have electronic equipment that permits us to monitor the patient through the night. In fact, if you're interested, why don't you come and spend a night in the clinic?

Connie: Maybe I should do that. . . .

Exercise 4 (Student's Book, page 297). *Juan went to a headache clinic. Listen to the conversation to find out what he learned there. Then listen again and check the appropriate column to show what they told him to do, what they told him not to do, and what they didn't mention.*

Ann: Hi, Juan. How are you doing?

Juan: Oh, well actually not that great. I've been having a lot of headaches lately. In fact, I just got back from a headache clinic.

Ann: Really? What did they tell you?

Juan: Let's see. . . . They said to get regular exercise. Oh, and they also told me to get eight hours' sleep. They said fatigue causes headaches.

Ann: That's interesting. You work at a sleep clinic and you haven't been getting enough sleep. Did they give you some pain killers?

Juan: No. They told me not to take pain killers right now. They said to try to treat the headaches without medication first.

Ann: That sounds good. What did they suggest?

Juan: Uhmm. They said to use an ice pack.

Ann: That's a good idea. How about massaging around your eyes?

Juan: They didn't tell me to do that. Does it help?

Ann: I think so. What else did they say about preventing headaches?

Juan: Oh, they said not to eat three big meals a day. They told me to eat several small meals instead.

Ann: Do you have to avoid certain foods?

Juan: Yeah. Chocolate. They said not to eat chocolate.

Ann: How about cheese? I've heard that cheese can cause headaches.

Juan: They didn't tell me to avoid cheese. Hey, you seem to know a lot about this.

Ann: Oh, I've been going to a headache clinic for a long time. Let me show you how to massage around your eyes. That really helps me.

UNIT 24

Introduction (Student's Book, page 300). *Read and listen to this excerpt from an article about job interviews.*

The Stress Interview

A few weeks ago, Melissa Morrow had an unusual job interview. First, the interviewer asked Melissa why she couldn't work under pressure. Before she could answer, he asked if she had cleaned out her car recently. Then he wanted to know who had written her application letter for her. Melissa was shocked, but she handled herself well. She asked the interviewer whether he was going to ask her serious questions. Then she politely ended the interview.

Melissa had had a stress interview, a type of job interview that features tough, tricky questions, long silences, and negative evaluations of the candidate. To the candidate, this strategy may seem like unnecessary nastiness on the part of the interviewer. However, some positions require an ability to handle just this kind of pressure. If there is an accident in a nuclear power plant, for example, the plant's public relations officer must remain poised when unfriendly reporters ask how the accident could have occurred.

The hostile atmosphere of a stress interview gives the employer a chance to watch a candidate react to pressure. In one case, the interviewer ended each interview by telling the candidate, "We're really not sure that you're the right person for this job." One very promising candidate asked the interviewer angrily if he was sure he knew how to conduct an interview. She clearly could not handle the pressure she would encounter as a television news anchor—the job she was interviewing for.

Stress questioning has its limitations, however. It's an appropriate technique only for positions which feature extreme on-the-job pressure. Accountants, secretaries, and computer programmers all experience job pressures, but not enough to merit a stress interview. Even when the job warrants it, this strategy can backfire and alienate good candidates. Melissa Morrow came through her interview with flying colors but later asked herself if she really wanted to work for that company. Her answer was no.

A word of warning to job candidates: Not all tough questioning constitutes a legitimate stress interview. Some questions are just illegal unless the answers are directly related to the job. If your interviewer asks how old you are, whether you are married, or how much money you owe, you can refuse to answer. If you think a question is improper, you should ask the interviewer how the answer specifically relates to that job. If you don't get a satisfactory explanation, you don't have to answer the question.

When an interviewer introduces pressure to create a reaction, it's easy to lose your composure. Remember that all interviews create stress. If you expect it and learn to control your response, you can remain poised, even in a stress interview.

Exercise 5 (Student's Book, page 309). *You are going to hear a job interview that takes place in the United States. Before you listen, read the chart about equal employment opportunity laws in the United States. Then listen to the interview and check the topics the interviewer asks about. The interviewer asks seven illegal questions. Listen again and note the illegal questions.*

Interviewer: Your résumé is very impressive, Ms. . . . uhm . . . Tsourikov.

Tsourikov: That's Tsourikov.

Interviewer: Tsourikov. So, tell me, Ms. Tsourikov, why did you leave your job at Q & L Enterprises?

Tsourikov: Well, I had worked there for more than fifteen years. Two years ago, I went back to school and got my degree in accounting. I want a position that uses my new skills, and there's nothing available at Q & L.

Interviewer: Fifteen years. Hmmm. That's a pretty long time. How old are you?

Tsourikov: [clearing her throat and laughing nervously] Let's just say that I'm old enough to have a lot of valuable experience and still young enough to bring a lot of energy to the job.

Interviewer: I'm sure you are. Are you married?

Tsourikov: Er, yes. I'm married and I have two grown children.

Interviewer: I see. What do you know about this company? I mean, why do you want to work for us?

Tsourikov: I know you're one of the three leading producers of household appliances and that your products have a reputation for excellence. I would like to be part of your company, and I know I could make a significant contribution.

Interviewer: Tsourikov. That's an unusual name. What nationality are you?

Tsourikov: Well, I took my husband's last name . . .

Interviewer: Oh, yes. What does your husband do, Mrs. Tsourikov? [mispronounced]

Tsourikov: Tsourikov. [corrected] He's a data processor.

Interviewer: Do you owe anyone any money?

Tsourikov: Er . . . We owe some money on our credit cards . . . , and uhm, we do still have a mortgage on our home . . .

Interviewer: OK . . . Tell me, what computer programs are you familiar with?

Tsourikov: I've used Lotus 123, Excel, and WordPerfect.

Interviewer: Have you ever been arrested?

Tsourikov: Excuse me?

Interviewer: Have you ever been arrested?

Tsourikov: Er, no. Why do you ask?

Interviewer: Just checking. We have to be very careful who we hire these days. . . . Why don't you tell me a little more about yourself. Do you consider yourself successful?

Tsourikov: Yes. I was very successful at my last job, as I'm sure my employer would tell you.

Interviewer: Good. How tall are you, Mrs. Tsourikov?

Tsourikov: How tall am I? I'm sorry, but before I answer that question, can you tell me how it specifically relates to this job?

[Interviewer is buzzed, and he picks up the phone.]

Interviewer: Yes? . . . Uhm, would you excuse me a moment? I have to take this call.

UNIT 25

Introduction (Student's Book, page 312). *Read and listen to this magazine article and interview.*

The Tip

In China it's illegal. In Australia it's not customary. In Germany it's included in the bill. In the United States and Canada it's common but follows no logical pattern: You tip the person who delivers you flowers, but not the person who delivers you a package. And in restaurants, you tip according to the amount of your bill, but not according to the amount of labor involved in bringing you your meal. So, what's a person to do?

Our correspondent, Marjorie Fuchs, interviewed Irene Frankel, author of *Tips on Tipping* (New Jersey, 1990) to help sort through the tipping maze.

Fuchs: Tell me why you decided to write a book about tipping.

Frankel: Well, I was working with a lot of people who were living here from abroad and who I thought needed to have a book on tipping because they had come from cultures where tipping wasn't a custom. But when I started talking to people about the book, I found that the people I was speaking to, who were mostly Americans, had a lot of questions about tipping also. So what started out as a book primarily for people living here from abroad became a book primarily for anybody living here.

Fuchs: That's very interesting. It's true that a lot of people get very nervous when it comes to tipping. Does your book explain who to tip?

Frankel: Oh, absolutely. It tells you who to tip in a variety of situations: in restaurants, hotels, taxis. It also tells you how much to tip and when to tip. Equally important, it tells you when not to tip.

Fuchs: Yes. That is important to know. Now, I've always wondered when the custom of tipping began.

Frankel: Well, actually it's a very old custom, and it started in England in the late 1700s. There was a box in coffee houses that was labeled *T I P. T I P* stood for "to insure promptness," and the box was placed by the door to let people put money in before they got service to ensure that they got good service. So it used to be that tipping was done *before* service was given, and then gradually it became reversed so that today tipping is done afterwards.

Fuchs: Now, what about bad service? I'd really like to know what to do when I get bad service. Should I still tip?

Frankel: I recommend that you tip *something* when you get bad service so that the person who gave you the bad service is aware that you didn't just forget to leave a tip. But I don't think you should tip the ordinary amount.

Fuchs: Now, suppose I don't know whether to tip someone, and I left your book at home. Is it OK to ask?

Frankel: Absolutely. If you don't know whether or not to tip someone, the best thing to do is to ask. Most people will probably say, "It's up to you." They won't tell you exactly what to do, but they will tell you what most people do.

Fuchs: Is there any reason why we tip a restaurant server but not a flight attendant?

Frankel: The rules for tipping in this country are very illogical, and there are often contradictions in who we tip. A flight attendant serves beverages and meals, just like a server in a restaurant. But we tip only the servers. In fact, flight attendants aren't allowed to accept tips.

Fuchs: I see. Now, when the waiter or waitress brings me my change, I never know if it's OK to leave pennies. What's the word on pennies?

Frankel: Well, there are a couple of things about pennies. If you're taking a taxi somewhere and you want to know how much to tip the taxi driver, you don't figure out 15 percent to the penny and then tip with pennies. But if you're in a restaurant, and the change comes back with some pennies, it's fine to leave them as part of the tip.

Fuchs: Before we leave the topic of restaurants, can you explain why a restaurant tip is tied to the amount of the bill rather than the amount of labor involved? After all, bringing out a $10 dish of food involves the same amount of work as carrying out a $2 plate.

Frankel: Can I explain why? No. And you're right. It makes no sense. It's just the way it is. But, I guess you could look at other occupations and compare the amount of labor somebody does in two occupations, and there are inequities in those kinds of things as well. So, the answer is: Nothing is fair.

Fuchs: One last question. Suppose I'm planning a trip to, let's say, Egypt, for example. Tell me how I can learn about tipping customs in that country—or any other country, for that matter.

Frankel: OK. Well, as you know, tipping isn't international, and so it's really important to find out before you go abroad what the tipping customs are. Usually travel agents are aware of what the rules are for tipping in each country, or you can get the information from a travel book. If you're really not sure, and you don't have a travel agent or you don't want to buy a book or go to the library, you can call up the consulate and they'll let you know.

Fuchs: Well, thanks for all the good tips. I know our readers will find them very helpful. I certainly did.

Frankel: Thank you.

Exercise 5 (Student's Book, page 321). *A travel agent is being interviewed on a call-in radio show. The topic is tipping. Listen to the callers' questions. Then listen again and for each question decide on an appropriate response.*

Host: Good morning. You're listening to RAP talk radio. I'm your host, Ed Collins, and our topic this morning is tipping—when, who, where, and how much. For those of you who have just tuned in, we've been talking to Alicia Marksen, who owns and operates a travel agency. Ms. Marksen is now ready to answer any and all of your questions about tipping. Caller number 1, you're on the air.

Caller 1: In Norway, where I come from, restaurants add a service charge to restaurant bills, so we usually don't leave a tip. Can you tell me how much to tip in a U.S. restaurant?

Host: Caller number 2, go ahead.

Caller 2: I don't take taxis very much, and I never know exactly how much to tip the driver. Sometimes I think I overtip.

Host: Caller number 3, you're on the air.

Caller 3: I just got to this country, and I've been eating out a lot in restaurants where, you know, you pay at the cashier. My problem is this—I'm never sure where to leave the tip.

Host: Caller number 4, you're on the air.

Caller 4: I'm going to France on business, and I'll probably go to the theater. Someone told me something about tipping in a French theater. Can you tell me who I'm supposed to tip?

Host: Caller number 5, please ask your question.

Caller 5: I just had an awful experience in a restaurant. Our server was slow, forgot things, and on top of it all, wasn't even polite. Please tell me what to do if I don't like the service in a restaurant.

Host: We have time for just one more question. Caller number 6, please go ahead.

Caller 6: I recently started going to a hairdresser. I know I'm also supposed to tip the person who washes my hair, but when I'm ready to leave, she's often busy with another customer, and I don't want to interrupt. Besides, her hands are all wet! Can you tell me where I should leave the tip?

Host: Thank you, callers, and thank you, Alicia Marksen. That's all the time we have right now. Please tune in tomorrow for more talk radio. Until then, this is Ed Collins, wishing you a good day.

UNIT 26

Introduction (Student's Book, page 329). *Read and listen to this excerpt from a psychology magazine.*

Self-Talk

Recent studies show that self-talk, or the way we explain a problem to ourselves, can affect our performance and even our health. To illustrate, one researcher tells the story of co-workers Tom and Sara. Both lost their jobs last fall, but their responses to this loss were very different. Before they left the job, they took each other's telephone numbers so that they could keep in touch during the winter. Sara called Tom and other friends often, continued her leisure-time activities, and kept herself fit. She encouraged Tom to do the same, but he couldn't take her advice. In fact, if Sara hadn't kept in touch with him, Tom would have had almost no contact with friends. He isolated himself, deprived himself of his hobbies, and even made himself sick with a bad cold all winter.

What made their responses so different from one another? Since both Tom and Sara were laid off, the job loss itself can't explain Tom's problems. One major difference was the way Tom and Sara explained the problem to themselves. Sara told herself that her problem was temporary and that she herself could change it. Tom saw himself as helpless and permanently unemployed.

In the spring, Tom and Sara both got their jobs back. Their responses when they talked to each other were similar to the way they explained things to themselves. "They finally realized that they needed me," said Sara the optimist. Tom grumbled, "I guess they were really desperate."

Exercise 5 (Student's Book, page 335). *Listen to the conversations at the office party. Then listen again and circle the pronouns that you hear.*

1.

A: Mark's department did a great job this year.

B: I know. They should be really proud of each other.

2.

A: What's wrong? You look upset.

B: I just heard Ed and Jeff talking. You know Ed blames himself for everything.

3.

A: I hear you're going to Japan on vacation this year. Are you going by yourself or with a tour?

B: Oh, with a tour.

4.

A: Hillary looks happy tonight. Did Meredith give her the promotion?

B: No, not yet. Meredith keeps asking herself if she can do the job.

5.

A: How do you like the new computer system?

B: I'm not sure. In our department, we're still teaching ourselves how to use it.

6.

A: So long, now. Thanks for coming. It was good to see you.

B: Oh, it was a great party.

A: I'm glad you enjoyed yourselves.

UNIT 27

Introduction (Student's Book, page 338). *Read and listen to the magazine article.*

Say *inventor,* and many people think of a professional scientist working in a laboratory full of modern equipment. However, creativity is a universal quality. We are all potential inventors, regardless of age, education, or situation. Inventions have been dreamed up and developed in kitchens as well as in laboratories, by elementary school children as well as by trained scientists. The first personal computer was put together in a garage by two young college students who had dropped out of school.

If higher education and an expensive laboratory aren't required, what is? People who come up with new ideas do have some special qualities. Curiosity comes first. Inventors are people who want to find out why things happen the way they do. For example, when George de Mestrel, a Swiss inventor, took his dog for walks in the mountains, burrs would get stuck in the dog's coat. De Mestrel wondered why they were so hard to remove. Acting on his curiosity, he examined the burrs through a microscope. When he saw the many tiny hooks on each burr, he realized that he was looking at the perfect fastener. Years later, de Mestrel developed this idea into Velcro®, now used to fasten everything from sneakers to space suits.

Imagination is also crucial for an inventor. This quality helps inventors put things together in a new way. One U.S. sixth grader invented a solar-powered light by combining solar cells and a bicycle. When he rides his bike during the day, the sunlight charges up two batteries. Then at night, when he needs the light, he switches it on. Imagination can also mean seeing a new use for a common object. The original Frisbee was a pie pan that two truck drivers were tossing to each other in a parking lot. As he watched the two men playing around, Walter Morrison came up with his idea for a new toy that became popular all over the world.

Inventors are often problem solvers. When fifteen-year-old Chester Greenwood's ears got frostbitten during Maine's bitter winters, he didn't give up and stay indoors. Instead, he attached fur cups to the ends of a piece of wire, and wrapped the wire around his head. His friends made fun of him at first, but soon the idea caught on, and they wanted earmuffs too. The Greenwood family had to work hard to keep up with the orders. Chester patented his invention when he was only nineteen.

After an inventor says Eureka! (Greek for *I've found it!*), there's still a lot of work to do. Another quality found in successful inventors is tenacity—the ability to stick with a project until it is completed. This usually involves looking up information related to the idea. George Eastman, inventor of the Kodak® camera and film, spent years researching chemicals and photography. Tenacity also involves trying out different materials and designs. De Mestrel experimented with many kinds of materials before he perfected Velcro®.

Finally, inventors need a lot of self-confidence. They have to believe in their ideas and be willing to learn from their failures. Gail Borden, who developed a process for condensing and canning milk, was turned down when he first applied for a patent. He kept on trying to perfect his method, and after years he finally succeeded. His invention probably saved many lives at a time when there was no way to refrigerate milk. Borden's motto is engraved on his tombstone: "I tried and failed; I tried again and again and succeeded."

Exercise 6 (Student's Book, page 348). *Listen to a teacher explain how to make a simple camera. Then listen again and in the boxes number the pictures to show the correct order. Listen a third time and complete each caption with the correct phrasal verb.*

Today in class, we're going to find out how to make a very simple camera, using objects that you can find around the house. I'll show you how to do it today, and after we do it in class, you can go home and try it out yourself.

OK! We're ready to start. First, take a cereal box like this one and empty it out. Don't throw away the cereal! You can put it into another container.

Second step . . . Cut out a small hole in the bottom of the box. The hole should be about one centimeter in diameter. It doesn't have to be perfect . . . there . . . just don't make it too big.

Now, for the third step, use some tape and cover up the hole with a small square of aluminum foil, like this one. . . . Can everyone see that? . . . The square makes a little flap over the hole.

OK, now, take a pin, like this. This is the fourth step. With the pin, punch a hole through the center of the foil. There . . . can you see the hole?

Fifth—you turn the box up. Now we'll work on the other side.

Now, for number six, you see these flaps at the top of the box? Cut them off. There'll be a big hole.

Cover up the opening with tissue paper, like this. Just put it right over the opening. That's the seventh step.

Eight—Use some tape to hold the tissue paper on . . .

. . . And your camera is finished. It doesn't look like much, does it? But it really is a camera. To prove it, we're going to light something up and look at it through the camera. That's step nine. Let's use that chair over there. You can all come up here and look. See that? You can see a picture of the chair on the tissue paper. It's upside-down. That's exactly how a camera works. . . .

Why don't we take a break now, and after the break, we'll talk about how to take a picture with your camera.

Answer Key to the Diagnostic and Final Tests

The contracted form is used in this answer key. You may choose to accept the uncontracted (full) form as well.

PART 1: Diagnostic Test

I.

2. What are you doing? **3.** 'm reading **4.** 're always reading **5.** watch **6.** Is the water boiling **7.** explains **8.** is setting **9.** does the sun set **10.** do people name **11.** is naming **12.** knits **13.** 'm knitting

II.

2. looks **3.** doesn't resemble **4.** Is . . . crying **5.** don't hear **6.** isn't sleeping **7.** have **8.** contains **9.** are . . . looking **10.** looks **11.** tastes **12.** 's eating

III.

2. didn't hear, called **3.** was singing, was taking **4.** turned off, started **5.** was talking, was dripping **6.** were going to move, changed **7.** decided, found **8.** was mowing, was working/mowed, worked **9.** started, looked **10.** finished, walked **11.** was going to swim, was

IV.

2. have been born, opened **3.** has lived **4.** came, was **5.** didn't know, arrived **6.** changed **7.** didn't have **8.** has read **9.** has been reading **10.** hasn't finished **11.** 's been studying **12.** have . . . owned **13.** Have . . . cooked **14.** Did . . . meet, came **15.** hasn't called . . . started

V.

2. had learned **3.** had shown **4.** hadn't decided **5.** hadn't acted **6.** had applied

VI.

2. Had . . . ridden, No, he hadn't
3. Had . . . read, Yes, I had
4. Had . . . planned, No, she hadn't
5. Had . . . said, No, he hadn't
6. Had . . . made, No, he hadn't

VII.

2. had . . . decided **3.** had . . . done **4.** had . . . acted **5.** had . . . considered **6.** had happened

VIII.

2. had been playing **3.** hadn't been getting together **4.** had been looking **5.** hadn't been feeling **6.** had been snowing

IX.

2. had . . . been talking
3. Had . . . been studying, Yes, she had
4. Had . . . been complaining, No, he hadn't
5. Had . . . been treating, Yes, they had
6. had . . . been doing

X.

2. b **3.** a **4.** a **5.** a **6.** b **7.** b **8.** b **9.** a **10.** a

XI.

2. Since he *started* two years ago, he's met a lot of actors and entertainers.
3. Last week, he *interviewed* Jessica Wood, a popular talk-show host.
4. When Bruce *arrived* at the studio for the interview, she was taping her show.
5. When Bruce *saw* her, Wood and her producers had just been arguing.
6. Jessica Wood *appeared* very calm in spite of the problem.
7. The producers *were going* to change some material, but Wood refused.
8. By the time the two started talking, Bruce *had been waiting* more than an hour.
9. Wood had studied psychology in college, and at first she *wasn't* going to be an entertainer.
10. She was performing at comedy clubs when the network *discovered* her.
11. When the interview ended, Bruce *went* home to write his article.

PART 1: Final Test

I.

2. eats **3.** is studying **4.** are you leaving **5.** do you leave **6.** name **7.** do they put **8.** are you putting **9.** tells **10.** is telling **11.** are you thinking **12.** 's Marcia going? **13.** goes

II.

2. need **3.** does . . . cost **4.** doesn't seem **5.** is wearing **6.** doesn't look **7.** feels **8.** Do . . . remember **9.** see **10.** don't like **11.** weighs **12.** Are . . . going

III.

2. were playing, got **3.** began, closed **4.** stopped, went **5.** saw, were walking **6.** were going to walk, seemed **7.** went, turned on **8.** came, were eating **9.** heard, got **10.** dialed, answered **11.** were thinking, rang

IV.

2. made **3.** have been coming **4.** have visited **5.** heard, were **6.** has been increasing/has increased **7.** have been causing/have caused **8.** have become **9.** Did . . . see, were **10.** 's been taking **11.** 's used, arrived **12.** Have . . . been **13.** 've booked **14.** tried **15.** 've been planning/'ve planned, studied

V.

2. had learned **3.** hadn't heard **4.** hadn't mailed **5.** hadn't told **6.** had knocked

VI.

2. Had . . . seen, No, I hadn't **3.** Had . . . studied, Yes, she had
4. Had . . . swum, No, they hadn't **5.** Had . . . eaten, Yes, she had **6.** Had . . . gotten, Yes, they had

VII.

2. had . . . applied **3.** had . . . learned **4.** had . . . told
5. had . . . read **6.** had . . . thought about

VIII.

2. had been improving **3.** hadn't been growing **4.** had been buying **5.** had been searching **6.** had been blaring

IX.

2. Had . . . been gaining, Yes, he had
3. Had . . . been ringing, No, they hadn't
4. had . . . been shopping
5. Had . . . been writing, Yes, she had
6. had . . . been waking up

X.

2. b **3.** a **4.** b **5.** b **6.** a **7.** b **8.** a **9.** b **10.** a

XI.

2. By the time he appeared in *Home Alone,* he *had* already *been acting*/he *had* already *acted* in movies for several years.
3. Before he chose Culkin, the director *had auditioned* more than 100 children.
4. He *wasn't going* to give Culkin the part because there were so many lines to learn.
5. Macaulay has a good memory and always *memorizes* his parts very quickly.
6. Since Macaulay *became* a star, his father has been working as his agent.
7. The movie *came* out several years ago.
8. Macaulay *has* six siblings.
9. Since he became famous, he *hasn't had* much privacy.
10. While the writer John Hughes was preparing to take his family on a vacation, he *got* the idea for *Home Alone.*
11. When the movie became a huge success, everyone *was* surprised.

PART II: Diagnostic Test

I.

2. 'll be packing **3.** 'm not going to be doing **4.** is going to be attending **5.** won't be camping **6.** 'll be staying
7. 'll be driving **8.** camping **9.** 's not going to be coming
10. 'll be starting **11.** 's going to be doing

II.

2. Will . . . be living, Yes, they will
3. Are . . . going to be watching, No, they won't
4. Will . . . be talking, Yes, we will
5. is . . . going to be using
6. will . . . be seeing

III.

1. Frank is going to be playing softball while I do the shopping.
2. He'll be straightening/He's going to be straightening up the house while I run some errands.
3. Billy will be doing/is going to be doing his homework when I get home.
4. While Frank sets the table, I'll be preparing/I'm going to be preparing dinner.

5. I'll still be cooking/I'm still going to be cooking when the guests start to arrive.
6. They'll be talking/They're going to be talking to Frank while I finish cooking.
7. We won't be sitting/We're not going to be sitting down to eat until everyone is here.
8. The children will be playing/are going to be playing outside while the adults have coffee.

IV.

2. 'll have been selling **3.** 'll have jogged **4.** 'll have been jogging **5.** won't have gone **6.** 'll have been waiting
7. 'll have completed **8.** 'll have learned

V.

2. 'll have saved, does **3.** arrives, 'll have been driving/'ll have driven **4.** graduates, won't have found **5.** quits, 'll have completed **6.** won't have received, gets back

VI.

2. will . . . have been living/will . . . have lived **3.** Will . . . have submitted, No, I won't (have) **4.** will . . . have interviewed
5. Will . . . have received, Yes, he will (have) **6.** will . . . have learned

VII.

I started writing a journal when I turned eighteen. My birthday is next month, so in a few weeks I'll have been *keeping* my journal for five years. When I *finish* this entry, I'll have *filled up* another notebook. Recently I reread those old journals. I was surprised. I've already accomplished so many things that I wanted to do when I first started writing them. In my first journal I said I wanted to go back to school. Well, in September, I'll be starting at the university. I also said I wanted to quit my job and find something more interesting. By my birthday, *I'll have been* working at my new job for a year. (Maybe my boss will have decided to give me a raise by then.)

There are some things I won't have accomplished by then, though. I wanted to have my own car by the time I turned twenty-three. I won't *have* saved enough by next month. And I won't *have moved* into my own apartment by then either. Never mind. When my twenty-fourth birthday *arrives,* I'll be writing in my journal about my car and new apartment.

PART II: Final Test

I.

2. 'll be looking **3.** are going to be celebrating **4.** won't be playing **5.** will be closing **6.** 're going to be checking out **7.** 's going to be getting married **8.** 'm going to be developing **9.** 're not going to be talking **10.** 'll be driving **11.** won't be going

II.

2. Will . . . be visiting, Yes, they will **3.** Are . . . going to be doing, No, I'm not **4.** Is . . . going to be taking, No, she's not/No, she isn't **5.** will be driving **6.** will . . . be getting

III.

2. I'll be answering/I'm going to be answering your telephone while you eat lunch.
3. We'll be thinking/We're going to be thinking about you while you're away.
4. Paz will be studying/is going to be studying when you come.
5. Sumail will be typing/is going to be typing her research paper while Paz studies.

6. I'll be taking/I'm going to be taking a nap while you write letters.
7. We'll be freezing/We're going to be freezing here in Chicago while they sunbathe in Miami.
8. Nora and Ted will be clearing/are going to be clearing the table while you wash the dishes.

IV.

2. won't have painted 3. 'll have been reviewing 4. won't have gotten 5. won't have seen 6. 'll have been traveling 7. 'll have been playing 8. 'll have been learning

V.

2. won't have opened, call 3. completes, 'll have been
4. graduates, 'll have been working/'ll have worked
5. go back, 'll have been living/'ll have lived 6. finish, won't have been able

VI.

2. Will . . . have expired, Yes, it will (have) 3. will . . . have lived
4. will . . . have made 5. Will . . . have finished, Yes, I will (have) 6. Will . . . have come back, Yes, I will (have)

VII.

2. Their children will be *giving* them a big party.
3. A band *is going to be* playing/*will b*e playing music so that the guests can dance.
4. I'*m going* to be meeting Bob's parents at the party.
5. What *will he* have told them about me?
6. Bob will have *seen* this dress three times.
7. I want to buy a new one, but I'm afraid I *won't* have found anything by the party.
8. By the time we *get* to the party, the music will already have started.
9. Bob's parents will have *celebrated* their anniversary every year.
10. They won't *have* missed a single year.
11. Their best man will have *known* them for more than thirty years.

PART III: Diagnostic Test

I.

2. didn't you 3. hasn't she 4. did she 5. weren't they
6. had they 7. do you 8. shouldn't we 9. can we
10. will you 11. won't he 12. doesn't he 13. wasn't it
14. is she

II.

2. 're 3. hasn't written 4. plans 5. didn't grow up
6. 's living 7. 'll be 8. should make 9. can't put
10. hadn't heard 11. didn't appear 12. doesn't have

III.

2. Yes, they do 3. No, I didn't 4. No, I won't 5. Yes, we are
6. Yes, we should 7. No, he hasn't

IV.

2. a 3. c 4. c 5. a 6. c 7. b 8. a 9. c 10. a
11. b 12. a

V.

Dear Lynn,

It seems like a long time since I left Vancouver, *doesn't* it? I've had some problems finding an apartment and a job, but you warned me about that before I left, didn't you? Anyway,

everything seems to be working out now. I found an apartment, a job, and a boyfriend (his name is Mark) just last month. Things can happen fast sometimes, *can't* they?

I'm working at a local hospital, on the pediatrics floor. My supervisor is nice and *so* are my co-workers. I live near the water in Bayview Apartments, and so *does* Mark. My apartment has a view, but his doesn't, so we spend a lot of time at my place. Mark and I have a lot in common. He isn't at all shy, and neither *am* I. I enjoy noisy, crowded places, and so *does* he. We have some differences, though. I love taking long quiet walks, but he doesn't. I can work odd hours and weekends with no problem, but he *can't*. He says he needs to have his weekends free. So far, we've worked out our differences. One last thing—Mark's from Vancouver too. It's a small world, *isn't* it?

When are you coming for a visit? I really want to show you around Seattle.

Love,

Kim

PART III: Final Test

I.

2. didn't he 3. hasn't she 4. didn't she 5. wasn't he
6. had he 7. do we 8. shouldn't you 9. can't we
10. will they 11. won't she 12. don't they 13. wasn't it
14. is she

II.

2. 've been here 3. hasn't written 4. is 5. sat 6. should call 7. is staying 8. 'll meet 9. can't eat 10. hadn't said
11. didn't make 12. hasn't heard

III.

2. Yes, he is 3. Yes, we are 4. No, I don't 5. No, he won't
6. Yes, I can 7. No, I didn't

IV.

2. b 3. b 4. c 5. a 6. b 7. c 8. c 9. a 10. a
11. c 12. a

V.

Dear Karl,

Last summer vacation seems like yesterday, *doesn't* it? It's hard to believe that it's been almost a year since we saw you. I'm looking forward to your visit this year, *and so is* your Aunt Jennie. You told us you'd teach us that new computer game you got for Christmas. You haven't forgotten your promise, have you?

Your mom has told us that you had some problems with school this year. She's not worried, though, and *neither* are we. She's confident that you'll work it out by the end of the term. So are we. Writing a paper isn't easy, *is* it? I had problems with that when I was in school too, and so *did* a lot of my classmates.

When you come to visit in July, your cousin Todd will be here too. You haven't seen him for a while, but you two have a lot in common. I know you love sports, and he *does* too. Maybe we can take in a baseball game while you're here. He enjoys skate-boarding, and so *do you*. It's going to be a great summer, *isn't* it? See you in July.

Love,

Uncle Al

PART IV: Diagnostic Test

I.
2. to read   3. Learning   4. to buy   5. to get   6. not to wait   7. Not following   8. going   9. to take   10. driving   11. to find out   12. seeing   13. to look   14. to buy   15. adding

II.
1. them moving   2. us studying   3. their wanting   4. Pete's admitting/Pete admitting   5. him to make   6. us to work   7. his not helping/him not helping   8. Cora's not paying/Cora not paying   9. her forgetting   10. them to change

III.
1. won't help you to live
2. got her to change
3. helps people avoid/helps people to avoid
4. has a friend walk
5. make criminals think
6. doesn't let bushes grow
7. make people believe
8. have the police give
9. lets people think
10. get her friends to take
11. have someone teach

IV.
It's time to *take* action. You can get lawmakers and others to change the laws. Even a busy person can make a difference. Here are some things you can do.
1. Learn personal safety techniques, but don't buy a gun. *Having* a gun in the house is dangerous and adds to the problem.
2. Violence is a public health problem. Get your doctors *to display* information about the risks of owning guns. Urge *them* to talk to parents about the danger of guns. Compare it to the danger of *not* using seat belts.
3. When you see gun advertising, call or write to the publication. Tell them how you feel about their publishing this kind of advertising.
4. Teaching children early *is* important. Talk to educators about starting a program on solving problems peacefully.
5. When you write to a politician, send your letter to the newspaper. A published letter gets a politician *to pay* attention to an issue.

PART IV: Final Test

I.
2. to decrease   3. to eat   4. cutting   5. not to select   6. to study   7. Acquiring   8. buying   9. visiting   10. not to have   11. to see   12. to mention   13. doing   14. walking   15. Not doing

II.
2. appreciated their telling/appreciated them telling   3. tells him to stop   4. didn't mind your not coming/didn't mind you not coming   5. celebrate your/you winning   6. worry about her not finishing   7. advised them to let   8. enjoyed their being/enjoyed them being   9. promised them to keep   10. allowed her to watch

III.
2. got my family to hold   3. make us arrange   4. get us to plan   5. let their children make   6. gets them to participate   7. had her write   8. helped her understand/to understand   9. got her to start   10. 're going to get everyone to cooperate   11. have one person take

IV.
To the Editor:

 The conflict between professional baseball players and the team owners has dominated the news recently. I, for one, am fed up with *hearing* about the problems of professional baseball. Like many other fans, I enjoy *watching* my team (the Baltimore Orioles) on television. Every season, I look forward to attending a game or two in the stadium. I was sorry to *learn* that I won't be doing that this year.

 I'm disappointed, but don't expect me to be horrified that players might not be earning more than a million dollars per contract. And I'm not crying about the owners' *losing* control over a multimillion dollar sports industry.

 It's clear that neither side is interested in talking seriously about a solution. And no one is thinking about the loyal fans. *Playing* the game just doesn't seem important to either side anymore.

 At this point, I'm so disgusted that nothing could make *me* watch another baseball game. I'm considering changing sports. Soccer is beginning to *seem* better and better.

Sincerely,

Clarissa Framton

Baltimore, Maryland

PART V: Diagnostic Test

I.
2. are described   3. weren't notified   4. choose   5. isn't assigned   6. were mailed   7. received   8. was taught   9. took   10. enjoy   11. weren't added   12. is still offered

II.
2. wasn't reported   3. were expanded   4. are bought   5. was hired   6. will be finished   7. were corrected   8. are spoken   9. isn't published   10. is sold

III.
2. Where was the Battle of Waterloo fought?
3. When was the first satellite launched?
4. Where are giant pandas found?
5. Are they protected by the government?, Yes, they are
6. How were the Philippines discovered by Europeans?
7. Is curling played with a ball?, No, it isn't
8. How were zippers first used?
9. When was the planet Pluto first seen through a telescope?
10. Is Urdu spoken in Finland?, No, it isn't

IV.
Sentences with agents crossed out:
3. Corn is grown ~~by farmers~~ in Indiana.
4. Spanish is spoken ~~by speakers~~ in many countries.
6. Some strange laws were passed ~~by lawmakers~~ in the nineteenth century.

V.
2. will be spoken **3.** ought to be awarded **4.** will be sold **5.** must not be disturbed **6.** has got to be locked **7.** may be chosen **8.** can be cured **9.** might not be paid **10.** won't be flown

VI.
2. Is . . . going to be launched, No, it isn't **3.** Can . . . be seen, No, it can't **4.** Should . . . be applied, No, it shouldn't **5.** will . . . be made **6.** can . . . be kept **7.** will be used **8.** could . . . be flown **9.** Will . . . be joined, Yes, they will **10.** Do . . . have to be trained, Yes, they do

VII.
2. get it serviced **3.** has it painted **4.** 'm going to have them washed/'m having them washed/'ll have them washed **5.** get it cleaned **6.** didn't get them repaired **7.** haven't had it tuned

VIII.

For a relaxing and romantic vacation, Caribbean Palm Resort *is recommended* by many travelers. At Caribbean Palm, guests will *enjoy* gleaming white beaches and three large swimming pools. A number of activities *are offered* at the resort, including diving, wind-surfing, and water-skiing. Independent souls might be tempted by shopping in nearby villages or exploring the island on a motorbike. The beautiful scenery along the coast can't be described—it *has to be seen*. After a long day in the sun, relax and have your hair styled in Caribbean Palm's own salon. For the evening, come and enjoy live entertainment in our dining room, or have your meal *served* on your own balcony. Reservations must be made far in advance for this popular resort. But it will be worth planning ahead for—wonderful things can *happen* at Caribbean Palm.

PART V: Final Test

I.
2. was probably caused **3.** brought **4.** controlled **5.** will rain **6.** are advising **7.** break out **8.** are started **9.** is used **10.** volunteer **11.** don't always follow **12.** are made

II.
2. was completed **3.** was blamed/is blamed **4.** are displayed **5.** aren't affected **6.** is influenced **7.** are taxed **8.** is banned **9.** isn't prohibited **10.** was proven/was proved

III.
2. When was color television invented? **3.** Was lacrosse first played in Europe?, No, it wasn't **4.** Is our weather influenced by El Niño?, Yes, it is **5.** How are hailstones formed? **6.** Is Swahili spoken in North America?, No, it isn't **7.** Is oil found in Bolivia?, Yes, it is **8.** Are llamas raised in the United States?, Yes, they are **9.** How is food cooked in a microwave? **10.** Where are dingoes found?

IV.
Sentences with agents crossed out:
3. Native American languages are spoken widely ~~by speakers~~ in North and South America.
4. Tin is mined ~~by miners~~ in Bolivia.

V.
2. could be invited **3.** may be completed **4.** must be followed **5.** has to be learned **6.** has got to be passed **7.** might be taken **8.** must be understood **9.** can't be ignored **10.** will be sought

VI.
2. Will . . . be built, Yes, it will **3.** Could . . . be connected, Yes, they could **4.** should . . . be banned **5.** Can . . . be bought, Yes, they can **6.** Will . . . be permitted, No, they won't **7.** can . . . be developed **8.** should . . . be spent **9.** will be sent **10.** can . . . be started

VII.
2. won't have it waxed **3.** get them cleaned **4.** got it repaired **5.** 'm going to have her dipped/'m having her dipped **6.** doesn't get it trimmed **7.** have it delivered

VIII.

Dear Editor:

In my opinion, all cigarette advertising should be *banned,* even attractive designs on packages. Joe Camel and the Marlboro Man portray smokers as independent and powerful people. Adults can make their own decisions, but teenagers *can't resist* these images.

I think my own experience is typical. I started smoking when I was fourteen, and I smoked for five years. I was aware that many diseases could be caused by smoking, but I *was influenced* by advertising, especially the Virginia Slim ads. Then, in my senior year of high school, I started getting sick all the time. When this *happened,* my parents took me to a specialist and had me *checked* out. I *was ordered* to quit, and I did.

I urge everybody to write to Congress about this issue. Lawmakers have got *to be forced* to take a strong stand. Tobacco is a big industry, but we can *get* laws passed if we work at it.
Sincerely Yours,
Betty Litton, Mechanicsville, Virginia

PART VI: Diagnostic Test

I.
1. b. ought to have studied **c.** shouldn't have gone
2. a. could have called **b.** might have sent **c.** ought to have marked
3. a. shouldn't have played **b.** ought to have stayed **c.** should have gone
4. a. shouldn't have stopped **b.** could have bought **c.** might have called

II.
2. should . . . have studied **3.** should . . . have taken **4.** should . . . have told **5.** Should . . . have called **6.** Should . . . have rented

III.
2. must not have received **3.** couldn't have left **4.** could have changed **5.** had to have been **6.** may have gotten **7.** may not have heard **8.** might not have understood

IV.

2. Where could I have left my glasses?
3. Could Zena have forgotten our date?
4. Could they have moved?
5. How could I have done such a dumb thing?
6. What could have made Nick so angry?

V.

3. We must not have   **4.** She may have   **5.** She couldn't have been   **6.** They must have been

VI.

To everyone's surprise, Roy Cole lost his bid for re-election yesterday to a newcomer, Martha Gomez. "I couldn't *have* been more pleased to hear the news," said one voter. "We needed a change." Political analysts attribute the Gomez victory to several factors. First, Cole should *have* started campaigning earlier. He was too sure of his re-election. In addition, voters may *have* been disappointed in Cole's vote on the crime bill. "Cole might have *explained* his position better," complained one prominent businessperson. "In my opinion, he shouldn't have voted against the bill," grumbled another voter.

The new senator claims not to be surprised at her land-slide victory yesterday. "After twelve years of Cole, voters had to have been ready for a change," said Gomez. "I don't know why reporters seem to be shocked. They must not *have* talked to voters the way I did in this campaign."

PART VI: Final Test

I.

1. b. could have asked   **c.** might have told
2. a. ought to have asked   **b.** shouldn't have forgotten   **c.** could have hidden
3. a. ought not to have waited   **b.** should have applied   **c.** might have put
4. a. ought to have left   **b.** shouldn't have driven   **c.** could have known

II.

2. should . . . have taken   **3.** should . . . have gone   **4.** Should . . . have stayed   **5.** Should . . . have bought   **6.** should . . . have asked

III.

2. couldn't have committed   **3.** might have overbooked
4. must have shrunk   **5.** might have been   **6.** may have fired
7. could have quit   **8.** must not have put

IV.

2. Who could have told Rhoda about her surprise party?
3. Could the kids have eaten it all?
4. Could someone have taken it?
5. What could I have said to hurt her feelings?
6. Could the bank have made a mistake?

V.

3. She might have   **4.** He must not have been   **5.** I must not have   **6.** They couldn't have been

VI.

Our vacation was fun, but it should *have* gone more smoothly. I think we ought to *have* planned it better. For starters, we could have *asked* more questions about the package deal. The car we got was too small. At that price, I should have *known*. We got a bigger one, but that took some time. Then the travel agent must not *have* confirmed our hotel reservation in Santa Monica. They weren't expecting us. And it couldn't have *happened* at a worse time. It was one of their busiest weekends. Anyway, after we got that straightened out, the rest of the trip was great. The California coast had to *have* been the most beautiful place I've ever seen. We loved San Francisco—that may *have* been because Ted grew up there and knows the city so well. His brother invited us back next summer. We may have *started* a tradition.

PART VII: Diagnostic Test

I.

2. Unless I wear suntan lotion, I get a bad sunburn.
3. If you have a headache, you should lie down.
4. Get out of the swimming pool immediately whenever you hear thunder.
5. If they don't obey these warnings, they can get hurt.
6. You shouldn't use this equipment unless you know how to operate it.
7. Try La Trattoria if you like Italian food.
8. If the air pollution is bad, some people don't go outside.

II.

2. doesn't win, 's going to run   **3.** increase, won't improve
4. isn't, won't stay   **5.** register, isn't going to know   **6.** loses, 'll ask for   **7.** starts, won't recognize

III.

2. unless   **3.** Unless   **4.** If   **5.** unless   **6.** Unless   **7.** If   **8.** unless

IV.

2. Will . . . go, forecast, No, I won't   **3.** do . . . stay, visit
4. Do . . . order, travel, No, I don't   **5.** fly, should . . . rent, Yes, you should   **6.** leaves, will . . . get   **7.** Will . . . close, stays, Yes, they will

V.

2. could reheat, weren't   **3.** would do, went   **4.** weren't, could earn   **5.** would redecorate, had   **6.** wouldn't be, didn't make
7. were, 'd give   **8.** wouldn't be, didn't practice
9. didn't talk, 'd understand   **10.** didn't make, 'd sleep

VI.

2. would . . . be, were   **3.** Would . . . go, won, Yes, I would
4. had, would . . . wish   **5.** didn't know, would . . . get
6. asked, would . . . lend, No, he wouldn't   **7.** would . . . get, left
8. would happen, changed

VII.

2. hadn't passed, would have been   **3.** would have seen, had been   **4.** hadn't moved, wouldn't have met   **5.** hadn't met, wouldn't have become   **6.** hadn't been, wouldn't have left
7. wouldn't have broken, had seen   **8.** wouldn't have gotten, hadn't recommended   **9.** wouldn't have rented, had heard
10. wouldn't have let, hadn't paid

VIII.

2. hadn't majored, would . . . have studied
3. Would . . . have gone, hadn't told, Yes, I would have
4. hadn't discovered, would . . . have developed
5. had been, would . . . have waited, Yes, I would have
6. would have happened, hadn't mailed
7. would have taught, hadn't been

IX.

2. I wish I didn't have a lot to read tonight.
3. I wish I had gone shopping for food today.
4. I wish there were something to eat in the house.
5. I wish I had enough time to cook dinner.
6. I wish my car had started today.
7. I wish the telephone hadn't been out of order too.
8. I wish I weren't bored.
9. I wish I hadn't finished reading that murder mystery.
10. I wish there were something interesting to read.

X.

2. F 3. T 4. T 5. F 6. T 7. F 8. T

XI.

2. Paula wishes she *had* started college years ago.
3. If I *stay* with my family next summer, we'll have a great time together.
4. Whenever the air pollution is bad these days, I *cough* a lot.
5. If Marco *had* a million dollars, he would take a trip around the world.
6. If Sue *hadn't told* me, I wouldn't have heard the news.
7. If I had *known* about this class earlier, I would have registered for it.
8. Unless I *pass* English this semester, I won't graduate./If I don't pass English this semester, I won't graduate.
9. We wish you could *have* stayed a little longer last night.

PART VII: Final Test

I.

2. Unless I drink coffee in the morning, I can't wake up.
3. Walk for an hour every day if you want to get some exercise.
4. Whenever you feel tired, you should take a nap.
5. Please don't disturb me unless there's an emergency.
6. If you have to report a fire, call 911.
7. Unless they call right away, the fire could go out of control.
8. People don't get the benefits of exercise unless they exercise three times a week.

II.

2. gets, won't get 3. won't be able to, isn't working 4. won't send, call 5. find, isn't going to be 6. expands, 're going to need 7. 's going to start, has

III.

2. if 3. If 4. unless 5. If 6. Unless 7. If 8. unless

IV.

2. Can . . . join, bring 3. do . . . prepare, eat 4. do . . . call, need 5. ask, will . . . babysit, Yes, she will 6. Do . . . leave, go, Yes, I do 7. Will . . . misbehave, don't know, No, they won't

V.

2. didn't keep, could explain 3. drank, would feel
4. knew, would invite 5. would buy, didn't cost 6. wouldn't take, were 7. would cook, had 8. told, wouldn't believe
9. were, wouldn't have 10. wouldn't be, didn't share

VI.

2. could meet, would . . . want 3. had, would . . . wish
4. saw, would . . . recognize, No, I wouldn't 5. worked, would . . . finish, Yes, we would 6. would . . . get, broke down
7. Would . . . bother, opened, No, it wouldn't 8. would . . . go, bought

VII.

2. wouldn't have chosen, hadn't heard
3. wouldn't have annoyed, hadn't been
4. would have had, hadn't warned
5. wouldn't have trusted, hadn't told
6. had let, would have made
7. wouldn't have said, had known
8. had joined, would have received
9. had watched, would have heard
10. had been, would have left

VIII.

2. hadn't moved, would . . . have grown up
3. Would . . . have gotten, hadn't answered, No, he wouldn't have
4. Would . . . have finished, hadn't become, Yes, he would have
5. hadn't worked, would . . . have met
6. would . . . have called, had needed
7. had studied, would . . . have passed, Yes, she would have

IX.

2. I wish it didn't snow here every winter.
3. I wish we had taken a vacation this year.
4. I wish the concert weren't sold out.
5. I wish you could buy tickets.
6. I wish I had heard this group of musicians last year.
7. I wish I hadn't returned Bob's phone call late.
8. I wish Bob had been home.
9. I wish I could call him from my office.
10. I wish my best friend lived in this city.

X.

2. F 3. T 4. T 5. F 6. F 7. F 8. T

XI.

1. Plants die *if* they don't have enough water.
2. Peter wishes he *hadn't* gotten so angry last night.
3. If Loretta *doesn't* get enough sleep, she won't get a good grade on her test tomorrow.
4. Evita wishes she *could* go to the state college next fall.
5. Whenever Rene hears that song now, he *remembers* New Orleans.
6. If I *were* rich, I wouldn't be any happier than I am now.
7. If I had *known* about this class earlier, I would have registered for it.
8. We *wouldn't* have left early if we had seen you at the party.
9. If the police officer *hadn't* stopped us, we wouldn't have known about that broken signal light.

PART VIII: Diagnostic Test

I.

2. whose 3. that 4. which 5. whose 6. which 7. that
8. whose 9. that 10. which

II.

2. that 3. whose 4. where 5. whom 6. that 7. whose
8. when 9. which 10. that

III.

2. attend 3. recognizes 4. live 5. gets, roams 6. is
7. see 8. bothers 9. works 10. love

IV.

2. Crystal works in the Accounting Department, where she's been the secretary for years.

3. She started the job right after she got married, when she was about nineteen.
4. It was an exciting time when the department was growing rapidly.
5. Crystal and Beth, who started at the same time, grew up together.
6. Our company is a friendly place where everyone enjoys working.
7. Rohan, who(m) Crystal works for, has a very stressful job.
8. Rohan, whose job Crystal understands perfectly, travels a lot.
9. Crystal has a personality which is very suited to her job.
10. She takes responsibility for a lot of tasks that Rohan doesn't have time for.

V.

Sentences with possible deletions:

4. Someone ~~who~~ I really enjoy talking to is Chris's father.
5. Josi bought the book ~~which~~ she had heard about on TV.
7. She's someone ~~whom~~ I campaign for every four years.
9. Thanksgiving is a time ~~when~~ many families get together.
10. Will Rogers, a U.S. comedian, never met a person ~~whom~~ he didn't like.

VI.

2. She often performs her own songs, which she *sings* in a powerful, country-western style.
3. Gould, who grew up in New York City, studied classical music.
4. A friend invited her to a country music festival in West Virginia, *where* she heard real country music for the first time.
5. Gould, *whose* songs are often in the top ten these days, was too poor at the time to buy a good guitar.
6. She found a used guitar in a yard sale the day after the festival, *when* she was on her way back to New York City.
7. She still has that guitar, *which* she named Lynette after a famous country singer.
8. Lynette is like an old friend *who/whom* you don't want to leave behind when your fortunes improve.
9. Gould and Jim Elliott, *who/whom* she met on a tour last year, got married recently.
10. Eliott, with *whom* she often practices, is also a musician.

PART VIII: Final Test

I.

2. which 3. whose 4. whose 5. that 6. that 7. who
8. which 9. which 10. who

II.

2. which 3. whom 4. that 5. where 6. when
7. whom 8. when 9. where 10. that

III.

2. helps 3. remembers 4. exist 5. owes 6. means
7. knows 8. don't support 9. plays 10. spends

IV.

2. Alexander, who has received many prizes for his fiction, writes fantasies.
3. *The High King*, which is one of his most famous stories, received an important award.
4. Many of his stories take place in an imaginary country where evil is always lurking.
5. *The Black Cauldron* tells about a time when there was great danger in the country.
6. Gurgi, who is one of the most charming characters in the book, always speaks in rhymes.

7. Taran, whom Gurgi follows everywhere, becomes the hero.
8. Lloyd Alexander grew up in Philadelphia, where he still lives.
9. The Welsh legends that he read as a boy fascinated him.
10. Alexander, whose hobbies include playing the violin, wrote a book about music.

V.

Sentences with possible deletions:

2. The days ~~when~~ you're not home I usually eat out.
5. Jan often thinks about the years ~~when~~ he was growing up in Poland.
8. The computer ~~that~~ Mike bought three years ago doesn't have enough memory.
10. Don't tell Theo anything ~~that~~ you want to keep secret.

VI.

2. After twelve years, they all moved to Trenton, *where* Mike went to high school.
3. When he was twenty, Mike's parents told him about his twin brother, *who* was adopted by another family.
4. In 1995, *when* they were twenty-one, the two brothers finally met.
5. Finding his brother Pete, whom he hadn't *seen* since birth, changed Mike's life.
6. His brother, *who is/who's* a famous writer today, persuaded him to start writing also.
7. Mike wrote some articles about the neighborhood in *which* he had grown up./about the neighborhood *which* he had grown up in.
8. Those articles, which *were* published in the local newspaper, later became part of his first novel.
9. Writing, which *is* hard for a lot of people, comes easy to Mike.
10. He writes about things *that/which* have happened to him since he found his brother.

PART IX: Diagnostic Test

I.

2. wanted 3. had read 4. was going 5. had been
6. wouldn't speed 7. should read 8. had 9. must be
10. 's having

II.

2. said 3. told 4. said 5. told 6. said

III.

2. she, next month 3. his, the day before 4. they, this year
5. there, that evening 6. he, the previous month 7. there, then 8. we, our, there

IV.

2. told, not to drink 3. invited, to visit 4. ordered, to leave
5. ask, to give 6. says, to call

V.

2. where I work.
3. if/whether water freezes at 32° F.
4. how far he should run every day.
5. who drives their children to school.
6. if/whether it's going to rain.
7. if/whether I know how to use a computer.
8. how we like our new apartment.
9. if/whether we could help her with the dishes.
10. why she quit her job so soon.

VI.

2. Will you be home by 9:00?, Yes, I will.
3. Show me your license., What's wrong?
4. You forgot to signal., I'm sorry.
5. Can I help you?, I'm just looking.
6. Where are you going?, We're going to the movies.
7. Can you come with us?, I have to be home by 9:00.

VII.

2. where we should turn?
3. if/whether this is the right exit.
4. if/whether Willow Street runs east and west.
5. who(m) we should ask?
6. why this road is closed?
7. if/whether this is a dead end.
8. how long they're going to wait for us.
9. what time it is?
10. how long we should stay.

VIII.

2. where to buy Basmati rice.   3. when to file our income taxes.
4. who(m) to call about it?   5. what to wear.   6. how to get
this coffee stain out.

IX.

2. When I telephoned her, she said she was just sitting *there* reading.
3. Pamela told me she *had* lost her watch on the train the day before.
4. She said *she* had taken off the watch and put it on the seat.
5. A year ago, Pamela said she *would* be more careful with her things.
6. She said she really *must be* more careful in the future.
7. I wonder what time *it is*.
8. Can you tell me *whether* or not/Can you tell me *if* this train stops in Yonkers?
9. The train conductor told me where *to get* off.
10. He told me *not to* forget my camera.

PART IX: Final Test

I.

2. enjoyed   3. had left   4. was going   5. had been looking
6. wouldn't quit   7. should exercise   8. had to start   9. had to
use   10. is thinning

II.

2. said   3. told   4. said   5. told   6. said

III.

2. she, the following week   3. his, the day before   4. they,
their, this   5. there   6. he, the previous month   7. they, those
8. their, there

IV.

2. told, not to drive   3. invited, to stay   4. ordered, to prepare
5. ask, to water   6. says, to let

V.

2. where I'm staying.
3. if/whether helium is lighter than oxygen.
4. how long she should practice every day.
5. who repairs her television.
6. if/whether we're there yet.
7. if/whether I exercise regularly.

8. if/whether I like fajitas.
9. if/whether we could have the recipe.
10. why she's working so hard.

VI.

2. Is the teacher going to give a test next week?, Yes, he is.
3. How long will the test take?, You will need about one hour.
4. Are we allowed to use calculators?, Yes, you are.
5. When will you finish grading the tests?, I'm going to grade them tonight.
6. Where can I talk to you after class?, We'll meet here in the classroom.
7. You should study harder for the final., I'll put more effort into it.

VII.

2. what channel it's on?
3. if/whether I really want to watch this show.
4. how long the show is.
5. why we can't get any sound.
6. if/whether this show is rated for violence?
7. how long this commercial is going to last.
8. how to adjust the color/how you adjust the color?
9. what you're watching?
10. who to tell about this show/who(m) we should tell about this show.

VIII.

2. where to sell my handmade jewelry.   3. when to plant
tomatoes.   4. who(m) to call about it?   5. what to bring.
6. how long to cook the noodles?

IX.

2. He *said* he was busy tonight, but he could come some other time.
3. Jeff asked us *whether* or not/*if* we like comedies.
4. Sara asked who was going to make the popcorn.
5. She asked *if/whether* we like butter on our popcorn.
6. Frank said *he* couldn't hear the show with all that talking.
7. We told Sara *to please be quiet*/We told Sara, *"Please be quiet."*
8. I'm not sure how long *this movie is*.
9. Sara showed me how *to rewind* the tape.
10. The video store wants to know when *we're returning* the tape.

PART X: Diagnostic Test

I.

2. yourselves   3. myself   4. each other   5. himself
6. ourselves   7. herself   8. each other   9. yourselves
10. itself

II.

2. of   3. up   4. off   5. with   6. up   7. over   8. on   9. up
10. off   11. up   12. up   13. on   14. together   15. up

III.

2. wake him up   3. pass them out   4. drop in on him
5. call her back   6. did them over   7. ran into him   8. pick
her up   9. pay it back   10. filling it out

IV.

2. dropped out of   3. turned off   4. get off   5. put together
6. get together   7. stand up   8. blew up   9. show up
10. cut in   11. figured out   12. dream up   13. used up
14. picked out

2. In kindergarten, the children learned to share their toys and put them away by *themselves*.
3. It was a great idea, and Marv was pleased with himself for *coming up with it*.
4. Frank himself hates to dress *up*, but he let Cynthia talk him into wearing a suit for the party.
5. Sandra taught *herself* to use a computer, and now she's trying to dream up new ways to use it in her job.
6. When Brian introduced *himself* to me at the party, we found that we got along very well.
7. The committee members were able to work out their problems after everyone had talked to *each other/one another* and had expressed their opinions.
8. The bus driver let *us* off at the wrong stop.

PART X: Final Test

I.

2. herself   3. yourselves   4. myself   5. itself   6. each other
7. yourself   8. one another   9. himself   10. myself

II.

2. out   3. off   4. up   5. in   6. about   7. up   8. up
9. around   10. down   11. on   12. off   13. around
14. up   15. up

III.

2. fool around with it   3. tried it on   4. picked it out   5. laid them off   6. put it on   7. wrote it down   8. 'm getting along with her/I get along with her   9. put them away   10. point them out

IV.

2. Bringing up   3. come in   4. came up with   5. hand over
6. hang up   7. Look out for   8. looked over   9. put away
10. set up   11. tear down   12. eat out   13. get up
14. broke out

V.

2. Gary and I were talking to each other on the telephone when he suddenly hung *up* without saying goodbye.
3. When Craig's college application was turned down, he blamed *himself* for not handing it in sooner.
4. The committee chairperson herself called the meeting *off* and rescheduled it for the following week.
5. Flu broke out in the school, and everyone seemed to be catching it from *one another/each other*.
6. The lights were still on in the bedroom, so I shut *them off* and lay down.
7. The students couldn't figure out the problem *themselves,* but they knew they'd be able to work it out with some help from their teacher.
8. I hate eating out by *myself.*

Diagnostic and Final Tests

There are ten diagnostic and ten final tests, corresponding to the ten parts in the Student's Book. These exams test the material presented in the Grammar Charts, Grammar Notes, and the Focused Practice Exercises. The results of the Diagnostic Tests enable you to tailor your teaching to the needs of individual students. The format of both the Diagnostic and Final Tests is the same, and all but the final section of each test are labeled by grammar point. This labeling allows you to pinpoint each student's particular strengths and weaknesses within the unit. Students can concentrate on the sections in which they are weakest. They can work alone at their own pace or with others who need to practice the same areas. The final section of each test, called Synthesis: Error Correction, covers the grammar points of the entire part. The errors shown reflect the most common mistakes students make. As students correct these errors, they begin to correct their own.

Students who do well on a Diagnostic Test should feel good about their high scores, but they should also realize that knowledge of a language requires communication in open-ended situations. If these students are weak in comprehension or communication skills, they should concentrate on the Listening and Communication Practice exercises in the Student's Book.

Students who do not do well on a Diagnostic Test will want to divide their time between the Focused Practice and Communication Practice exercises.

Students of diverse skills and abilities can be divided into groups that concentrate on the kinds of exercises they need the most. You can work with the different groups and help each student to overcome his or her weaknesses.

Part I: Diagnostic Test

I. Contrast: Simple Present Tense and Present Progressive. *Circle the correct words to complete each sentence.*

1. The Johnsons (are expecting)/expect a baby.

2. Hi, Nicki. This is Jack. What do you do?/What are you doing?

3. I 'm reading/read a book about baby names at the moment.

4. You always read/'re always reading something.

5. I'm watching/watch television a lot too.

6. Is the water boiling/Does the water boil yet? I want some tea.

7. In this book, the writer explains/is explaining the meaning of some unusual names.

8. Look—the sun sets/is setting. Aren't the colors beautiful?

9. What time does the sun set/is the sun setting in December?

10. In your country, do people name/are people naming children after relatives?

11. Let's watch the press conference. The president names/is naming the new secretary of education right now.

12. My grandmother always knits/is knitting an afghan for each grandchild. It's a family tradition.

13. I knit/'m knitting a pair of baby booties. Do you like them?

II. Contrast: Action and Non-Action Verbs. *Complete each sentence with the correct form of the verb in parentheses. Use the simple present tense or the present progressive.*

1. How much _____ does _____ the baby _____ weigh _____ now?
   (weigh)

2. She _____ like her father.
   (look)

3. She _____ my side of the family at all.
   (not resemble)

4. Listen! _____ she _____?
   (cry)

5. I _____ anything.
   (not hear)

6. She _____ right now.
   (not sleep)

7. The Johnsons already _____ three boys.
   (have)

8. This bag _____ diapers and baby formula.
   (contain)

9. What's wrong? What _____ you _____ at?
   (look)

10. That baby food _____ awful.
    (look)

11. I guess it _____ good, though.
    (taste)

12. Look—she _____ it all. She's almost finished this whole jar.
    (eat)

III. Contrast: Past Progressive, Simple Past Tense, and *Was/Were going to.* *Complete each sentence with the correct form of the verb in parentheses. Use the past progressive, the simple past tense, or was/were going to.*

1. Where ___ *were* ___ you ___ *traveling* ___ to when you ___ *had* ___ the flat tire?
   (travel)   (travel)

2. I _____ the telephone when you _____ the first time.
   (not hear)   (call)

3. I _____ while I _____ my shower.
   (sing)   (take)

4. When I _____ the water, the phone _____ to ring again.
   (turn off)   (start)

5. While I _____ on the telephone, I _____ some water onto the carpet.
   (talk)   (drip)

6. We _____ to Toronto but we _____ our minds at the last minute.
   (move)   (change)

7. As soon as we _____ to sell our house, Jim _____ a good job here.
   (decide)   (find)

8. Gina _____ the lawn while Anne _____ in the garden.
   (mow)   (work)

9. I don't like to drive in bad weather. When it _____ to rain, I _____ for a
   (start)   (look)

   parking spot.

10. When we _____ lunch, we _____ to the beach.
    (finish)   (walk)

11. Agnes _____ , but the beach _____ closed because of the storm.
    (swim)   (be)

IV. Contrast: Present Perfect and Simple Past Tense. *Complete each sentence with the correct form of the verb in parentheses. Use the present perfect, the present perfect progressive, or the simple past tense.*

1. Dot's cousin ___ *was born* ___ in 1980.
   (be born)

2. A lot of children _____ in the new hospital since they _____ it.
   (be born)   (open)

3. Corinna _____ in several different countries. Next month she's moving again.
   (live)

4. She _____ to this country when she _____ fourteen.
   (come)   (be)

5. She _____ anyone here when she _____ .
   (not know)   (arrive)

6. Ray and Adam _____ schools last September.
                        (change)

7. They _____ many friends in their old school.
              (not have)

8. It's only November, and Sid _____ his whole history book already.
                                        (read)

9. For the past week, Karen _____ a book about European history.
                                    (read)

10. She _____ it yet.
          (not finish)

11. She _____ English for many years, and she plans to continue.
              (study)

12. How long _____ you _____ your present car?
                                           (own)

13. _____ you ever _____ kasha?
                                    (cook)

14. _____ you _____ my roommate when you _____ over
                              (meet)   (come)

    last week?

15. Paul _____ since he _____ his new job.
              (not call)   (start)

V. Past Perfect: Affirmative and Negative Statements. *Complete each sentence with the past perfect form of the verb in parentheses.*

1. By midnight, we still ___hadn't heard___ from them. We were really worried.
                              (hear)

2. Hua _____ English by the fourth grade. She spoke it very well.
            (learn)

3. Les _____ a lot of talent as a child. He won several music awards.
            (show)

4. By June, they _____ on a college yet.
                      (decide)

5. Ken _____ before appearing in the movie. This was his first role.
            (act)

6. Fran _____ for a number of jobs already.
              (apply)

VI. Past Perfect: *Yes/No* Questions and Short Answers. *Complete the questions and write short answers. Use the past perfect form of the verb in parentheses.*

1. **A:** I didn't see you at the party. ___Had___ you already ___left___ ?
                                                                  (left)

   B: ___Yes, I had___ . I left very early.

2. **A:** _____ Dan ever _____ a motorcycle before? He seemed scared.
                                              (ride)

   B: _____ . That was the first time.

3. **A:** _____ you already _____ the book?
                                                    (read)

   B: _____ . That's what made me want to see the movie.

4. **A:** _____ Nancy _____ to attend the meeting yesterday?
                                          (plan)

   B: _____ . No one had told her about it.

5. **A:** _____ Mark ever _____ anything like that before?
                                              (say)

   B: _____ . It was totally unexpected.

6. **A:** _____ the mayor already _____ his speech?
                                                      (make)

   B: _____ . The crowd was still waiting for him to start.

VII. Past Perfect: *Wh-* Questions. *Complete the questions. Use the past perfect form of the verb in parentheses.*

1. **A:** Where _____had_____ you and Vera _____met_____ before you started working together?
                                                      (meet)

   B: In high school. When we started this play, we'd already known each other for years.

2. **A:** Why _____ she _____ to become an actress?
                                          (decide)

   B: She'd always loved to perform.

3. **A:** What kind of work _____ she _____ before she started acting?
                                                          (do)

   B: She'd been a teacher for several years.

4. **A:** How many plays _____ she _____ in before she tried out for this one?
                                                        (act)

   B: Quite a few. She'd been in a lot of amateur productions.

5. **A:** Who _____ they _____ for the part before they hired her?
                                            (consider)

   B: I'm not sure. But a lot of people had already tried out for the role.

6. **A:** What _____ backstage before the show?
                    (happen)

   B: Nothing. Why?

VIII. Past Perfect Progressive: Affirmative and Negative Statements. *Complete the sentences with the past perfect progressive form of the verbs in parentheses.*

1. We _____ hadn't been watching _____ the news regularly before the Williams case. After that,
   (watch)

   we watched it every night.

2. Before her accident, Janet _____ soccer every weekend. She
   (play)

   had been the goalie all season.

3. I _____ with my friends because of my heavy schedule.
   (get together)

4. When you called, I _____ for my car keys. That's why I sounded so upset.
   (look)

5. Ben _____ well. That's why he made an appointment to see his doctor.
   (feel)

6. It _____ before our trip. The weather cleared just before we left.
   (snow)

IX. Past Perfect Progressive: Questions and Short Answers. *Complete the questions and write short answers where indicated. Use the past perfect progressive form of the verb in parentheses.*

1. **A:** _____ Had _____ you _____ been living _____ in Florida long before you started your business?
   (live)

   B: _____ No, we hadn't _____ . We had just moved here.

2. **A:** Who _____ you _____ to about opening a store?
   (talk)

   B: My lawyer.

3. **A:** _____ Annette _____ hard for the test?
   (study)

   B: _____ . Every night.

4. **A:** _____ Ben _____ about headaches?
   (complain)

   B: _____ . He never complains about anything.

5. **A:** _____ his doctors _____ him for the problem?
   (treat)

   B: _____ . Quite successfully.

6. **A:** What _____ Sheila _____ before she found this job?
   (do)

   B: Working in a factory.

X. Time Clauses in the Past: Meaning. *Circle the letter of the sentences closer in meaning to the numbered sentence.*

1. Bob was eating dinner when he heard the news.

    a. First Bob started dinner. Then he heard the news.

    b. First Bob heard the news. Then he ate dinner.

2. Laura was attending college while she was living on Elm Street.

    a. Laura moved away from Elm Street. Then she started college.

    b. Laura lived on Elm Street. At the same time, she attended college.

3. I was reading when you called.

    a. First I started reading. Then you called.

    b. I finished reading. Then you called.

4. When it started to rain, we left the park.

    a. First it started to rain. Then we left.

    b. First we left. Then it started to rain.

5. The Wangs were going to name their first child Edward, but they had a girl.

    a. The Wangs chose another name for their first child.

    b. The Wangs named their first child Edward.

6. When the storm began, the softball game had already ended.

    a. First the storm began. Then the game ended.

    b. First the game ended. Then the storm began.

7. When I turned on the television, the news had started.

    a. First I turned on the television. Then the news started.

    b. First the news started. Then I turned on the television.

8. By the time we got to the station, the train had left.

    a. First we got to the station. Then the train left.

    b. First the train left. Then we got to the station.

9. When rush hour started, it was raining.

    a. First it began to rain. Then rush hour started.

    b. First rush hour started, then it began to rain.

10. While we were taking the test, the lights went out.

    a. First we started taking the test. Then the lights went out.

    b. First the lights went out. Then we started taking the test.

XI. Synthesis: Error Correction. *Correct these sentences.*

1. Bruce Fenster, a writer for *TV View*, frequently is interviewing celebrities for the magazine.

    Bruce Fenster, a writer for *TV View*, frequently interviews celebrities for the magazine.

2. Since he has started two years ago, he's met a lot of actors and entertainers.

3. Last week, he has interviewed Jessica Wood, a popular talk-show host.

4. When Bruce was arriving at the studio for the interview, she was taping her show.

5. When Bruce sees her, Wood and her producers had just been arguing.

6. Jessica Wood was appearing very calm in spite of the problem.

7. The producers going to change some material, but Wood refused.

8. By the time the two started talking, Bruce been waiting more than an hour.

9. Wood had studied psychology in college, and at first she isn't going to be an entertainer.

10. She was performing at comedy clubs when the network has discovered her.

11. When the interview ended, Bruce had gone home to write his article.

Part I: Final Test

I. Contrast: Simple Present Tense and Present Progressive. *Circle the correct words to complete each sentence.*

1. Adam eats/(is eating) dinner right now. Can he call you back?

2. His family eats/is eating dinner every night at 6:00.

3. Alice studies/is studying nursing this semester.

4. Why are you leaving/do you leave so soon? The party just started.

5. What time are you leaving/do you leave for work every morning?

6. In my family, we usually name/are naming the first son after his father.

7. Why are they putting/do they put salt on the roads after a snowstorm?

8. Why are you putting/do you put so much salt into that soup? It's going to taste awful.

9. This movie review tells/is telling the whole plot of the movie. Now there won't be any surprises.

10. Listen. Jack tells/is telling that same joke again.

11. You look sad. What are you thinking/do you think about?

12. Where's Marcia going?/does Marcia go? She's all dressed up.

13. She goes/'s going to a concert every month.

II. Contrast: Action and Non-Action Verbs. *Complete each sentence with the correct form of the verb in parentheses. Use the simple present tense or the present progressive.*

1. Why _____ are _____ we _____ stopping _____ here? I thought we were finished shopping.

(stop)

2. I _____ a new coat.

(need)

3. How much _____ this coat _____?

(cost)

4. That _____ expensive.

(not seem)

5. Look! That woman _____ the same coat.

(wear)

6. It _____ very good on her.

(not look)

7. This one _____ nice and warm.

(feel)

8. _____ you _____ all the snow we had this year?

(remember)

9. I _____ some other nice coats over here.

(see)

10. I _____ any of those.

(not like)

11. This one _____ a ton.
    (weigh)

12. _____ we _____ in the right direction? I think I'm lost.
    (go)

III. Contrast: Past Progressive, Simple Past Tense, and *Was/Were going to.* *Complete each sentence with the correct form of the verb in parentheses. Use the past progressive, the simple past tense, or was/were going to.*

1. What _____were_____ you _____doing_____ when the storm _____started_____ last night?
   (do)   (start)

2. We _____ cards when it suddenly _____ very dark.
   (play)   (get)

3. As soon as it _____ to rain, we _____ all the windows.
   (begin)   (close)

4. When it _____ raining, we _____ outside.
   (stop)   (go)

5. We _____ a lot of fallen trees while we _____ around the neighborhood.
   (see)   (walk)

6. We _____ to the beach, but it _____ too dangerous.
   (walk)   (seem)

7. When we _____ inside, we _____ the radio.
   (go)   (turn on)

8. The weather forecast _____ on while we _____ dinner.
   (come)   (eat)

9. When we _____ the news, we _____ worried about you.
   (hear)   (get)

10. When we _____ your number, no one _____ .
    (dial)   (answer)

11. While we _____ about what to do, you _____ the doorbell.
    (think)   (ring)

IV. Contrast: Present Perfect and Simple Past Tense. *Complete each sentence with the correct form of the verb in parentheses. Use the present perfect, the present perfect progressive, or the simple past tense.*

1. Roy _____visited_____ Yellowstone National Park last year.
   (visit)

2. In 1872, Congress _____ the Yellowstone area a park.
   (make)

3. For more than 100 years, tourists _____ to Yellowstone. It's one of the most popular tourist
   (come)

   destinations in the United States.

4. Millions of people _____ it since the 1800s.
   (visit)

5. In the nineteenth century, when people first _____ about Yellowstone, they
   (hear)

   _____ amazed.
   (be)

6. Since then the number of visitors _____ year by year.
    (increase)

7. Visitors _____ a lot of damage to land and wildlife.
    (cause)

8. Some animals _____ rare.
    (become)

9. _____ you _____ any grizzly bears when you _____ in the
        (see)   (be)

park last year?

10. Look at Craig. He _____ pictures for hours.
        (take)

11. He _____ ten rolls of film since he _____ at the park.
        (use)   (arrive)

12. _____ you _____ to Yellowstone yet?
                        (be)

13. It's only January, and they _____ all the camping spots for the whole year already.
                                    (book)

14. Two years ago, we _____ to make a reservation.
                        (try)

15. We _____ to go since the children _____ it in school.
        (plan)   (study)

V. Past Perfect: Affirmative and Negative Statements. *Complete each sentence with the past perfect form of the verb in parentheses.*

1. By morning, they still _____ hadn't called _____ .
                            (call)

2. Steve _____ to ride a bike by the time he was five years old. He was a fast learner.
        (learn)

3. When I talked to him yesterday, Leif still _____ about last week's meeting.
                                                (hear)

4. By the holidays, we still _____ our greeting cards.
                            (mail)

5. Bernadette _____ me about the weather in Minneapolis. I arrived unprepared for the cold.
            (tell)

6. Vince _____ several times before opening the door.
        (knock)

VI. Past Perfect: *Yes/No* Questions and Short Answers. *Complete the questions and write short answers. Use the past perfect form of the verb in parentheses.*

1. **A:** _____ Had _____ you _____ moved _____ to New York City by 1990?
                            (move)

   B: _____ Yes, I had _____ . I came here in 1989.

2. **A:** _____ you ever _____ such a big city before?
   (see)

   B: _____ . Only small towns.

3. **A:** _____ Natalie _____ German before last year?
   (study)

   B: _____ . She'd taken a class in high school.

4. **A:** _____ your team members ever _____ so fast before?
   (swim)

   B: _____ . This was a new record for our team.

5. **A:** _____ Sasha ever _____ snails before you two went to Madrid?
   (eat)

   B: _____ . She tried them in Quebec last summer.

6. **A:** _____ the students _____ tired of studying by summer vacation?
   (get)

   B: _____ . They were ready for a break.

VII. Past Perfect: *Wh-* Questions. *Complete the questions. Use the past perfect form of the verb in parentheses.*

1. **A:** What ___*had*___ you ___*heard*___ about Tokyo by the time you moved there?
   (hear)

   B: Just that it was a very exciting city.

2. **A:** How many jobs _____ you _____ for by the time you got this one?
   (apply)

   B: Too many to count.

3. **A:** How much French _____ you _____ by the time you arrived in Paris?
   (learn)

   B: Unfortunately, not much. We started studying it seriously after we got settled.

4. **A:** Before you left, who _____ you _____ about your plans to be out
   (tell)

   of town?

   B: Everyone. It wasn't a secret.

5. **A:** How many reports _____ you _____ by the time the train got in?
   (read)

   B: Not many. I fell asleep.

6. **A:** Before Betty and Lou came to Montreal, where else _____ they _____ living?
   (think about)

   B: They'd considered Chicago.

VIII. Past Perfect Progressive: Affirmative and Negative Statements. *Complete the sentences with the past perfect progressive form of the verb in parentheses.*

1. We ___*hadn't been waiting*___ long before they arrived. They were only five minutes late.
   (wait)

2. Before the government cut spending, schools _____ rapidly. Now
   (improve)

   everyone is worried about the future of our schools.

3. Because of the drought, farmers _____ many vegetables.
   (grow)

4. Before we bought a car, we _____ our groceries at the corner store. Large
   (buy)

   supermarkets are great, but I miss the small local shop.

5. By the time I found my glasses, I _____ for them for days.
   (search)

6. The TV _____ for an hour before Chris woke up and turned it off.
   (blare)

IX. Past Perfect Progressive: Questions and Short Answers. *Complete the questions and write short answers where indicated. Use the past perfect progressive form of the verb in parentheses.*

1. **A:** Where ___*had*___ you ___*been staying*___ before you moved into your apartment?
   (stay)

   B: With friends.

2. **A:** _____ Stan _____ weight before he started exercising?
   (gain)

   B: _____ . He had become quite overweight.

3. **A:** _____ they _____ the doorbell for a long time?
   (ring)

   B: _____ . I answered it right away.

4. **A:** How long _____ Mrs. Nelson _____ at your store when it closed?
   (shop)

   B: At least ten years. She was one of our oldest customers.

5. **A:** _____ Sherry _____ her book since 1985?
   (write)

   B: _____ . I thought she'd never get it finished.

6. **A:** What time _____ the baby _____?

(wake up)

    B: Usually at around 5:00 in the morning.

X. Time Clauses in the Past: Meaning. *Circle the letter of the sentences closer in meaning to the numbered sentence.*

1. Sandy was making a phone call when the fire started.

    a. First Sandy started making a call. Then the fire started.

    b. First the fire started. Then Sandy started making a call.

2. Ethel was working at the hospital while she was going to nursing school.

    a. Ethel quit her job at the hospital and then she started school.

    b. Ethel was working at the hospital. At the same time, she was going to school.

3. I was doing homework when you told me dinner was ready.

    a. First I started doing my homework. Then you told me dinner was ready.

    b. I finished doing my homework. Then you told me dinner was ready.

4. When it got dark, we went home.

    a. First we went home. Then it got dark.

    b. First it got dark. Then we went home.

5. Sharon was going to cut her hair, but her friends liked it long.

    a. Sharon cut her hair.

    b. Sharon didn't cut her hair.

6. When the accident happened, the police closed the highway.

    a. First there was an accident. Then the police closed the highway.

    b. First the police closed the highway. Then there was an accident.

7. When we got to the theater, the movie had started.

    a. First we got to the theater. Then the movie started.

    b. First the movie started. Then we got to the theater.

8. By the time the tow truck came, we'd been waiting for two hours.

    a. First we waited for two hours. Then the tow truck came.

    b. First the tow truck came. Then we waited for two hours.

9. When the plane took off, it was raining.

    a. First the plane took off. Then it began to rain.

    b. First it began to rain. Then the plane took off.

10. While we were thinking about you, you called.

    a. First we started thinking about you. Then you called.

    b. First you called. Then we started thinking about you.

XI. Synthesis: Error Correction. *Correct these sentences.*

1. Macaulay Culkin, the star of *Home Alone*, has begun acting when he was four years old.

   Macaulay Culkin, the star of <u>Home Alone</u>, began acting when he was four years old.

2. By the time he appeared in *Home Alone*, he already acted in movies for several years.

3. Before he chose Culkin, the director has auditioned more than 100 children.

4. He not going to give Culkin the part because there were so many lines to learn.

5. Macaulay has a good memory and is always memorizing his parts very quickly.

6. Since Macaulay becomes a star, his father has been working as his agent.

7. The movie has come out several years ago.

8. Macaulay is having six siblings.

9. Since he became famous, he hadn't had much privacy.

10. While the writer John Hughes was preparing to take his family on a vacation, he was getting the idea for *Home Alone*.

11. When the movie became a huge success, everyone had been surprised.

Part II: Diagnostic Test

I. Future Progressive: Affirmative and Negative Statements with *Will* and *Be going to*.

Complete the conversation with the future progressive form of the words in parentheses.

A: Do you have plans for tomorrow afternoon?

B: I ___'m going to be working___ all afternoon. I have a project due on Monday.
   <small>1. (be going to / work)</small>

A: How about next Saturday, then?

B: Sorry. We're leaving for vacation in Florida next Sunday, so we _____ most of the
   <small>2. (will / pack)</small>

day on Saturday. But I _____ anything the week we get back. Let's make some
   <small>3. (be not going to / do)</small>

plans then, OK?

A: Sounds good. So, are you going camping again this year?

B: Only the second week. My wife _____ a sales conference in Sarasota, so we
   <small>4. (be going to / attend)</small>

_____ the first week. We _____ at the hotel. The second week,
   <small>5. (will not / camp)</small>   <small>6. (will / stay)</small>

we _____ along the Gulf Coast and _____ along the way.
   <small>7. (will / drive)</small>   <small>8. (camp)</small>

A: Your son enjoyed scuba diving there the last time you went.

B: That's right. Unfortunately, he _____ with us for that part of the trip.
   <small>9. (be not going to / come)</small>

A: Why not?

B: He _____ college that week. We're going to drop him off in Tallahassee and then
   <small>10. (will / start)</small>

go camping.

A: Poor kid. But I guess he _____ a lot of diving during the next four years.
   <small>11. (be going to / do)</small>

II. Future Progressive: *Wh-* Questions, *Yes/No* Questions, and Short Answers with *Will* and *Be going to*. Complete the questions and write short answers where indicated. Use the future progressive form of the verbs in parentheses.

1. **A:** Where ___will___ people ___be working___ in the future?
   <small>(will / work)</small>

   B: Many of them at home. Home offices will become more and more common in the next century.

2. A: _____ people _____ longer in the twenty-first century?
          (Will / live)

   B: _____ . Possibly 150 years or more.

3. A: _____ my great-grandchildren _____ the same kind of television that I
                                                   (be going to / watch)

   do now?

   B: _____ . There will be many changes in home entertainment in the near future.

4. A: _____ we still _____ on telephones in 2010?
                                     (Will / talk)

   B: _____ . But they'll be tiny ones, worn in necklaces and pins.

5. A: What sources of energy _____ the world _____ in the future?
                                                              (be going to / use)

   B: Probably a variety, including solar, wind, and nuclear energy.

6. A: When _____ we _____ some of these changes?
                                    (will / see)

   B: Very soon. In fact, some are already here.

III. Future Progressive with Time Clauses. *Write sentences with the words in parentheses. Use the simple present tense and the future progressive with* will *or* be going to.

1. (Frank/play softball/while/I/do the shopping)

   Frank will be playing softball while I do the shopping.

   _____

2. (He/straighten up the house/while/I/run some errands)

   _____

   _____

3. (Billy/do his homework/when/I/get home)

   _____

   _____

4. (While/Frank/set the table/I/prepare dinner)

   _____

   _____

5. (I/still/cook/when/the guests/start to arrive)

   _____

   _____

6. (They/talk to Frank/while/I/finish cooking)

_____

_____

7. (We/not sit down/to eat/until/everyone/be here)

_____

_____

8. (The children/play outside/while/the adults/have coffee)

_____

_____

IV. Future Perfect and Future Perfect Progressive: Affirmative and Negative Statements.

Complete the conversations with the correct form of the verb in parentheses. Use the future perfect or the future perfect progressive.

A: By New Year's you ___'ll have been working___ at Spratt's for five years.
   1. (work)

B: Don't remind me. I _____ cars for half a decade.
   2. (sell)

A: There goes Wilma again. By the time she gets to the corner, she _____ around
   3. (jog)

the block six times.

B: You can set your clock by her. By the end of this week, she _____ every morning
   4. (jog)

for six months.

A: We're two hours late. I'm not going to call Mom and Dad when we get home. They'll be asleep.

B: No, they _____ to sleep yet. Anyway, I promised we'd call when we got home.
   5. (not go)

They _____ for more than two hours.
   6. (wait)

A: We _____ this book by the end of the year.
   7. (complete)

B: And we _____ some interesting new verb tenses.
   8. (learn)

V. Future Perfect and Future Perfect Progressive with Time Clauses. *Complete each sentence with the correct form of the verb in parentheses. Use the future perfect, the future perfect progressive, and the simple present tense.*

1. Tom's in his third year of college. By the time he and Lisa ___get___ married next
   (get)

month, he ___won't have graduated___ yet.
   (not graduate)

2. Lisa has been saving $50 a month since January. She _____ $600 by the time she
(save)

_____ her holiday shopping in December.
(do)

3. Tom's driving to Washington for a job interview. He's going to leave New York City at 5:00 A.M. By the

time he _____ in Washington, he _____ for five hours without
(arrive)   (drive)

a break.

4. Lisa wants a new job too, but she's too busy to look for one. By the time Tom _____ ,
(graduate)

she probably _____ one yet.
(not find)

5. By the time Lisa _____ her job, she _____ several training
(quit)   (complete)

courses.

6. Tom's sending Lisa a postcard from Washington. She _____ it by the time he
(not receive)

_____ to New York City.
(get back)

VI. Future Perfect and Future Perfect Progressive: *Wh-* Questions, *Yes/No* Questions, and Short Answers. *Complete the questions and write short answers where indicated. Use the verbs in parentheses and the future perfect or the future perfect progressive.*

1. **A:** ____Will____ you __have finished__ the newspaper by 10:00? I want to take it with me on
(finish)

the train.

B: ____Yes, I will____ . I'm almost finished with it now.

2. **A:** Tuition is much cheaper for residents of the state. How long _____ you

_____ here by September?
(live)

B: Two years.

3. **A:** The staff meeting is on Wednesday. _____ you _____ your report by then?
(submit)

B: _____ . I'm going to need another week.

4. **A:** How many applicants _____ Sharon _____ by 5:00?
(interview)

B: At least five. She's been seeing people all day.

5. **A:** Mark's birthday is the twelfth. _____ he _____ our gift by then?
(receive)

   B: _____ . I sent it express mail.

6. **A:** What _____ you _____ from your experience living in the United States?
(learn)

   B: I'm not sure. I'll know better after I get home.

VII. Synthesis: Error Correction. *Find and correct seven errors with the future.*

I started writing a journal when I turned eighteen. My birthday is next month, so in a few weeks I'll have
been ~~keep~~ keeping my journal for five years. When I will finish this entry, I'll have been filling up another notebook.
Recently I reread those old journals. I was surprised. I've already accomplished so many things that I wanted
to do when I first started writing them. In my first journal I said I wanted to go back to school. Well, in
September, I'll be starting at the university. I also said I wanted to quit my job and find something more
interesting. By my birthday, I've been working at my new job for a year. (Maybe my boss will have decided
to give me a raise by then.)

   There are some things I won't have accomplished by then, though. I wanted to have my own car by
the time I turned twenty-three. I won't had saved enough by next month. And I won't moving into my own
apartment by then either. Never mind. When my twenty-fourth birthday arrived, I'll be writing in my journal
about my car and new apartment.

Part II: Final Test

I. Future Progressive: Affirmative and Negative Statements with *Will* and *Be going to*.

Complete the conversation with the future progressive form of the words in parentheses.

A: Jim <u>'s not going to be working</u> with that client anymore. He was just promoted.
  1. (be not going to / work)

B: I guess you _____ for someone to take over his job.
  2. (will / look)

A: Probably.

A: Baseball fans _____ in Toronto tonight. The Toronto Blue Jays just won against
  3. (be going to / celebrate)

the Chicago White Sox.

B: That means the White Sox _____ in the World Series this year.
  4. (will not / play)

A: You're right.

A: The library _____ in half an hour.
  5. (will / close)

B: Can I still check out books?

A: Sure. We _____ books for another fifteen minutes.
  6. (be going to / check out)

A: How's your daughter?

B: Fine. She _____ in June.
  7. (be going to / get married)

A: That's wonderful. Congratulations!

A: Do you want to put anything on the agenda for our next meeting?

B: I _____ a marketing plan over the next month. Should we discuss it at
  8. (be going to / develop)

the meeting?

A: Let's wait. We _____ about marketing until the following month.
  9. (be not going to / talk)

A: I _____ into town tomorrow. Can I pick up anything for you while I'm there?
  10. (will / drive)

B: Could you take these books back to the library for me? I _____ that way for
  11. (will not / go)

another week.

II. Future Progressive: *Wh-* Questions, *Yes/No* Questions, and Short Answers with *Will* and *Be going to.* Complete the questions and write short answers. Use the future progressive form of the verbs in parentheses.

1. **A:** Where _____*are*_____ you *going to be moving* ?
   (be going to / move)

   B: Atlanta.

   A: Oh, really? I hear it's a nice city.

2. **A:** _____ the Paytons _____ us this summer?
   (Will / visit)

   B: _____ . In July.

3. **A:** _____ you _____ anything next Friday night?
   (be going to / do)

   B: _____ . I don't have any plans. Why?

4. **A:** _____ Rosa _____ any more computer courses?
   (be going to / take)

   B: _____ . She's already taken all the courses they offer.

5. **A:** Who _____ tomorrow?
   (will / drive)

   B: It's my turn. You drove today.

6. **A:** When _____ you _____ your new furniture?
   (will / get)

   B: They promised to deliver it next week.

III. Future Progressive with Time Clauses. Write sentences with the words in parentheses. Use the simple present tense and the future progressive with *will* or *be going to.*

1. (We/look for a new receptionist/before/Cora/leave)

   <u>We'll be looking for a new receptionist before Cora leaves.</u>

   _____

2. (I/answer your telephone/while/you/eat lunch)

   _____

   _____

3. (We/think about you/while/you/be away)

   _____

   _____

4. (Paz/study/when/you/come)

   _____

   _____

5. (Sumail/type her research paper/while/Paz/study)

   _____

   _____

6. (I/take a nap/while/you/write letters)

   _____

   _____

7. (We/freeze/here in Chicago/while/they/sunbathe in Miami)

   _____

   _____

8. (Nora and Ted/clear the table/while/you/wash the dishes)

   _____

   _____

IV. Future Perfect and Future Perfect Progressive: Affirmative and Negative Statements.

Complete the conversations with the correct form of the verbs in parentheses. Use the future perfect or the future perfect progressive.

A: By next summer, I ___'ll have been living___ in this apartment for ten years.
   1. (live)

B: And you _____ it for at least three. I think it's time for some interior decorating.
   2. (not paint)

A: Dan got up at six this morning to study. By lunchtime, he _____ his notes for six hours.
   3. (review)

B: He's sure to get an A for the course.

A: Which means he _____ any grade lower than a B in four years.
   4. (not get)

A: What are your plans for summer vacation?

B: I think I'll go home. By that time, I _____ my family for more than a year.
   5. (not see)

A: Should we take Bekah out for dinner when she arrives?

B: I don't think so. She _____ for two days. She'll probably just want to stay home.
   6. (travel)

A: Tamika spends a lot of time on computer games. By dinner time she _____ that one
   7. (play)

all afternoon.

B: Well, at least she _____ geography that way.
   8. (learn)

V. Future Perfect and Future Perfect Progressive with Time Clauses. *Complete each sentence with the correct form of the verb in parentheses. Use the future perfect, the future perfect progressive, and the simple present tense.*

1. **A:** I think we should tell Monica we can't come tonight.

   B: Maybe you're right. By the time we _____arrive_____ (arrive), they _____'ll have started_____ (start) eating already.

2. **A:** I think I mailed the wrong material to my client yesterday.

   B: Call them right away and tell them to send it back. They _____ (not open) the package by the time

   you _____ (call) .

3. **A:** I wonder if Grayson will run for re-election.

   B: I hope not. By the time he _____ (complete) this term, he _____ (be) mayor for

   sixteen years.

4. **A:** Manny started working at McDonald's when he was sixteen.

   B: By the time he _____ (graduate) , he _____ (work) there for eight years.

5. **A:** How long have you and Jamil been roommates?

   B: Let's see. He moved in last September. By the time we _____ (go back) to school again, he

   _____ (live) here for one year.

6. **A:** How long have they been doing road work on your street?

   B: Since June, and they won't be done until October. By the time they _____ (finish) , I

   _____ (not be able) to use my driveway for five months.

VI. Future Perfect and Future Perfect Progressive: *Wh-* Questions, *Yes/No* Questions, and Short Answers. *Complete the questions and write short answers. Use the verbs in parentheses and the future perfect or the future perfect progressive.*

1. **A:** I have to go out at 7:00. _____Will_____ we _____have eaten_____ (eat) dinner by then?

   B: _____No, we won't have_____ . We're starting late. But you can leave if you have to.

2. **A:** _____ our lease _____ by June 1?
   (expire)

   B: _____. It'll expire at the end of May. Why?

   A: I saw a great apartment today. It's going to be available in June.

3. **A:** How long _____ we _____ here by then?
   (live)

   B: Three years.

4. **A:** How many sales calls _____ you _____ by 5:00?
   (make)

   B: About fifteen. I've been on the telephone all day.

5. **A:** I'll need the computer at 2:00. _____ you _____ by then?
   (finish)

   B: _____. I only need a few more minutes.

6. **A:** The workload is going to be heavy in July. _____ you _____ from
   (come back)

   vacation by then?

   B: _____. I'll be back by June 20.

VII. Synthesis: Error Correction. *Correct these sentences.*

1. Next month Bob's parents will been married for thirty years.

   Next month Bob's parents will have been married for thirty years.

   _____

2. Their children will be give them a big party.

   _____

   _____

3. A band will going to be playing music so that the guests can dance.

   _____

   _____

4. I going to be meeting Bob's parents at the party.

   _____

   _____

5. What he'll have told them about me?

   _____

   _____

6. Bob will have been seeing this dress three times.

   _____

   _____

7. I want to buy a new one, but I'm afraid I don't have found anything by the party.

   _____

   _____

8. By the time we'll get to the party, the music will already have started.

   _____

   _____

9. Bob's parents will have been celebrating their anniversary every year.

   _____

   _____

10. They won't had missed a single year.

    _____

    _____

11. Their best man will have been knowing them for more than thirty years.

    _____

    _____

Part III: Diagnostic Test

I. Tag Questions: Affirmative and Negative. *Complete the questions with a pronoun and the correct form of the verb.*

1. You're not from Boston originally, _____are you_____ ?

2. You lived in Atlanta before, _____ ?

3. Irene's been to Japan, _____ ?

4. She didn't go last year, _____ ?

5. The Aguirres were going to buy a house, _____ ?

6. They hadn't planned to move into the city, _____ ?

7. You don't know them, _____ ?

8. We should leave soon, _____ ?

9. We can't be late, _____ ?

10. You won't tell anyone, _____ ?

11. Steve will be at the party, _____ ?

12. He always comes a little late, _____ ?

13. That was a big surprise, _____ ?

14. Eva isn't working now, _____ ?

II. Tag Questions: Affirmative and Negative. *Complete each question with the correct form of the verb in parentheses.*

1. You _____'ve read_____ Brian Frank's books, haven't you?
      (read)

2. They _____ interesting, aren't they?
      (be)

3. He _____ very many books, has he?
      (write)

4. He _____ to write more, doesn't he?
      (plan)

5. He _____ in England, did he?
   (grow up)

6. He _____ in the United States now, isn't he?
   (live)

7. He _____ famous someday, won't he?
   (be)

8. They _____ a movie of *Redfern,* shouldn't they?
   (make)

9. Once you start one of his books, you _____ it down, can you?
   (put)

10. I _____ of him before last year, had you?
    (heard)

11. His last book _____ on the best-seller lists, did it?
    (appear)

12. The library _____ it yet, does it?
    (have)

III. Tag Questions: Short Answers. *Write the short answer to each question.*

1. **A:** You're from the United States, aren't you?

   B: ___No, I'm not___. I'm from Canada.

2. **A:** The Behlers don't like living in Los Angeles, do they?

   B: _____. They love it there.

3. **A:** You didn't buy coffee, did you?

   B: _____. I forgot. Sorry.

4. **A:** You won't forget to call, will you?

   B: _____. I promise.

5. **A:** We're leaving soon, aren't we?

   B: _____. In about five minutes.

6. **A:** We should bring a small gift, shouldn't we?

   B: _____. Flowers would be nice.

7. **A:** Lars hasn't seen this movie yet, has he?

   B: _____. He hasn't even heard of it.

IV. Additions with *So, Too, Neither, Not either,* and *But.* *Circle the letter of the correct way to correct each sentence.*

1. Mark is very outgoing, and
   a. so does Kim.   b. Kim isn't either.   (c.) so is Kim.

2. Kim sometimes likes to spend time alone, but
   a. Mark doesn't.   b. Mark does.   c. Mark isn't.

3. She didn't use to live in Seattle and,
   a. so did Mark.   b. so was Mark.   c. Mark didn't either.

4. She lived in Vancouver for years, and
   a. Mark had too.   b. neither did Mark.   c. so did Mark.

5. Mark hadn't met her then, but
   a. I had.   b. I had too.   c. I hadn't.

6. When she moved to Seattle, she was looking for an apartment, and
   a. Mark wasn't either.   b. so did Mark.   c. so was Mark.

7. After three months, she still hadn't found anything nice,
   a. and neither was he.   b. and neither had he.   c. but he hadn't.

8. Then she found a great apartment facing the water, and
   a. he did too.   b. so does he.   c. he does.

9. It was the same apartment. She wanted it right away,
   a. and neither did he.   b. but he did.   c. and so did he.

10. Luckily, he found another apartment in the same building. Kim was glad, and
    a. I was too.   b. me neither.   c. but I was.

11. Kim's had some problems here in Seattle,
    a. and Mark hasn't either.   b. and so has Mark.   c. but Mark did.

12. I know she won't give up,
    a. and neither will Mark.   b. and so will Mark.   c. but Mark won't.

V. Synthesis: Error Correction. *Find and correct seven errors with tag questions, additions, and responses.*

Dear Lynn,

It seems like a long time since I left Vancouver, ~~isn't~~ *doesn't* it? I've had some problems finding an apartment and a job, but you warned me about that before I left, didn't you? Anyway, everything seems to be working out now. I found an apartment, a job, and a boyfriend (his name is Mark) just last month. Things can happen fast sometimes, don't they?

I'm working at a local hospital, on the pediatrics floor. My supervisor is nice and either are my co-workers. I live near the water in Bayview Apartments, and so is Mark. My apartment has a view, but his doesn't, so we spend a lot of time at my place. Mark and I have a lot in common. He isn't at all shy, and neither do I. I enjoy noisy, crowded places, and so did he. We have some differences, though. I love taking long quiet walks, but he doesn't. I can work odd hours and weekends with no problem, but he didn't. He says he needs to have his weekends free. So far, we've worked out our differences. One last thing—Mark's from Vancouver too. It's a small world, doesn't it?

When are you coming for a visit? I really want to show you around Seattle.

Love,

Kim

Part III: Final Test

I. Tag Questions: Affirmative and Negative. *Complete the questions with a pronoun and the correct form of the verb.*

1. They're not teachers, ___are they___ ?

2. He worked for Comcrest, _____ ?

3. Anna's seen that movie, _____ ?

4. She went with you, _____ ?

5. Mike was going to change jobs, _____ ?

6. When you talked to him, he hadn't quit yet, _____ ?

7. We don't have to go yet, _____ ?

8. You should start to get ready, _____ ?

9. We can still apply to school, _____ ?

10. If we're late, they won't mind, _____ ?

11. Sharon will call back, _____ ?

12. They always break the rules, _____ ?

13. That was nice of them, _____ ?

14. Eva isn't working anymore, _____ ?

II. Tag Questions: Affirmative and Negative. *Complete each question with the correct form of the verb in parentheses.*

1. This restaurant ___looks___ familiar, doesn't it?
   (look)

2. We _____ here before, haven't we?
   (be)

3. She _____ to you yet, has she?
   (write)

4. The plane _____ very late, isn't it?
   (be)

5. It _____ on the runway for an hour, didn't it?
(sit)

6. We _____ Selma, shouldn't we?
(call)

7. Pietro _____ with you, isn't he?
(stay)

8. He _____ us at the airport, won't he?
(meet)

9. You really _____ just one potato chip, can you?
(eat)

10. He _____ anything like that before, had he?
(say)

11. It _____ sense, did it?
(make)

12. Sue _____ about it yet, has she?
(not hear)

III. Tag Questions: Short Answers. *Write the short answer to each question.*

1. **A:** You're a doctor, aren't you?

   B: ____No, I'm not____ . I'm a lawyer.

2. **A:** Bob's not doing well this semester, is he?

   B: _____ . He's getting straight A's.

3. **A:** We're going to invite the Corio's to our barbecue, aren't we?

   B: _____ . We invite them every year.

4. **A:** You don't mind cooking tonight, do you?

   B: _____ . It's OK with me.

5. **A:** Bobby won't eat spinach, will he?

   B: _____ . He never touches it.

6. **A:** You can ride a bike, can't you?

   B: _____ . I learned years ago.

7. **A:** You didn't buy gas, did you?

   B: _____ . You'd better get some soon.

IV. Additions with *So, Too, Neither, Not either,* and *But.* *Circle the letter of the correct way to complete each sentence.*

1. Mr. Santos gives a lot of homework,

   (a.) and so does Ms. Kovak.   b. and Ms. Kovak doesn't either.   c. but Ms. Kovak does.

2. Ms. Kovak doesn't give weekly quizzes, but

   a. Mr. Santos doesn't.   b. Mr. Santos does.   c. Mr. Santos didn't.

3. He didn't use to give a final exam,

   a. but she didn't.   b. but she did.   c. and she did too.

4. He requires a term paper for his course,

   a. and neither does she.   b. but she does.   c. and she does too.

5. I took Mr. Santos's course last year,

   a. and my friend Karl did too.   b. but my friend Karl did.   c. and my friend Karl didn't either.

6. I had never written a term paper before, and

   a. so had Karl.   b. neither had Karl.   c. neither did Karl.

7. Karl's a fairly good writer,

   a. but I am.   b. and neither do I.   c. and I am too.

8. He's always had trouble using the library,

   a. and I haven't either.   b. but I have.   c. and so have I.

9. He couldn't find information about his topic,

   a. and neither could I.   b. and neither did I.   c. but I couldn't.

10. Finally, I asked the librarian for help.

    a. but Karl didn't.   b. and neither did Karl.   c. but Karl doesn't.

11. The computers aren't hard to figure out, and

    a. the indexes didn't either.   b. the indexes don't either.   c. neither are the indexes.

12. My paper turned out pretty good,

    a. but Karl's didn't.   b. and Karl's didn't either.   c. and neither did Karl's.

V. Synthesis: Error Correction. *Find and correct eight errors with tag questions, additions, and responses.*

Dear Karl,

           Last summer vacation seems like yesterday, ~~isn't~~ *doesn't* it? It's hard to believe that it's been almost a year since we saw you. I'm looking forward to your visit this year, but so is your Aunt Jennie. You told us you'd teach us that new computer game you got for Christmas. You haven't forgotten your promise, have you?

Your mom has told us that you had some problems with school this year. She's not worried, though, and either are we. She's confident that you'll work it out by the end of the term. So are we. Writing a paper isn't easy, does it? I had problems with that when I was in school too, and so had a lot of my classmates.

When you come to visit in July, your cousin Todd will be here too. You haven't seen him for a while, but you two have a lot in common. I know you love sports, and he is too. Maybe we can take in a baseball game while you're here. He enjoys skateboarding, and so you do. It's going to be a great summer, won't it? See you in July.

Love,

Uncle Al

Part IV: Diagnostic Test

I. Contrast: Gerunds and Infinitives. *Circle the correct form of the verb.*

1. (Collecting)/To collect coins is a popular hobby.

2. It's important <u>to read/reading</u> about each coin's history.

3. <u>To learn/Learning</u> about each coin makes it even more fascinating.

4. Kehinde decided <u>to buy/buying</u> a silver World Cup coin.

5. His father advised him <u>to get/getting</u> one right away.

6. He warned him <u>not to wait/not waiting</u>.

7. <u>Not to follow/Not following</u> his father's advice was a big mistake.

8. Kehinde postponed <u>to go/going</u> to the store.

9. His brother offered <u>to take/taking</u> him.

10. He didn't mind <u>to drive/driving</u> him there.

11. Kehinde was disappointed <u>to find out/finding out</u> that there were none left.

12. Then his brother remembered <u>to see/seeing</u> one in another store.

13. On the way home, they stopped <u>to look/looking</u> in that store.

14. They were lucky. They managed <u>to buy/buying</u> the last one in the store.

15. Kehinde was excited about <u>to add/adding</u> the coin to his collection.

II. Object Pronouns and Possessives. *Complete each sentence with the correct form of the words in parentheses.*

1. Did we mention _____their moving_____ to Texas?

(they / move)

2. The teacher would like _____us to study_____ more.

(we / study)

3. We don't understand _____ to leave.

(they / want)

4. The police were surprised at _____ to the crime.

(Pete / admit)

5. They allowed _____ a telephone call.

(he / make)

6. Mrs. Aguirre always encourages _____ harder.

(we / work)

7. Many people resent _____.

(he / not help)

8. Sadie won't tolerate _____ her own share of their expenses.
   (Cora / not pay)

9. She's fed up with _____ her appointments.
   (she / forget)

10. She persuaded _____ their minds.
    (they / change)

III. *Make, Have, Help, Get,* and *Let.* *Complete each sentence with the correct form of the words in parentheses.*

1. Crime is a problem, but experts say that owning a gun ___won't help you live___

   (not help / you / live)

   any more safely. In fact, it will make things a lot more dangerous.

2. Sarah Metaski attended some classes on personal safety. The classes _____

   (get / she / change)

   a lot of habits.

3. Knowing danger areas _____ becoming crime victims.
   (help / people / avoid)

4. Parking lots are favorite spots for muggers. Sarah always _____ with her to

   (have / a friend / walk)

   her car after work.

5. Sarah keeps a pair of men's basketball shoes on her back seat. The shoes _____

   (make / criminals / think)

   that an athletic man owns the car.

6. Sarah _____ more than two feet high around her house. Sometimes burglars

   (not let / bushes / grow)

   hide in the bushes near a house.

7. She bought an alarm that sounds like a barking dog. She wants to _____

   (make / people / believe)

   she owns a dog because that's a big crime deterrent.

8. Next week, she's going to _____ her home a free security inspection.

   (have / the police / give)

9. When she's in an unfamiliar neighborhood, she always walks briskly. She never

   _____ she's lost or confused.
   (let / people / think)

10. Now Sarah wants to _____ the course.

    (get / her friends / take)

11. She thinks her company should _____ personal safety to its employees.

    (have / someone / teach)

IV. Synthesis: Error Correction. *Find and correct seven errors with gerunds and infinitives in this article about gun control.*

         take

It's time to ~~taking~~ action. You can get lawmakers and others to change the laws. Even a busy person can make a difference. Here are some things you can do.

1. Learn personal safety techniques, but don't buy a gun. Has a gun in the house is dangerous and adds to the problem.

2. Violence is a public health problem. Get your doctors display information about the risks of owning guns. Urge they to talk to parents about the danger of guns. Compare it to the danger of don't using seat belts.

3. When you see gun advertising, call or write to the publication. Tell them how you feel about their publishing this kind of advertising.

4. Teaching children early are important. Talk to educators about starting a program on solving problems peacefully.

5. When you write to a politician, send your letter to the newspaper. A published letter gets a politician pays attention to an issue.

Part IV: Final Test

I. Contrast: Gerunds and Infinitives. *Circle the correct form of the verb.*

1. To eat/(Eating) properly is important for good health.

2. Most doctors advise their patients to decrease/decreasing the amount of fat in their diets.

3. They urge everyone to eat/eating at least five servings of fruits and vegetables every day.

4. Some nutritionists advise to cut/cutting down on the amount of meat in your diet.

5. They say not to select/not selecting as much refined food.

6. It's not necessary to study/studying nutrition, though.

7. To acquire/Acquiring good habits is a matter of common sense and small changes.

8. My friend Moira stopped to buy/buying whole milk, for example. She only uses skim milk now.

9. I remember to visit/visiting my parents a few months ago.

10. I was surprised not to have/not having a steak for dinner. They served meatless spaghetti instead.

11. I was happy to see/seeing that they had changed their habits.

12. I almost forgot to mention/mentioning exercise.

13. Some people don't believe in to do/doing strenuous aerobics anymore.

14. Maybe to walk/walking around the block once in a while is enough.

15. Not to do/Not doing any kind of exercise is a big mistake.

II. Object Pronouns and Possessives. *Complete each sentence with the correct form of the words in parentheses.*

1. We ___complained about Jana's making___ noise after 10:00.
   (complain about / Jana / make)

2. We _____ us when they changed their plans.
   (appreciate / they / tell)

3. Every year, Fritz's doctor _____ working long hours.
   (tell / he / stop)

   Fritz should take the advice.

4. I _____ to the meeting yesterday.
   (not mind / you / not come)

5. We should _____ the marathon.
   (celebrate / you / win)

6. Nanci's parents used to _____ her homework.
   (worry about / she / not finish)

7. Then the teacher _____ her do it at the kitchen table.
   (advise / they / let)

8. From the first day, Nanci _____ close by to help her.

(enjoy / they / be)

9. Yesterday, she _____ trying.

(promise / they / keep)

10. Last week, they _____ television after dinner.

(allow / she / watch)

III. *Make, Have, Help, Get,* and *Let.* *Complete each sentence with the correct form of the words in parentheses.*

1. Time management techniques can ___help families keep___ running smoothly.

(help / families / keep)

2. Last year, I _____ weekly meetings.

(get / my family / hold)

3. We still have the meetings because they _____ our schedules better.

(make / we / arrange)

4. They _____ ahead and avoid problems.

(get / we / plan)

5. Families should _____ suggestions.

(let / their children / make)

6. Making suggestions _____ in the meetings more.

(get / they / participate)

7. When Tom's daughter was a teenager, he _____ the checks for the household bills.

(have / she / write)

8. This _____ the cost of basic expenses.

(help / she / understand)

9. It also _____ saving for college.

(get / she / start)

10. Next year, we _____ with chores.

(get / everyone / cooperate)

11. We don't want to _____ too much responsibility.

(have / one person / take)

IV. Synthesis: Error Correction. *Find and correct seven errors in this letter to the editor.*

To the Editor:

The conflict between professional baseball players and the team owners has dominated the news recently. I, for one, am fed up with ~~hear~~ *hearing* about the problems of professional baseball. Like many other fans, I enjoy to watch my team (the Baltimore Orioles) on television. Every season, I look forward to attending a game or two in the stadium. I was sorry to learned that I won't be doing that this year.

I'm disappointed, but don't expect me to be horrified that players might not be earning more than a million dollars per contract. And I'm not crying about the owners' to lose control over a multimillion dollar sports industry.

It's clear that neither side is interested in talking seriously about a solution. And no one is thinking about the loyal fans. Play the game just doesn't seem important to either side anymore.

At this point, I'm so disgusted that nothing could make I watch another baseball game. I'm considering changing sports. Soccer is beginning to seems better and better.

Sincerely,

Clarissa Framton,

Baltimore, Maryland

Part V: Diagnostic Test

I. Contrast: Active and Passive. *Circle the correct form of the verb.*

1. Students advise / (are advised) to see their faculty advisors before they register.

2. Courses describe / are described in the bulletin.

3. We didn't notify / weren't notified of any changes.

4. Students usually choose / are chosen their majors during their second year.

5. Homework doesn't assign / isn't assigned during the first week of classes.

6. Grades mailed / were mailed to students last week.

7. I received / was received my grades yesterday.

8. Last year, that course taught / was taught by Professor Russo.

9. I took / was taken one of his courses two years ago.

10. A lot of students enjoy / are enjoyed taking language courses.

11. New language courses weren't added / didn't add last year.

12. Russian still offers / is still offered.

II. Passive: Affirmative and Negative Statements. *Complete each sentence with the correct passive form of the verb in parentheses.*

1. City Bank ___was robbed___ yesterday afternoon.
   (rob)

2. The crime _____ until today.
   (not report)

3. Our offices _____ in 1990.
   (expand)

4. New computers _____ every year.
   (buy)

5. A well-known sportswriter _____ a few weeks ago.
   (hire)

6. His first article _____ in time for next month's issue.
   (finish)

7. The mistakes in this memo _____ yesterday.
   (correct)

8. Both French and English _____ in Quebec.
   (speak)

9. The magazine *Le Cercle* _____ in English, though.
   (not publish)

10. It _____ on newsstands all over the province.
    (sell)

III. Passive *Wh-* Questions, *Yes/No* Questions, and Short Answers. *Write questions and short answers where indicated. Use the passive.*

1. **A:** _____ Was the Sears Tower completed in 1963? _____
   (the Sears Tower / complete / in 1963)

   B: _____ No, it wasn't. _____ . They finished it in 1973.

2. **A:** _____
   (Where / the Battle of Waterloo / fight)

   B: In Belgium, near the village of Waterloo.

3. **A:** _____
   (When / the first satellite / launch)

   B: In 1957, by the former Soviet Union.

4. **A:** _____
   (Where / giant pandas / find)

   B: Only in China. These large black and white animals look like bears.

5. **A:** _____
   (they / protect / by the government)

   B: _____ . The Chinese government wants to save them

   from extinction.

6. **A:** _____
   (How / the Philippines / discover / by Europeans)

   B: Magellan found them when he sailed across the Pacific Ocean from South America.

7. **A:** _____
   (curling / play / with a ball)

   B: _____ . Players of this Scottish game use large flat stones.

8. **A:** _____
   (How / zippers / first use)

   B: To fasten shoes. Before zippers, shoes were fastened with buttons.

9. **A:** _____
   (When / the planet Pluto / see through a telescope)

   B: In 1930. Clyde W. Tombaugh found it.

10. **A:** _____
    (Urdu / speak / in Finland)

    B: _____ . People in Pakistan speak it.

IV. Passives with and without an Agent. *Cross out any unnecessary agents in the following sentences.*

1. This magazine is published ~~by its publisher~~ in California.

2. I was told by Mrs. Jones to order that textbook.

3. Corn is grown by farmers in Indiana.

4. Spanish is spoken by speakers in many countries.

5. These mistakes weren't made by our editors.

6. Some strange laws were passed by lawmakers in the nineteenth century.

V. Passives with Modals. *Complete each sentence with the words in parentheses. Use the passive.*

1. The space station ___couldn't be completed___ last year. They hope to complete it this year.
   (couldn't / complete)

2. English _____ by all the scientists on board.
   (will / speak)

3. Mariel _____ a prize for her work.
   (ought to / award)

4. Tickets _____ at the door of the theater.
   (will / sell)

5. The class _____. The teacher is still lecturing. Please be quiet.
   (must not / disturb)

6. This room _____. All the lab equipment is here.
   (have got to / lock)

7. Martin's science project _____ for the state fair. The judges are going to
   (may / choose)

   decide next week.

8. Many diseases _____ by plants found in the rain forest.
   (can / cure)

9. Smith's debt _____ for several years. He's looking for a second job now.
   (might not / pay)

10. The rescue helicopter _____ by inexperienced pilots.
    (will not / fly)

VI. Passives with Modals: *Wh-* Questions, *Yes/No* Questions, and Short Answers. *Complete the questions and write short answers where indicated. Use the passive form of the verbs in parentheses.*

1. A: ___Will___ an international space program ___be developed___ soon?
                                                 (Will / develop)

   B: ___Yes, it will___. In fact, it's already started.

2. A: _____ it _____ by 1999?
                       (be going to / launch)

   B: _____. The target date is 2020.

3. **A:** _____ Pluto _____ without a telescope?

(Can / see)

   B: _____ . It's not bright enough.

4. **A:** _____ heat _____ to a sprained ankle?

(Should / apply)

   B: _____ . Use ice instead.

5. **A:** When _____ space flight _____ available to ordinary people?

(will / make)

   B: Maybe by 2005.

6. **A:** How _____ costs _____ down in commercial space flight?

(can / keep)

   B: All parts of the ship will be reusable.

7. **A:** What kind of fuel _____ ?

(will / use)

   B: A combination of hydrogen and oxygen.

8. **A:** How often _____ each ship _____ ?

(could / fly)

   B: Every few days.

9. **A:** _____ Asia and North America ever _____ by land transportation?

(Will / join)

   B: _____ . There are plans now for a railroad across the Bering Strait.

10. **A:** _____ scientists _____ to work in space?

(have to be / train)

    B: _____ . There's a long training process.

VII. Passive Causatives: _Have_ and _Get_. _Complete each conversation with an object pronoun and the correct form of the verbs in parentheses._

1. **A:** Your hair looks great.

   B: Thanks. I ___ had it cut ___ at a new place last time.

(have / cut)

2. **A:** The car's making a funny noise.

   B: We really should _____ more often.

(get / service)

3. **A:** Maureen's apartment looks great.

   B: She _____ every year.

(have / paint)

4. **A:** The windows are getting kind of dirty.

   B: I called the window cleaner yesterday. I _____ early next week.
   (have / wash)

5. **A:** I'm tired, and the house is a mess.

   B: Let's _____ by a professional.
   (get / clean)

6. **A:** You're not planning to wear those shoes, are you?

   B: I guess not. I _____ last week like I should have.
   (not get / repair)

7. **A:** The piano sounds awful.

   B: We _____ since 1975.
   (not have / tune)

VIII. Synthesis: Error Correction. *Find and correct six errors with passives,* have, *and* get *in this advertisement.*

For a relaxing and romantic vacation, Caribbean Palm Resort is ~~are~~ recommended by many travelers. At Caribbean Palm, guests will be enjoyed gleaming white beaches and three large swimming pools. A number of activities offer at the resort, including diving, wind-surfing, and water-skiing. Independent souls might be tempted by shopping in nearby villages or exploring the island on a motorbike. The beautiful scenery along the coast can't described—it has to be seen. After a long day in the sun, relax and have your hair styled in Caribbean Palm's own salon. For the evening, come and enjoy live entertainment in our dining room, or have your meal serves on your own balcony. Reservations must be made far in advance for this popular resort. But it will be worth planning ahead for—wonderful things can be happen at Caribbean Palm.

Part V: Final Test

I. Contrast: Active and Passive. *Circle the correct form of the verb.*

1. Volunteer firefighters (were notified)/notified about a new forest fire last night.

2. The fire was probably caused/probably caused by lightning.

3. Helicopters were brought/brought firefighters into the area from many parts of the state.

4. By late this afternoon, they had not been controlled/controlled the blaze.

5. Everyone is hoping that it will rain/be rained tonight.

6. Officials are advising/are advised local ranchers to leave the area at once.

7. Fires break out/are broken out in national parks every year.

8. Sometimes fires start/are started by careless campers.

9. Modern equipment is used/uses to fight the fires.

10. Many people volunteer/are volunteered when a fire occurs.

11. Hurried firefighters don't always follow/aren't always followed safety rules.

12. Sometimes dangerous mistakes make/are made.

II. Passive: Affirmative and Negative Statements. *Complete each sentence with the correct passive form of the verb in parentheses.*

1. Today, a lot of cigarette advertisements _____*are aimed*_____ at teenagers.
   (aim)

2. A study of teenage smokers _____ by the government last year.
   (complete)

3. In the study, advertising _____ for the increase in teenage smokers.
   (blame)

4. Now signs _____ in most stores about the effects of smoking.
   (display)

5. However, young people _____ by these signs.
   (not affect)

6. Often, a teenager _____ by a catchy ad.
   (influence)

7. Cigarettes _____ heavily in some areas.
   (tax)

8. Smoking _____ in most public buildings now.
   (ban)

9. Shoppers can still smoke in shopping malls. It _____ there.
   (not prohibit)

10. Years ago, nicotine _____ to be very addictive.
    (prove)

III. Passive: *Wh-* Questions, *Yes/No* Questions, and Short Answers. *Write questions and short answers where indicated. Use the passive.*

1. **A:** _____ Why are tennis balls made with a fuzzy surface? _____
(Why / tennis balls / make / with a fuzzy surface)

   B: To slow the ball down and give the player more control.

2. **A:** _____
(When / color television / invent)

   B: In 1922. A Scottish engineer built the first one.

3. **A:** _____
(lacrosse / first / play / in Europe)

   B: _____ . It's a Native American game.

4. **A:** _____
(our weather / influence / by El Niño)

   B: _____ . This warming of the Pacific Ocean has

   many effects on the weather.

5. **A:** _____
(How / hailstones / form)

   B: Water droplets bounce back up into the clouds and freeze.

6. **A:** _____
(Swahili / speak / in North America)

   B: _____ . It's a major language in Africa.

7. **A:** _____
(oil / find / in Bolivia)

   B: _____ . In the lowlands.

8. **A:** _____
(llamas / raise / in the United States)

   B: _____ . They are becoming popular pets in the

   United States.

9. **A:** _____
(How / food / cook / in a microwave)

   B: Tiny energy waves penetrate the food and cook it.

10. **A:** _____
(Where / dingoes / find)

   B: In Australia. They're a kind of wild dog.

IV. Passives with and without an Agent. *Cross out any unnecessary agents in the following sentences.*

1. The article on Argentina was written ~~by a writer~~ last year.

2. We were advised by our geography teacher to read the article.

3. Native American languages are spoken widely by speakers in North and South America.

4. Tin is mined by miners in Bolivia.

5. The storm was predicted by several local forecasters yesterday.

6. This medicine wasn't prescribed by my regular doctor.

V. Passives with Modals. *Complete each sentence with the words in parentheses. Use the passive.*

1. Some U.S. scientists _____may be trained_____ in Star City, the Russian Cosmonaut Center.
   (may / train)

2. A U.S. scientist _____ to conduct experiments on *Mir,* the Russian space station, soon.
   (could / invite)

3. His training _____ by next spring.
   (may / complete)

4. Strict training schedules _____ every day.
   (must / follow)

5. The Russian language _____ by the U.S. scientists.
   (have to / learn)

6. An oral exam _____ by all cosmonauts, both Russian and foreign.
   (have got to / pass)

7. A U.S. space shuttle _____ to *Mir* by a U.S.–Russian team.
   (might / take)

8. Life in space _____ better.
   (must / understand)

9. Chances for international cooperation _____ .
   (can't / ignore)

10. Scientists hope that researchers from many countries _____ for future projects.
    (will / seek)

VI. Passives with Modals: *Wh-* Questions, *Yes/No* Questions, and Short Answers. *Complete the questions and write short answers where indicated. Use the passive form of the verbs in parentheses.*

1. **A:** How _____can_____ animals _____be taught_____ to communicate with humans?
   (can / teach)

   B: Some primates learn International Sign Language.

2. **A:** _____ a new airport _____ for Hong Kong?
   (Will / build)

   B: _____ . They plan to build one on an island in the harbor.

3. **A:** _____ Africa and Europe ever _____ by a bridge or a tunnel?
   (Could / connect)

   B: _____ . Engineers are working on this project now.

4. **A:** Why _____ cigarettes _____ in public places?
   (should / ban)

   B: Because even second-hand smoke is dangerous.

5. **A:** _____ tickets _____ for the tunnel from France to England yet?
   (Can / buy)

   B: _____ . Travel agents are selling them now.

6. **A:** _____ travelers _____ to drive their cars through the tunnel?
   (Will / permit)

   B: _____ . Trains will carry cars through instead.

7. **A:** How _____ colonies _____ on Mars?
   (can / develop)

   B: People could live underground.

8. **A:** Why _____ money _____ for space exploration?
   (should / spend)

   B: There could be many benefits, such as new technologies.

9. **A:** What signals _____ to beings in other galaxies?
   (will / send)

   B: One scientist has suggested music.

10. **A:** When _____ the Mars project _____ ?
    (can / start)

    B: As soon as transportation problems are solved.

VII. Passive Causatives: *Have* and *Get*. *Complete each conversation with an object pronoun and the correct form of the verbs in parentheses.*

1. **A:** You look different. Did you do something with your hair?

   B: I ___ had it colored ___ . Do you like it?
   (have / color)

2. **A:** They made a big scratch on the car when they waxed it yesterday.

   B: Wow. We _____ there anymore.
   (not have / wax)

3. **A:** I want to shampoo the carpets before the party.

   B: That's a big job. Let's _____ by a service instead.
   (get / clean)

4. **A:** The television is broken. Who should I take it to?

   B: Last year I _____ at Ace's. They did a good job.
   (get / repair)

5. **A:** The cat must have fleas. She's scratching like crazy.

   B: I called the animal clinic. I _____ first thing tomorrow.
   (have / dip)

6. **A:** John's hair is always too long. He _____ often enough.
   (not get / trim)

   B: I guess that's his own business now. He's eighteen years old.

7. **A:** I'd like to buy this bicycle.

   B: Are you taking it with you or would you like to _____?
   (have / deliver)

VIII. Synthesis: Error Correction. *Find and correct eight errors with passives,* have, *and* get *in this letter to the editor.*

Dear Editor:

                                                    banned
In my opinion, all cigarette advertising should be ~~ban~~, even attractive designs on packages. Joe Camel and the Marlboro Man portray smokers as independent and powerful people. Adults can make their own decisions, but teenagers can't be resisted these images.

I think my own experience is typical. I started smoking when I was fourteen, and I smoked for five years. I was aware that many diseases could be caused by smoking, but I influenced by advertising, especially the Virginia Slim ads. Then, in my senior year of high school, I started getting sick all the time. When this was happen, my parents took me to a specialist and had me check out. I am ordered to quit, and I did.

I urge everybody to write to Congress about this issue. Lawmakers have got to forced to take a strong stand. Tobacco is a big industry, but we can gets laws passed if we work at it.

Sincerely yours,

Betty Litton

Mechanicsville, Virginia

Part VI: Diagnostic Test

I. Advisability and Obligation in the Past: Affirmative and Negative Statements. *Read each situation. Then complete each sentence with the correct form of the words in parentheses.*

1. Marta got a low grade on the midterm exam.

   a. She _____should have talked_____ to her teacher before the test.
   (should / talk)

   b. She _____ more.
   (ought to / study)

   c. She _____ out the night before the test.
   (should / go)

2. I forgot to buy a gift for my sister's birthday.

   a. I _____ her.
   (could / call)

   b. I _____ her a card.
   (might / send)

   c. I _____ my calendar.
   (ought to / mark)

3. Lynn has a bad cold.

   a. She _____ football in the rain.
   (should / play)

   b. She _____ home when she first felt sick.
   (ought to / stay)

   c. She _____ to the doctor by now.
   (should / go)

4. The Chens missed their plane this morning.

   a. They _____ to buy film.
   (should / stop)

   b. They _____ it at the airport, instead.
   (could / buy)

   c. They _____ us to say they'd be late.
   (might / call)

II. Advisability and Obligation in the Past: Questions. *Complete the questions. Use the words in parentheses.*

1. **A:** I feel bad about not helping Minna move.

   B: How _____could_____ you _____have known_____ ? She didn't tell anyone she was moving.
   (could / know)

2. **A:** Lisa was bored with her classes last year.

   B: What _____ she _____ instead?
   (should / study)

   A: Maybe languages.

3. **A:** My parents couldn't eat anything on the menu at The Golden Bowl last night. Where

   _____ I _____ them instead?
   (should / take)

   B: Maxi's has good, simple food.

4. **A:** Who _____ we _____ about the mistake on this bill? The sales
   (should / tell)

   clerk couldn't help us at all.

   B: Customer Service.

5. **A:** Look at these crowds. _____ I _____ for a reservation?
   (Should / call)

   B: Probably. We'll wait an hour for a table.

6. **A:** _____ we _____ a car for this trip?
   (Should / rent)

   B: I don't think so. I enjoyed the flight, didn't you?

III. Speculations and Conclusions about the Past: Affirmative and Negative Statements.
Complete each sentence with the correct form of the words in parentheses.

1. Jack __must have been__ exhausted yesterday. He had worked late the night before.
   (must / be)

2. Frieda _____ my message. She never called back.
   (must / receive)

3. Derek _____ already. It's only 10:00, and his flight isn't until 3:00.
   (could / leave)

4. He _____ his reservation. He sometimes has to leave earlier than he planned.
   (could / change)

5. Myra's only worked here for six months. She _____ surprised by that raise.
   (had to / be)

6. Ernie _____ laid off. He hasn't been to work for a while.
   (may / get)

7. Could you repeat that? The students in the back of the room _____ you.
   (may / hear)

8. Abbas _____ the teacher's explanation. He still looks puzzled.
   (might / understand)

IV. Speculations and Conclusions about the Past: Questions. *Write questions with* could have. *Use the words in parentheses.*

1. **A:** <u>Who could have left the door open?</u>
   (Who / leave / door open)

   B: I think I did. Sorry.

2. **A:** _____
   (Where / I / leave / my glasses)

   B: They're on the coffee table.

3. **A:** _____
   (Zena / forget / our date)

   B: I don't think so. She mentioned it to me this afternoon.

4. **A:** I never see Sam and Terry anymore. _____
   (they / move)

   B: Maybe, Sam had been complaining about the neighborhood.

5. **A:** I just locked my keys in the car. _____
   (How / I / do / such a dumb thing)

   B: Everybody has done that at least once.

6. **A:** _____
   (What / make / Nick / so angry)

   B: I don't know. Should we ask?

V. Speculations and Conclusions about the Past: Short Answers with and without *Be*. *Write short answers using the words in parentheses.*

1. **A:** Did it rain last night?

   B: <u>It might have</u>. The streets are wet.
   (might)

2. **A:** Were the runners tired when they got to the finish line?

   B: <u>They may not have been</u>. They'd been training for a long time.
   (may not)

3. **A:** Did we ever give the Galarragas our new address?

   B: _____. We haven't heard from them in months.
   (must not)

4. **A:** Did Sandra grow up in Mexico?

   B: _____. She speaks Spanish fluently.
   (may)

5. **A:** Was Annmarie at the party last night?

   B: _____ . I was there all evening, and I didn't see her.

(couldn't)

6. **A:** Were the peaches I bought yesterday any good?

   B: _____ . There aren't any left.

(must)

VI. Synthesis: Error Correction. *Find and correct five errors with modals in the following article.*

To everyone's surprise, Roy Cole lost his bid for re-election yesterday to a newcomer, Martha Gomez. "I couldn't ~~had~~ *have* been more pleased to hear the news," said one voter. "We needed a change." Political analysts attribute the Gomez victory to several factors. First, Cole should has started campaigning earlier. He was too sure of his re-election. In addition, voters may been disappointed in Cole's vote on the crime bill. "Cole might have explain his position better," complained one prominent businessperson. "In my opinion, he shouldn't have voted against the bill," grumbled another voter.

The new senator claims not to be surprised at her landslide victory yesterday. "After twelve years of Cole, voters had to have been ready for a change," said Gomez. "I don't know why reporters seem to be shocked. They must not talked to voters the way I did in this campaign."

Part VI: Final Test

I. Advisability and Obligation in the Past: Affirmative and Negative Statements. *Read each situation. Then complete each sentence with the correct form of the words in parentheses.*

1. Bob Simm's store went out of business last month.

   a. He _____ shouldn't have given up _____ so soon.

(should / give up)

   b. He _____ the bank for a loan.

(could / ask)

   c. He _____ his relatives that he needed help.

(might / tell)

2. I locked myself out of my apartment today.

   a. I _____ my neighbor to keep a key for me.

(ought to / ask)

   b. I _____ to have an extra key made.

(should / forget)

   c. I _____ a key somewhere outside.

(could / hide)

3. The college turned down Sana's application.

   a. She _____ so long to apply.

(ought to / wait)

   b. She _____ to several schools.

(should / apply)

   c. They _____ her on a waiting list.

(might / put)

4. Carl was late for work today. His boss was angry.

   a. Carl _____ the house earlier.

(ought to / leave)

   b. He _____ in such bad weather.

(should / drive)

   c. His boss _____ that the weather would cause delays.

(could / know)

II. Advisability and Obligation in the Past: Questions. *Complete the questions. Use the words in parentheses.*

1. **A:** Bob just lost his job. It's too bad no one warned him.

   B: How _____ could _____ we _____ have warned _____ him? He wouldn't listen to anyone.

(could / warn)

2. **A:** Dana didn't do well in her tennis class last summer. What _____ she

_____ instead?

(should / take)

   B: I think swimming would be a good sport for her.

3. **A:** The heat in Mexico bothered the Clarks. Where _____ they _____ instead?

(should / go)

   B: Bolivia would have been better. It's always cool in the altiplano.

4. **A:** Everyone was still at the party when we left. _____ we _____ a

(Should / stay)

   little longer?

   B: Probably. We were having a good time.

5. **A:** I'm not sure I like this shirt I just bought. _____ I _____ another color?

(Should / buy)

   B: No. It looks good on you.

6. **A:** I wasted that ticket by asking Bart to the concert. He hated it.

   B: Who _____ you _____?

(should / ask)

   A: You. You like classical music, don't you?

III. Speculations and Conclusions about the Past: Affirmative and Negative Statements.

Complete each sentence with the correct form of the words in parentheses.

1. I ___ must not have bought ___ enough bread. There's just a little left.

(must / buy)

2. Allison _____ the crime. She was in another city when it happened.

(could / commit)

3. They _____ this flight. It's getting very crowded at the gate.

(might / overbook)

4. These jeans _____ in the wash. I can't get them on.

(must / shrink)

5. That _____ an unmarked police car. They go very fast sometimes.

(might / be)

6. They _____ Steve. He hasn't been at work for a while.

(may / fire)

7. He _____. He was looking for another job.

(could / quit)

8. I _____ light bulbs on the shopping list. You didn't buy any.

(must / put)

IV. Speculations and Conclusions about the Past: Questions. *Write questions with* could have. *Use the words in parentheses.*

1. **A:** Those people know me, but I don't remember them. <u>When could I have met them?</u>
   (When / I / meet / them)

   B: They were at the Smiths' anniversary party last year.

2. **A:** _____
   (Who / tell / Rhoda / about her surprise party)

   B: No one. She overheard us making plans.

3. **A:** There's no pizza left. _____
   (the kids / eat / it all)

   B: Easily. I've seen them eat two large ones.

4. **A:** My wallet isn't in my bag. _____
   (someone / take / it)

   B: No. Your bag was closed. Look again.

5. **A:** Sandra's upset. _____
   (What / I / say / to hurt / her feelings)

   B: Why don't you ask her?

6. **A:** My checkbook just won't balance. _____
   (the bank / make / a mistake)

   B: Sure. It happens all the time.

V. Speculations and Conclusions about the Past: Short Answers with and without *BE*. *Write short answers using the words in parentheses.*

1. **A:** Do you think George got lost?

   B: <u>He must have</u>. He left more than an hour ago, and it's only a fifteen-minute trip.
   (must)

2. **A:** Was Phyllis upset about not getting her promotion?

   B: <u>She may have been</u>. She looked kind of depressed.
   (may)

3. **A:** Did Janice move?

   B: _____. I haven't seen her for quite a while.
   (might)

4. **A:** Was Jamie home when you called last night?

   B: _____. I got his answering machine.
   (must not)

5. **A:** We just got a second notice from the telephone company. Did you pay the bill last month?

B: _____ . Sorry.
(must not)

6. **A:** Were the kids hungry at lunchtime?

B: _____ . They hardly ate anything.
(couldn't)

VI. Synthesis: Error Correction. *Find and correct eight errors with modals in the following diary entry.*

                                                 have
Our vacation was fun, but it should ~~had~~ gone more smoothly. I think we ought to of planned it better. For starters, we could have ask more questions about the package deal. The car we got was too small. At that price, I should have knew. We got a bigger one, but that took some time. Then the travel agent must not has confirmed our hotel reservation in Santa Monica. They weren't expecting us. And it couldn't have happen at a worse time. It was one of their busiest weekends. Anyway, after we got that straightened out, the rest of the trip was great. The California coast had to been the most beautiful place I've ever seen. We loved San Francisco—that may have been because Ted grew up there and knows the city so well. His brother invited us back next summer. We may have start a tradition.

Part VII: Diagnostic Test

I. Present Factual Conditional: Affirmative and Negative Statements. *Combine each pair of sentences into one present factual conditional sentence. Use the words in parentheses and keep the same order of sentences.*

1. Brian reads in the car. He gets carsick. (whenever)

   Whenever Brian reads in the car, he gets carsick.

   _____

2. I wear suntan lotion. I get a bad sunburn. (unless)

   _____

   _____

3. You have a headache. You should lie down. (if)

   _____

   _____

4. Get out of the swimming pool immediately. You hear thunder. (whenever)

   _____

   _____

5. They don't obey these warnings. They can get hurt. (if)

   _____

   _____

6. You shouldn't use this equipment. You know how to operate it. (unless)

   _____

   _____

7. Try La Trattoria. You like Italian food. (if)

   _____

   _____

8. The air pollution is bad. Some people don't go outside. (if)

   _____

   _____

II. Future Factual Conditional: Affirmative and Negative Sentences. *Circle the correct form of the verb to complete each future factual conditional sentence.*

1. If Craig will win/wins the election next month, she will work for/works for better education in this state.

2. If she won't win/doesn't win this year, she's going to run/runs again in four years.

3. Unless we will increase/increase teachers' salaries, schools won't improve/don't improve by the year 2000.

4. If our transportation system isn't/won't be reliable, businesses don't stay/won't stay in this area much longer.

5. Unless you <u>will register/register</u> to vote, the next governor <u>isn't going to know/ doesn't know</u> your opinion.

6. If Craig's opponent <u>will lose/loses</u>, she<u>'ll ask for/asks for</u> his ideas about improving the state.

7. Unless she <u>will start/starts</u> appearing on television, voters <u>won't recognize/don't recognize</u> her.

III. Contrast: *If* and *Unless*. *Complete these sentences with* if *or* unless.

1. _____If_____ you don't succeed the first time, try again.

2. We usually drive to the city _____ the car isn't working.

3. _____ Sasha calls soon, I'm going to call her. I'm worried because I haven't heard from

    her in a week.

4. _____ the server brings the wrong food this time, we should complain.

5. I usually take the bus _____ I'm very late for work. Then I take a cab.

6. _____ Tom knows who is at the door, he doesn't open it right away.

7. _____ customers don't pay by the fifteenth, another bill is sent out.

8. George usually answers the telephone _____ he doesn't hear it.

IV. Present and Future Factual Conditional: Questions and Short Answers. *Complete the questions and write short answers. Use the words in parentheses and the present or future factual conditional.*

1. **A:** What _____will_____ you _____do_____ if you _____don't work_____ next weekend?
   (do)   (not work)

   B: Go to the beach, I guess.

2. **A:** _____ you _____ if they _____ rain?
                              (go)   (forecast)

   B: _____ . In that case, I'll stay home.

3. **A:** Who _____ you _____ with whenever you _____ L.A.?
                              (stay)   (visit)

   B: My sister. She lives there.

4. **A:** _____ you _____ a special meal whenever you _____
                              (order)   (travel)

    by plane?

   B: _____ . I always eat the regular meal.

5. **A:** If we _____ to the coast, _____ we _____ a car?
(fly)   (should / rent)

   B: _____ . We're going to need one.

6. **A:** If Sandra _____ at 6:00 tomorrow evening, when _____ she
(leave)

   _____ to the airport?
(get)

   B: Probably around 7:30.

7. **A:** _____ they _____ the airport tonight if the weather _____
(close)   (stay)

   like this?

   B: _____ . It's too dangerous to take off in a storm like this.

V. Present Unreal Conditional: Affirmative and Negative Statements. *Complete each present unreal conditional sentence with the correct form of the verbs in parentheses.*

1. If we ___*won*___ the lottery, we ___*'d buy*___ a new house.
(win)   (buy)

2. We _____ the pizza quickly if the microwave _____ broken.
(can / reheat)   (not be)

3. Jaime _____ well if he _____ back to school now.
(do)   (go)

4. If I _____ so busy, I _____ my degree in nursing.
(not be)   (can earn)

5. Karen _____ her apartment if she _____ enough money.
(redecorate)   (have)

6. Our phone bill _____ so high if we _____ so many long distance calls.
(not be)   (not make)

7. If I _____ you, I _____ that decision a lot more thought.
(be)   (give)

8. You _____ such a good tennis player if you _____ .
(not be)   (not practice)

9. If Matilde _____ so much in class, she _____ a lot more.
(not talk)   (understand)

10. If my neighbors _____ so much noise, I _____ a lot better.
(not make)   (sleep)

VI. Present Unreal Conditional: Questions and Short Answers. *Complete the questions and write short answers. Use the verbs in parentheses and the present unreal conditional.*

1. **A:** If you ___*could be*___ a famous person for one day, who ___*would*___ you ___*choose*___ to be?
(can / be)   (choose)

   B: Probably the president.

2. **A:** What _____ school _____ like if there _____ no teachers?
(be)$$(be)

   B: Students would have to work with computers and video presentations.

3. **A:** _____ you _____ to college if you _____ a scholarship?
(go)$$(win)

   B: _____ . That would be great.

4. **A:** If you _____ one wish, what _____ you _____ for?
(have)$$(wish)

   B: A cure for AIDS.

5. **A:** If you _____ how to drive, how _____ you _____
(not know)$$(get)

   to work?

   B: By bus.

6. **A:** If I _____ him nicely, _____ he _____ me his computer?
(ask)$$(lend)

   B: _____ . He uses it all the time himself.

7. **A:** What time _____ we _____ home if we _____ at noon?
(get)(leave)

   B: Not until about 10:00 P.M.

8. **A:** What _____ if the climate _____ drastically?
(happen)$$(change)

   B: A lot of species would die out.

VII. Past Unreal Conditional: Affirmative and Negative Statements. *Complete each past unreal conditional sentence with the correct form of the verb in parentheses.*

1. I _would have told_ you if I _had known_ the answer.
(tell)$$(know)

2. If the Senate _____ the crime bill last year, voters _____ very angry.
(not pass)$$(be)

3. We _____ him if he _____ at the party.
(see)$$(be)

4. If you _____ here, I _____ you.
(not move)$$(not meet)

5. If I _____ you, we _____ such good friends.
(not meet)$$(not become)

6. If Tom _____ in such a rush, he _____ his keys in the car.
(not be)$$(not leave)

7. The robbers _____ into that store if they _____ the warning sign about the
      (not break)   (see)

burglar alarm.

8. Carlos _____ the promotion if his boss _____ him.
          (not get)   (not recommend)

9. I _____ this apartment if I _____ the noise in the street first.
      (not rent)   (hear)

10. The library _____ him borrow any more books if he _____ his fine.
                  (not let)   (not pay)

VIII. Past Unreal Conditional: Questions and Short Answers. *Complete the questions and write short answers where indicated. Use the verbs in parentheses and the past unreal conditional.*

1. **A:** _____Would_____ Gregor ____have been____ better off if he ____hadn't taken____ that job?
                                       (be)   (not take)

   B: __No, he wouldn't have__ . He really needed it.
              (not pay)

2. **A:** If you _____ in business, what _____ you _____?
                  (not major)   (study)

   B: Probably art history.

3. **A:** _____ you _____ to work if the doctor _____ you to
                              (go)   (not tell)

   stay home?

   B: _____ . I felt fine.

4. **A:** If Fleming _____ penicillin by accident, how _____ scientists
                      (not discover)

   _____ antibiotics?
        (develop)

   B: Maybe through another accidental discovery.

5. **A:** If my train _____ late, _____ you _____ ?
                        (be)   (wait)

   B: _____ . I knew you were coming.

6. **A:** What _____ if Cora _____ the letters yesterday?
               (happen)   (not mail)

   B: There would have been big problems.

7. **A:** Who _____ this class if Professor Karlen _____ here this semester?
               (teach)   (not be)

   B: I'm not sure. They might have canceled it.

IX. Wishes: Past and Present. *Rewrite the statements as wishes.*

1. I don't like to study.

   I wish I liked to study.

   _____

2. I have a lot to read tonight.

   _____

   _____

3. I didn't go shopping for food today.

   _____

   _____

4. There's nothing to eat in the house.

   _____

   _____

5. I don't have enough time to cook dinner.

   _____

   _____

6. My car didn't start today.

   _____

   _____

7. The telephone was out of order too.

   _____

   _____

8. I'm bored.

   _____

   _____

9. I finished reading that murder mystery.

   _____

   _____

10. There's nothing interesting to read.

    _____

    _____

X. Conditional Sentences and Sentences with *Wish:* Meaning. *Read each sentence. Then write* T *(True) or* F *(False).*

1. Ted wishes he hadn't told Sandra his problems.

   ___T___ Ted told Sandra his problems.

2. If Sonja called the Shanghai office, she could solve this problem.

   _____ Sonja has already called the Shanghai office.

3. If Beth's grandmother had been at the graduation, she would have been very proud of Beth.

   _____ Beth's grandmother didn't attend the graduation.

4. Whenever Sam is near cats, he sneezes.

   _____ Sam is sometimes near cats.

5. Tom wishes he lived in the country.

   _____ Tom lives in the country.

6. If the Yangs had the money, they'd buy a new computer.

   _____ The Yangs don't have enough money for a new computer.

7. If I have jet lag, I try to go to sleep at the normal time.

   _____ The speaker never experiences jet lag.

8. Jeanine wishes she had studied French.

   _____ Jeanine didn't study French.

XI. Synthesis: Error Correction. *Correct these sentences.*

1. I wish I have a better job.
   I wish I had a better job.
   _____

2. Paula wishes she has started college years ago.
   _____
   _____

3. If I will stay with my family next summer, we'll have a great time together.

_____

_____

4. Whenever the air pollution is bad these days, I coughed a lot.

_____

_____

5. If Marco has a million dollars, he would take a trip around the world.

_____

_____

6. If Sue hadn't had told me, I wouldn't have heard the news.

_____

_____

7. If I had knew about this class earlier, I would have registered for it.

_____

_____

8. Unless I don't pass English this semester, I won't graduate.

_____

_____

9. We wish you could stayed a little longer last night.

_____

_____

Part VII: Final Test

I. Present Factual Conditional: Affirmative and Negative Statements. *Combine each pair of sentences into one present factual conditional sentence. Use the words in parentheses and keep the same order of sentences.*

1. He watches TV. He gets a headache. (whenever)

   Whenever he watches TV, he gets a headache.

2. I drink coffee in the morning. I can't wake up. (unless)

3. Walk for an hour every day. You want to get some exercise. (if)

4. You feel tired. You should take a nap. (whenever)

5. Please don't disturb me. There's an emergency. (unless)

6. You have to report a fire. Call 911. (if)

7. They call right away. The fire could go out of control. (unless)

8. People don't get the benefits of exercise. They exercise three times a week. (unless)

II. Future Factual Conditional: Affirmative and Negative Sentences. *Circle the correct form of the verb to complete each future factual conditional sentence.*

1. Sally is/will be late for work unless she will leave/leaves right now.

2. Unless she gets/will get there on time, she doesn't get/won't get her work done.

3. We aren't able to/won't be able to print your letter if the printer won't be working/isn't working.

4. They don't send/won't send a repairperson unless you will call/call them by 1:00.

5. Unless they <u>are going to find/find</u> the problem, the printer <u>isn't/isn't going to be</u> ready by tomorrow.

6. If the company <u>will expand/expands</u>, we <u>need/'re going to need</u> more computers.

7. Don's <u>going to start/starts</u> his own company if he <u>has/will have</u> the chance.

III. Contrast: *If* and *Unless.* *Complete these sentences with* if *or* unless.

1. _____<u>If</u>_____ you don't understand, ask questions.

2. We usually call the Chinese restaurant _____ we want to order take-out food.

3. _____ Joyce has guests, she always cooks for them.

4. I don't want you to go _____ I can come too. I'll miss you too much.

5. _____ the television is too loud, just tell me and I'll turn it down.

6. _____ it rains soon, we could have a serious drought.

7. _____ you see Bill, tell him we said Hello.

8. Barry usually has dinner with us on Friday _____ he's out of town.

IV. Present and Future Factual Conditional: Questions and Short Answers. *Complete the questions and write short answers. Use the words in parentheses and the present or future factual conditional.*

1. **A:** What _____<u>will</u>_____ you _____<u>do</u>_____ if you _____<u>don't go</u>_____ out tomorrow?
                                                 (do)   (not go)

   B: Cook dinner and watch a movie.

2. **A:** _____ I _____ you if I _____ the video?
                              (Can / join)   (bring)

   B: That sounds like fun.

3. **A:** What kind of food _____ you _____ when you _____
                                           (prepare)   (eat)

   at home?

   B: Sometimes I make pasta. How about you?

   A: I usually order take-out. I don't know how to cook.

4. **A:** Who _____ you usually _____ if you _____ a babysitter?
                                      (call)   (need)

   B: My mother usually babysits for us. She lives in the building.

5. **A:** If I _____ her, _____ she _____ for us sometime?
(ask)   (babysit)

   B: _____ . She likes your daughter very much.

6. **A:** _____ you _____ emergency numbers whenever you
(leave)

   _____ out?
   (go)

   B: _____ . I tape them to the refrigerator door.

7. **A:** _____ the kids _____ tomorrow night if they _____
(misbehave)   (not know)

   their babysitter?

   B: _____ . They're very polite.

V. Present Unreal Conditional: Affirmative and Negative Statements. *Complete each present unreal conditional sentence with the correct form of the verbs in parentheses.*

1. If Jennifer ___woke up___ earlier, she ___wouldn't be___ late for work.
   (wake up)   (not be)

2. If they _____ interrupting the teacher, he _____ the problem.
   (not keep)   (can / explain)

3. If you _____ some juice, you _____ better.
   (drink)   (feel)

4. If we _____ Karl better, we _____ him to the party.
   (know)   (invite)

5. Selma _____ those shoes if they _____ so much.
   (buy)   (not cost)

6. I _____ that job if I _____ you.
   (not take)   (be)

7. I _____ this dish every week if I _____ the recipe.
   (cook)   (have)

8. If I _____ you the truth, you _____ me.
   (tell)   (not believe)

9. If Roberto _____ more careful, he _____ so many accidents.
   (be)   (not have)

10. Maria and Paz _____ such good friends if they _____ so many interests.
    (not be)   (not share)

VI. Present Unreal Conditional: Questions and Short Answers: *Complete the questions and write short answers. Use the verbs in parentheses and the present unreal conditional.*

1. **A:** ___Would___ Jalil ___move___ if he ___found___ a new job?
   (move)   (find)

   B: ___Yes, he would___ . He's willing to go almost anywhere.

2. **A:** If you _____ any famous person, whom _____ you _____
(can / meet)   (want)

to talk to?

B: I think I'd like to meet Maya Angelou.

3. **A:** If you _____ three wishes, what _____ you _____ for?
(have)   (wish)

B: More wishes.

4. **A:** If you _____ those bank robbers again, _____ you _____
(see)   (recognize)

them?

B: _____ . The whole thing happened too fast.

5. **A:** If we _____ faster, _____ we _____ the project in time?
(work)   (finish)

B: _____ . There isn't that much more to do.

6. **A:** How _____ you _____ to work if your car _____?
(get)   (break down)

B: By bus.

7. **A:** _____ it _____ you if I _____ a window?
(bother)   (open)

B: _____ . Go right ahead.

8. **A:** Where _____ you _____ if you _____ an around-the-world
(go)   (buy)

airline ticket?

B: First to Hawaii.

VII. Past Unreal Conditional: Affirmative and Negative Statements. *Complete each past unreal conditional sentence with the correct form of the verb in parentheses.*

1. Habeeb __would have changed__ his mind if we __had talked__ to him.
(change)   (talk)

2. I _____ this school if I _____ about it from my friends.
(not choose)   (not hear)

3. Chris's little sister _____ him so much if he _____ so tired.
(not annoy)   (not be)

4. Jana _____ an accident if you _____ her about that truck.
(have)   (not warn)

5. Rene's boss _____ (not trust) her anymore if she _____ (not tell) him the truth

   yesterday.

6. If you _____ (let) us know you were coming, we _____ (make) some plans

   together.

7. I _____ (not say) that if I _____ (know) Paul was listening.

8. If Sophie _____ (join) the book club, she _____ (receive) a free dictionary.

9. If you _____ (watch) the news, you _____ (hear) about the robbery.

10. If the service _____ (be) better, Ayadele _____ (leave) a bigger tip.

VIII. Past Unreal Conditional: Questions and Short Answers. *Complete the questions and write short answers where indicated. Use the verbs in parentheses and the past unreal conditional.*

1. **A:** _____Would_____ the Bulls ___have won___ (win) the game if Sam ___hadn't dropped___ (not drop)

   the ball in the last quarter?

   B: _No, they wouldn't have_. They were too far behind by that time.

2. **A:** If you _____ (not move) to Cincinnati ten years ago, where _____ you

   _____ (grow up) ?

   B: Probably in Toronto. That's where we were living before we moved.

3. **A:** _____ Yuri _____ (get) angry if you _____ (not answer) his letter?

   B: _____ . He knows I've been very busy lately.

4. **A:** _____ Chris _____ (finish) college if he _____ (not become) a

   professional athlete?

   B: _____ . He was very interested in teaching history.

5. **A:** If Lena and Harry _____ (not work) together, how _____ they _____ (meet) ?

   B: Probably at a party. They have a lot of mutual friends.

6. **A:** Who _____ you _____ if you _____ help?
                              (call)   (need)

   B: My family.

7. **A:** If Petra _____ for her final, _____ she _____ ?
                        (study)   (pass)

   B: _____ . She's a good student.

IX. Wishes: Past and Present. *Rewrite the statements as wishes.*

1. I hate to exercise.

   I wish I didn't hate to exercise.

   _____

2. It snows here every winter.

   _____

   _____

3. We didn't take a vacation this year.

   _____

   _____

4. The concert is sold out.

   _____

   _____

5. You can't buy tickets.

   _____

   _____

6. I didn't hear this group of musicians last year.

   _____

   _____

7. I returned Bob's phone call late.

   _____

   _____

8. Bob wasn't home.

   _____

   _____

9. I can't call him from my office.

   _____

   _____

10. My best friend doesn't live in this city.

_____

_____

X. Conditional Sentences and Sentences with *Wish*: Meaning. *Read each sentence. Then write* T *(True) or* F *(False).*

1. Andrea wishes she hadn't moved.

   ___T___ Andrea moved.

2. If Ted talked to his boss, they'd be able to find a solution to this problem.

   _____ Ted has already talked to his boss.

3. If they had seen that movie, they would have cried too.

   _____ They didn't see the movie.

4. Whenever Beth is out late, her mother waits up for her.

   _____ Beth sometimes stays out late.

5. Fabiana wishes she had a job as a translator.

   _____ Fabiana has a job as a translator.

6. Van would buy a new car if he had the money.

   _____ Van has enough money for a new car.

7. If I feel nervous, I take ten deep breaths.

   _____ The speaker never feels nervous.

8. Jeanine wishes she knew how to drive.

   _____ Jeanine doesn't know how to drive.

XI. Synthesis: Error Correction. *Correct these sentences.*

1. Plants die unless they don't have enough water.
   Plants die unless they have enough water.

   _____

   _____

2. Peter wishes he doesn't get so angry last night.

_____

_____

3. If Loretta won't get enough sleep, she won't get a good grade on her test tomorrow.

_____

_____

4. Evita wishes she can go to the state college next fall.

_____

_____

5. Whenever Rene hears that song now, he remembered New Orleans.

_____

_____

6. If I am rich, I wouldn't be any happier than I am now.

_____

_____

7. If I had knew about this class earlier, I would have registered for it.

_____

_____

8. We won't have left early if we had seen you at the party.

_____

_____

9. If the police officer hadn't had stopped us, we wouldn't have known about that broken signal light.

_____

_____

Part VIII: Diagnostic Test

I. Relative Pronouns in Subject Position. *Circle the correct word to complete each sentence.*

1. A friend (who)/whose has known you a long time can almost read your mind.

2. Someone that/whose interests are very different from yours is interesting to talk to.

3. Friends are people that/which choose to spend time together.

4. Disloyalty is a problem which/who ruins many friendships.

5. Henry and Lars, who/whose families live next door to each other, have been friends since childhood.

6. Friendship is a subject whose/which concerns everyone.

7. It's a relationship that/who changes from culture to culture.

8. Mary Fried is an acquaintance that/whose opinions often differ from mine.

9. Politics is a topic that/whose often divides friends.

10. *Psychology Today,* that/which is a popular magazine, published a survey about friendship recently.

II. Relative Pronouns in Object Position, *Where,* and *When.* *Circle the correct word.*

1. I loved the book whose/(that) you gave me.

2. It was the best biography where/that I've read in a long time.

3. Eva Hoffman, whose/whom articles I always enjoy, is one of my favorite authors.

4. I keep the book in the living room, when/where I read it every evening.

5. It was nice of you to remember someone whom/which you don't see very often.

6. Language is a subject where/that I'm very interested in.

7. Eva Hoffman reminds me of my friend Karla, who/whose daughter you met when you were here last year.

8. We enjoy her stories about the time where/when she was living in Brazil.

9. Rio, that/which she describes beautifully, sounds like a fascinating place.

10. Homesickness is one of the problems that/whose she faces now.

III. Adjective Clauses: Subject-Verb Agreement. *Complete each sentence with the correct form of the verb in parentheses.*

1. The letters that he ___'s___ mailing now will probably arrive next week.
   (be)

2. Ivan enjoys meeting the people who _____ his neighborhood association meeting every month.
   (attend)

3. He always learns the names of a few people whose faces he _____ from around the

neighborhood.

4. Jan and Marty are his neighbors who _____ across the street.
(live)

5. They own a big dog that sometimes _____ free and _____ the neighborhood.
(get)   (roam)

6. The dog, whose name _____ Boomer, barks loudly but never bites.
(be)

7. The neighborhood children who _____ him always get frightened.
(see)

8. It's a problem that _____ Jan and Marty a lot.
(bother)

9. Now Ivan, who _____ at home, plans to call Jan at her office the next time Boomer gets free.
(work)

10. Jan and Marty, who _____ Boomer a lot, appreciate Ivan's help.
(love)

IV. Identifying and Non-Identifying Adjective Clauses. *Combine the two sentences using the word in parentheses. Use commas where necessary.*

1. Yesterday we met Phil Mungo. His wife, Crystal, works in my office. (whose)

    Yesterday we met Phil Mungo, whose wife, Crystal, works in my office.

    _____

2. Crystal works in the Accounting Department. She's been the secretary there for years. (where)

    _____

    _____

3. She started the job right after she got married. She was about nineteen then. (when)

    _____

    _____

4. It was an exciting time. The department was growing rapidly then. (when)

    _____

    _____

5. Crystal and Beth grew up together. Beth started at the same time. (who)

    _____

    _____

6. Our company is a friendly place. Everyone enjoys working there. (where)

    _____

    _____

7. Rohan has a very stressful job. Crystal works for Rohan. (whom)

    _____

    _____

8. Rohan travels a lot. Crystal understands Rohan's job perfectly. (whose)

_____

_____

9. Crystal has a personality. It is very well suited to her job. (which)

_____

_____

10. She takes responsibility for a lot of tasks. Rohan doesn't have time for them. (that)

_____

_____

V. Relative Pronouns and *When*: Deletions. *Wherever possible, delete the relative pronouns and* when.

1. Georgina's the person ~~whom~~ I told you about yesterday.
2. I don't like movies that have a lot of violence.
3. Centralia, the town in which I grew up, is in a rural area.
4. Someone who I really enjoy talking to is Chris's father.
5. Josi bought the book which she had heard about on TV.
6. Frieda is a politician whose views I respect.
7. She's someone whom I campaign for every four years.
8. I don't know anyone who agrees with you.
9. Thanksgiving is a time when many families get together.
10. Will Rogers, a U.S. comedian, never met a person whom he didn't like.

VI. Synthesis: Error Correction. *Correct these sentences.*

1. Stephie Gould is a song writer whom music appeals to all kinds of people.
   Stephanie Gould is a song writer whose music appeals to all kinds of people.

   _____

2. She often performs her own songs, which she sings them in a powerful, country-western style.

   _____

   _____

3. Gould who grew up in New York City studied classical music.

   _____

   _____

4. A friend invited her to a country music festival in West Virginia, which she heard real country music for the first time.

   _____

   _____

5. Gould, who's songs are often in the top ten these days, was too poor at the time to buy a good guitar.

    _____

    _____

6. She found a used guitar in a yard sale the day after the festival, that she was on her way back to New York City.

    _____

    _____

7. She still has that guitar, that she named Lynette after a famous country singer.

    _____

    _____

8. Lynette is like an old friend whose you don't want to leave behind when your fortunes improve.

    _____

    _____

9. Gould and Jim Elliott, which she met on a tour last year, got married recently.

    _____

    _____

10. Elliott, with who she often practices, is also a musician.

    _____

    _____

Part VIII: Final Test

I. Relative Pronouns in Subject Position. *Circle the correct word.*

1. Karina, which/(who) is interested in music, is studying in New York City.

2. Her school, which/that has an excellent reputation, is near a concert center.

3. A teacher that/whose son studied there recommended the school.

4. Karina, who/whose family always encourages her to finish her education, wants to find a job as a teacher after graduation.

5. A friend that/which is teaching now suggested working part time in a school.

6. The course that/whose appeals to her most is music history.

7. Her friend Zena, who/that is also her roommate, plays the piano.

8. They both practice on Zena's piano, that/which was a gift from her grandmother.

9. The concert center, whose/which is close to their apartment, gives a lot of free tickets to students.

10. Zena, who/which once performed there, wants to become a concert musician.

II. Relative Pronouns in Object Position, *Where,* and *When.* *Circle the correct word.*

1. Edna, (who)/whose the school named Student of the Year, wants to study social work.

2. The college whose/which she wants to apply to is close to her home.

3. The person from who/whom she has received the most support is her father.

4. An accident that/when he had several years before had changed his life.

5. Her father had been a school bus driver in a rural area which/where the roads are very narrow.

6. One afternoon at 2:00, that/when he was starting his route, his bus had a flat tire.

7. When he went to look at the tire, he was hit by a drunk driver, whose/whom he hadn't seen coming.

8. During his recovery, when /which he had a lot of time to think, he decided to change jobs.

9. He went to college and became a guidance counselor in the school district when/where Edna was attending high school.

10. The reason whose/that he gave for this decision was his desire to help others.

III. Adjective Clauses: Subject-Verb Agreement. *Complete each sentence with the correct form of the verb in parentheses.*

1. The shows that Henry _____watches_____ are all family sitcoms.
   (watch)

2. Schools should offer a course that _____ students find jobs.
   (help)

3. Many cities that Bill _____ visiting had unemployment problems.
   (remember)

4. These problems, which still _____ , don't have easy solutions.
   (exist)

5. The person to whom Marta _____ the most thanks is her teacher.
   (owe)

6. Two people whose help _____ a great deal to me are my parents.
   (mean)

7. They're inviting Kelly, who _____ a lot about elementary school education, to speak at the
   (know)

   Parent-Teachers Association meeting.

8. Senator Ruiz, whose voters _____ the new law, is opposing it.
   (not support)

9. For his birthday, Steve got two computer games, which he _____ all the time.
   (play)

10. Angie's brothers, with whom she _____ a lot of time, are teaching her how to play baseball.
    (spend)

IV. Identifying and Non-Identifying Adjective Clauses. *Combine the two sentences using the word in parentheses. Use commas where necessary.*

1. Lloyd Alexander is a writer. Many children love his books. (whose)

   Lloyd Alexander is a writer whose books many children love. _____

   _____

2. Alexander writes fantasies. He has received many prizes for his fiction. (who)

   _____

   _____

3. *The High King* is one of his most famous stories. It received an important award. (which)

   _____

   _____

4. Many of his stories take place in an imaginary country. Evil is always lurking there. (where)

   _____

   _____

5. *The Black Cauldron* tells about a time. There was great danger in the country then. (when)

   _____

   _____

6. Gurgi always speaks in rhymes. Gurgi is one of the most charming characters in the book. (who)

   _____

   _____

7. Taran becomes the hero. Gurgi follows Taran everywhere. (whom)

   _____

   _____

8. Lloyd Alexander grew up in Philadelphia. He still lives there. (where)

   _____

   _____

9. The Welsh legends fascinated him. He read the legends as a boy. (that)

   _____

   _____

10. Alexander wrote a book about music. His hobbies include playing the violin. (whose)

    _____

    _____

V. Relative Pronouns and *When*: Deletions. *Wherever possible, delete the relative pronouns and* when.

1. Everything ~~that~~ he says is true.
2. The days when you're not home I usually eat out.
3. Have you ever met anyone that has lived in Montreal?
4. Lloyd Alexander dedicated his book *Westmark* to "those who regret their many imperfections . . ."
5. Jan often thinks about the years when he was growing up in Poland.
6. Ten years ago, when he first came here, he couldn't speak English at all.
7. Corinne's favorite dish, which I'm going to cook for her tonight, is fettucini.
8. The computer that Mike bought three years ago doesn't have enough memory.
9. We enjoyed the restaurant where we ate last night.
10. Don't tell Theo anything that you want to keep secret.

VI. Synthesis: Error Correction. *Correct these sentences.*

1. When he was a baby, Mike was adopted by a young couple whom lived in Pittsburgh.

   When he was a baby, Mike was adopted by a young couple who lived in Pittsburgh.

   _____

2. After twelve years, they all moved to Trenton, when Mike went to high school.

   _____

   _____

3. When he was twenty, Mike's parents told him about his twin brother, whom was adopted by another family.

   _____

   _____

4. In 1995, which they were twenty-one, the two brothers finally met.

   _____

   _____

5. Finding his brother Pete, whom he hadn't seen him since birth, changed Mike's life.

_____

_____

6. His brother, whose a famous writer today, persuaded him to start writing also.

_____

_____

7. Mike wrote some articles about the neighborhood in that he had grown up.

_____

_____

8. Those articles, which was published in the local newspaper, later became part of his first novel.

_____

_____

9. Writing, which it's hard for a lot of people, comes easy to Mike.

_____

_____

10. He writes about things what have happened to him since he found his brother.

_____

_____

Part IX: Diagnostic Test

I. Indirect Speech: Tense Changes. *Circle the correct form of the verb.*

1. Ahmed says that Laila left/(leaves) the television on all the time these days.

2. Bob told me that he wants/wanted to stay home last night.

3. I told my teacher that I had read/have read the chapter before class.

4. When the police officer stopped him, Marty said that he was going/is going home.

5. The officer said that Marty has been/had been exceeding the speed limit.

6. Last year Marty told me that he won't speed/wouldn't speed anymore.

7. My teacher told me that I should have read/should read more next year.

8. Two years ago, Sylvia's doctor told her that she has/had to do something about her weight.

9. I followed the instructions, which said that the safety switch must be/must have been on at all times for the equipment to work.

10. Cindy tells me that she's having/was having some trouble at college these days.

II. Contrast: *Tell* and *Say*. *Complete each sentence with* told *or* said.

1. I _____told_____ Marty that the class was starting in five minutes.

2. A year ago I _____ we'd have problems with this software.

3. Last semester, some teachers _____ their students to type their papers on the computer.

4. They _____ that the computer lab was open every night except Sunday.

5. A student _____ Mr. Hall that he was working at night.

6. Mr. Hall _____ he could submit handwritten papers.

III. Indirect Speech: Changes in Pronouns and Time Phrases. *Read the direct speech. Circle the words to correctly complete the indirect speech.*

Direct Speech:	Indirect Speech:
Conversations at lunch in New Orleans on January 1	Reports of those conversations in New Jersey on February 1
1. "We want to visit you next week."	Mandy and Vic told us that we/(they) wanted to visit (us)/you (the following week)/next week.
2. "I'm going to move to San Juan next month."	Mrs. Hillman told me that I/she is going to move to San Juan this month/next month.

3. "My electricity went out yesterday."

Frank said that <u>my/his</u> electricity had gone out <u>the day before/yesterday</u>.

4. "We're buying a house this year."

Bill and Jenny told me that <u>we/they</u> were buying a house <u>this year/next year</u>.

5. "Ken Melzer is here this evening."

Don said that Ken Melzer was <u>here/there</u> <u>that evening/this evening</u>.

6. "I met him last month."

He said that <u>I/he</u> had met him <u>last month/the previous month</u>.

7. "No one is sitting here right now."

He said that no one was sitting <u>here/there</u> right <u>then/now</u>.

8. "You should think about moving your office down here."

He said that <u>you/we</u> should think about moving <u>your/our</u> office down <u>here/there</u>.

IV. Indirect Instructions. *Circle the correct words.*

1. The doctor (advised)/said me (to get)/getting more sleep.

2. She <u>said/told</u> me <u>not to drink/didn't drink</u> coffee at night.

3. Last year, my friends <u>invited/ordered</u> us <u>to visit/visited</u> them at the beach.

4. When the fire started, a police officer <u>invited/ordered</u> everyone <u>leave/to leave</u> the building.

5. When my husband needs the car, I sometimes <u>ask/advise</u> Marcia <u>to give/gives</u> me a ride to school.

6. Marcia <u>says/tells</u> <u>calling/to call</u> her in advance.

V. Indirect Questions: Word Order. *Write indirect questions using the direct questions in parentheses. Do not change verb tenses.*

1. She asked ____ if I live on Monroe Street. ____
   ("Do you live on Monroe Street?")

2. He asked ____
   ("Where do you work now?")

3. The teacher asked ____
   ("Does water freeze at 32°F?")

4. Khaleel asked his coach ____
   ("How far should I run every day?")

5. I asked my neighbors ____
   ("Who drives your children to school?")

6. Jeff always asks ____
   ("Is it going to rain?")

7. The interviewer asked me ____
   ("Do you know how to use a computer?")

8. Last night Gene asked us _____
   ("How do you like your new apartment?")

9. We asked her _____
   ("Could we help you with the dishes?")

10. Ann's friends asked her _____
    ("Why did you quit your job so soon?")

VI. Direct Speech. *Read the indirect speech. Write the direct speech.*

1. Vera asked Bill where he was going. Bill told her he was going to the mall.

   Vera: Where are you going? _____

   Bill: I'm going to the mall. _____

2. Vera asked him if he would be home by 9:00. Bill said that he would.

   Vera: _____

   Bill: _____

3. A police officer ordered Bill to show her his license. Bill asked her what was wrong.

   Police officer: _____

   Bill: _____

4. She said that he had forgotten to signal. Bill told her that he was sorry.

   Police officer: _____

   Bill: _____

5. At the mall, a clerk in the shoe store asked Bill if he could help him. Bill told him that he was just looking.

   Clerk: _____

   Bill: _____

6. Then Bill saw some of his friends. He asked them where they were going. They told him that they were

   going to the movies.

   Bill: _____

   Friends: _____

7. They asked whether he could come with them. Bill said that he had to be home by 9:00.

   Friends: _____

   Bill: _____

VII. Embedded Questions: Word Order and Punctuation. *Write embedded questions using the questions in parentheses. Use the correct punctuation for statements and questions.*

1. I wonder _____ how far the expressway is. _____
   (How far is the expressway?)

2. Can you tell us _____
   (Where should we turn?)

3. I'm not sure _____
   (Is this the right exit?)

4. It doesn't say _____
   (Does Willow Street run east and west?)

5. Do you know _____
   (Who should we ask?)

6. Would you find out _____
   (Why is this road closed?)

7. We can't tell _____
   (Is this a dead end?)

8. I wonder _____
   (How long are they going to wait for us?)

9. Could you tell me _____
   (What time is it?)

10. We're not sure _____
    (How long should we stay?)

VIII. Question Words with Infinitives. *Rewrite the questions with a question word and an infinitive. Use the correct end punctuation (period or question mark).*

1. **A:** It's hot in here. Do you know _____ how to turn on the air conditioner? _____
   (How can I turn on the air conditioner?)

   B: Use the knob on the lower left.

2. **A:** I wish I knew _____
   (Where can I buy Basmati rice?)

   B: There's an Indian grocery store on Broad Street that sells it.

3. **A:** I don't know _____
   (When do we have to file our income taxes?)

   B: By April 15.

4. **A:** There's a mistake on our phone bill. Can you tell me _____
   (Who should I call about it?)

   B: There's a customer service number on the first page of your bill.

5. **A:** I'm going to attend Sylvia's wedding reception, and I'm not sure _____
   (What am I supposed to wear?)

   B: Either a suit or a dress would be fine.

6. **A:** I wish I knew _____
   (How can I get this coffee stain out?)

   B: Try Stain Buster. It really works.

IX. Synthesis: Error Correction. *Correct these sentences.*

1. Last night, I invited Pamela to having dinner with us this weekend.

   Last night, I invited Pamela to have dinner with us this weekend.
   _____

2. When I telephoned her, she said she was just sitting here reading.

   _____

   _____

3. Pamela told me she has lost her watch on the train the day before.

   _____

   _____

4. She said I had taken off the watch and put it on the seat.

   _____

   _____

5. A year ago, Pamela said that she will be more careful with her things.

   _____

   _____

6. She said she really must have been more careful in the future.

   _____

   _____

7. I wonder what time is it.

   _____

   _____

8. Can you tell me if or not this train stops in Yonkers?

   _____

   _____

9. The train conductor told me where get off.

_____

_____

10. He told me to don't forget my camera.

_____

_____

Part IX: Final Test

I. Indirect Speech: Tense Changes. *Circle the correct form of the verb.*

1. Laurel says that her daughter studied/(studies) too much these days.

2. Vic told me that he enjoys/enjoyed the concert last night.

3. I told my boss that I had left/have left her a message on her voice mail.

4. When I saw her in the lobby, Corinne said that she was going/'s going out to dinner.

5. I said that we have been looking/had been looking for her.

6. Last year Daisy told me that she won't quit/wouldn't quit for at least six months.

7. My doctor told me that I should have exercised/should exercise more in the future.

8. Two years ago Scott's parents told him that he has to start/had to start saving for college.

9. The technician told me that I had to use/had to have used a 150-watt bulb from now on.

10. Scientists say that the ozone is thinning/was thinning more rapidly now.

II. Contrast: *Tell* and *Say.* *Complete each sentence with* told *or* said.

1. I _____told_____ David that dinner would be ready in a half hour.

2. I _____ Jim was coming over to eat with us.

3. Last week, some of our friends _____ us that they were moving.

4. They _____ that their company had relocated to the suburbs.

5. We _____ Amy that she should look for another job.

6. Amy _____ she was already looking.

III. Indirect Speech: Changes in Pronouns and Time Phrases. *Read the direct speech. Circle the words to correctly complete the indirect speech.*

Direct Speech:	Indirect Speech:
Conversations at a meeting in New York City on March 1	Reports of those conversations in Atlanta on April 1
1. "We'll send you a copy of our report by next month."	They told us that we/(they) would send (us/you) a copy of our/(their) report (this month)/next month.
2. "I'm going to start working in Corporate Communications next week."	Grace Conti told me that I/she was going to start working in Corporate Communications next week/the following week.

3. "My computer was down yesterday."

Frank said that <u>my/his</u> computer had been down <u>the day before/</u><u>yesterday</u>.

4. "We're expanding our company this year."

Bonnie and Dita told me that <u>we/they</u> were expanding <u>our/their</u> company <u>this year/next year</u>.

5. "Julie Mason is here."

Clyde said that Julie Mason was <u>here/there</u>.

6. "I saw her at the seminar last month."

He said that <u>I/he</u> had seen her at the seminar <u>last month/the previous month</u>.

7. "We prefer these offices to our old ones."

He said that <u>we/they</u> preferred <u>these/those</u> offices to their old ones.

8. "Our company is new here in New York City."

He said that <u>their/our</u> company was new <u>here/there</u> in New York City.

IV. Indirect Instructions. *Circle the correct words.*

1. His accountant (advised)/said him (to close)/closing his business.

2. Dr. Thomas <u>said/told</u> Bob <u>not to drive/didn't drive</u> more than five hours a day.

3. Last year, my cousin <u>invited/ordered</u> me <u>to stay/stayed</u> with them when I went to Washington.

4. The sergeant <u>invited/ordered</u> her troops <u>preparing/to prepare</u> to leave.

5. When we go on vacation, I usually <u>ask/advise</u> my neighbor <u>to water/waters</u> my plants for me.

6. My neighbor always <u>says/tells</u> <u>letting/to let</u> her know whenever I need someone to help.

V. Indirect Questions: Word Order. *Write indirect questions using the direct questions in parentheses. Do not change verb tenses.*

1. He asked ———— if I work for Vulcan Metals. ————
("Do you work for Vulcan Metals?")

2. She asked ————
("Where are you staying?")

3. The professor asked ————
("Is helium lighter than oxygen?")

4. Gloria asked her piano teacher ————
("How long should I practice every day?")

5. I asked Nita ————
("Who repairs your television?")

6. Dee always asks ————
("Are we there yet?")

7. My doctor asked ————
("Do you exercise regularly?")

8. Last night Bill asked me ————
("Do you like fajitas?")

9. We asked him _____
("Could we have the recipe"?)

10. Ann's friends asked her _____
("Why are you working so hard?")

VI. Direct Speech. *Read the indirect speech. Write the direct speech.*

1. Jane asked Ann if she had been in class on Tuesday. Ann said she had been.

   Jane: Were you in class on Tuesday? _____

   Ann: Yes, I was. _____

2. Jane asked her if the teacher was going to give a test the following week. Ann said that he was.

   Jane: _____

   Ann: _____

3. One student asked the teacher how long the test took. The teacher told her she needed about one hour.

   Student: _____

   Teacher: _____

4. Another student asked whether they were allowed to use calculators. The teacher said that they were.

   Student: _____

   Teacher: _____

5. After the test, several students wanted to know when the teacher would finish grading the tests. He told

   them that he was going to grade them that night.

   Students: _____

   Teacher: _____

6. Anna asked the teacher where she could talk to him after class. The teacher told her they would meet

   there in the classroom.

   Anna: _____

   Teacher: _____

7. The teacher told Anna that she should study harder for the final. Anna told him she would put more effort into it.

Teacher: _____

Anna: _____

VII. Embedded Questions: Word Order and Punctuation. *Write embedded questions using the questions in parentheses. Use the correct punctuation for statements and questions.*

1. I wonder ___what time the news starts.___
(What time does the news start?)

2. Can you tell us _____
(What channel is it?)

3. I'm not sure _____
(Do I really want to watch this show?)

4. It doesn't say _____
(How long is the show?)

5. Let's ask _____
(Why can't we get any sound?)

6. Do you know _____
(Is this show rated for violence?)

7. I wonder _____
(How long is this commercial going to last?)

8. Does anybody know _____
(How do you adjust the color?)

9. Could I ask _____
(What are you watching?)

10. I wonder _____
(Who should we tell about this show?)

VIII. Question Words with Infinitives. *Rewrite the questions with a question word and an infinitive. Use the correct end punctuation (period or question mark).*

1. **A:** Do you know ___how to defrost the refrigerator?___
(How can I defrost the refrigerator?)

   B: Set the temperature knob to *defrost*.

2. **A:** I wish I knew _____
(Where can I sell my handmade jewelry?)

   B: There's a craft fair at the city center every year.

3. **A:** I want to start a garden. I don't know _____
(When should I plant tomatoes?)

   B: Wait until May 1.

4. **A:** Our landlord wants extra money for repairs, and we don't think that's fair. Can you tell us

   _____

   (Who should we call about it?)

   B: Here's the number of the city agency that deals with housing.

5. **A:** I'm going to a baby shower next week. I'm not sure _____

   (What am I supposed to bring?)

   B: You can ask the host for a list of things that the parents need for the baby.

6. **A:** I've never made lasagna. Do you know _____

   (How long should I cook the noodles?)

   B: Check the instructions. They're right on the package.

IX. Synthesis: Error Correction. *Correct these sentences.*

1. Last night, we invited our neighbor over watched a movie.

   Last night, we invited our neighbor over to watch a movie.

   _____

2. He told he was busy tonight, but he could come some other time.

   _____

   _____

3. Jeff asked us if or not we like comedies.

   _____

   _____

4. Sara asked who was going to make the popcorn?

   _____

   _____

5. She asked do we like butter on our popcorn.

   _____

6. Frank said I couldn't hear the show with all that talking.

   _____

   _____

7. We told Sara, "to please be quiet."

   _____

   _____

8. I'm not sure how long is this movie.

   _____

   _____

9. Sara showed me how rewind the tape.

_____

_____

10. The video store wants to know when are we returning the tape.

_____

_____

Part X: Diagnostic Test

I. Reflexive and Reciprocal Pronouns. *Circle the correct word.*

1. Jenny is very proud of herself/itself for getting straight A's this semester.

2. Will you kids please behave yourself/yourselves? You're disturbing other people in the library.

3. I learned how to take care of myself/himself when I went away to college.

4. The Gilberts must have had an argument with their neighbors. The two families aren't talking to each other/themselves any more.

5. Tom should do well in the game today. He really believes in himself/yourself.

6. Thanks for your help. We couldn't have painted this apartment by ourselves/myself.

7. Diane just cut herself/itself on the playground.

8. Francois and his pen pal wrote to each other/himself for years before they met.

9. You and Luke really have to take better care of yourself/yourselves.

10. The gift itself/myself isn't important. It's the thought that counts.

II. Phrasal Verbs: Particles. *Circle the correct word.*

1. We've used through/up all the milk, so there's none left for breakfast.

2. Barbara got sick and had to drop out from/of school this semester.

3. Our company came over/up with a new product that is selling very well.

4. Turn off/in the lights. You're wasting electricity.

5. George stuck on/with his project until it was finished.

6. Sara's French class worked so quickly that she couldn't keep through/up.

7. Don't get angry. Let's talk things over/back.

8. Where are the dressing rooms? I'd like to try up/on this sweater.

9. Three students set on/up the experiment for the class.

10. Our plane took off/up in a rainstorm. I was scared.

11. Successful inventors never give up/about.

12. If you can't guess the meaning of a word, look it up/off in a dictionary.

13. Quick! We'd better get on/up the bus before it leaves.

14. Chin bought a new lawn mower. He's putting it together/with this weekend.

15. We thought our cat was lost. Then it just turned up/out on the front porch one night.

III. Phrasal Verbs: Object Pronouns. *Complete each sentence with a phrasal verb and an object pronoun.*

1. **A:** Angie still hasn't gotten over losing her job.

   B: She'll ___*get over it*___ as soon as she finds another one.

2. **A:** Did Tom wake up yet?

   B: Not yet. I'm going to _____ now.

3. **A:** I have a lot of tests to pass out to the class.

   B: Let me help you _____ .

4. **A:** Let's drop in on Phil. I haven't seen him in a while.

   B: I'd rather call first. I don't want just to _____ .

5. **A:** Martha called. She said to call back.

   B: I can't _____ until after lunch.

6. **A:** You had a lot of mistakes in your math homework yesterday. Why don't you do over the problems in

   this chapter?

   B: I _____ last night. Here they are.

7. **A:** Do you ever run into Sam Phipps anymore?

   B: Yes, I do. As a matter of fact I _____ yesterday.

8. **A:** Who's going to pick up Tracey after her dentist appointment?

   B: I'll _____ on my way home from work.

9. **A:** I haven't paid back that dollar I owe you.

   B: You don't have to _____ . You bought lunch today.

10. **A:** Have you filled out the application for the apartment?

    B: I'm _____ now.

IV. Phrasal Verbs: Meaning. *Complete each sentence with the phrasal verb closest in meaning to the word in parentheses. Remember to use the correct form of the verb.*

dream up	turn off	show up
lie ~~down~~	pick out	get together
use up	get off	blow up
drop out of	put together	stand up
figure out		cut in

1. Marie's _____lying down_____ in her room. She has a headache.
   (reclining)

2. Mark _____ school to work for a few years.
   (quit)

3. I read until midnight and then _____ the light.
   (extinguished)

4. George was talking to a friend on the bus and didn't _____ at his stop.
   (leave)

5. Russ can't _____ the model airplane kit he bought yesterday.
   (assemble)

6. When can we _____ ?
   (meet)

7. You have to _____ when the judge enters the courtroom.
   (rise)

8. The police officer disarmed the explosive just before it _____ .
   (exploded)

9. Phil will be late, but don't worry. He'll _____ eventually.
   (appear)

10. Can I _____ for a moment? There's an important call for you.
    (interrupt)

11. Inspector Poirot _____ the mystery when no one else could.
    (solved)

12. How did Walt Disney _____ all those characters?
    (invent)

13. Have we _____ all the ketchup? I don't see any in the refrigerator.
    (consumed)

14. Marv _____ a ripe tomato for the salad.
    (selected)

V. Synthesis: Error Correction. *Correct these sentences.*

1. When Kay was in town, I called up her myself to ask her to dinner.

   When Kay was in town, I called her up myself to ask her to dinner.

_____

2. In kindergarten, the children learned to share their toys and put them away by theirselves.

_____

_____

3. It was a great idea, and Marv was pleased with himself for coming it up with.

_____

_____

4. Frank himself hates to dress over, but he let Cynthia talk him into wearing a suit for the party.

_____

_____

5. Sandra taught itself to use a computer, and now she's trying to dream up new ways to use it in her job.

_____

_____

6. When Brian introduced hisself to me at the party, we found that we got along very well.

_____

_____

7. The committee members were able to work out their problems after everyone had talked to themselves and had expressed their opinions.

_____

_____

8. The bus driver let ourselves off at the wrong stop.

_____

_____

Part X: Final Test

I. Reflexive and Reciprocal Pronouns. *Circle the correct words.*

1. Teamwork is great in this department. We all help ourselves/one another.

2. Eileen talks to herself/himself when she gets nervous. It calms her down.

3. All of you will have successful interviews if you'll just relax and be yourselves/each other.

4. I myself/itself don't know the answer, but I'll find it out for you.

5. Our canary sings to itself/each other in its little mirror.

6. Please work with a partner and correct the homework for themselves/each other.

7. Listen Bob, if you want to pass your road test this time, you're going to have to prepare yourself/yourselves by driving more.

8. On the first night of class, the students exchanged telephone numbers with ourselves/one another.

9. Steve gave each other/himself a pat on the back for working so hard.

10. I know people can act friendly in this city. I've seen it happen many times themselves/myself.

II. Phrasal Verbs: Particles. *Circle the correct word.*

1. Mr. Taylor cut out/through pictures from a magazine for his class's bulletin board.

2. This math problem is too hard to figure out/over.

3. The game was called back/off because of rain.

4. The children dressed up/about as ghosts and goblins for Halloween.

5. I forgot to fill up/in my name on the application.

6. The railroad brought down/about great changes in the United States.

7. Cynthia couldn't pass up/on the opportunity to go to college.

8. Vic and Susan are teaming with/up for the science project.

9. Could you ask around/over to see if there are any apartments available in your building?

10. Ted's car broke through/down several times last year.

11. The idea of car pools caught on/back years ago in the suburbs.

12. A button came off/out my coat while I was buttoning it.

13. Don't play around/over with the fire extinguisher. It could go off.

14. Chris used to be able to stay up/on all night and study.

15. Agnes wants to be a doctor when she grows up/about.

III. Phrasal Verbs: Object Pronouns. *Complete each sentence with a phrasal verb and an object pronoun.*

1. **A:** You left on your headlights.

   B: Thanks for telling me. The last time I ___left them on___ the battery went dead.

2. **A:** The kids are fooling around with the computer.

   B: I don't mind their using it, but I don't want them to _____ .

3. **A:** Are you going to try on this shirt?

   B: I _____ a few minutes ago. It's too big.

4. **A:** You picked out the perfect gift for Cindy.

   B: Actually, she _____ herself. She told me what book she wanted, and I just bought

   it for her.

5. **A:** Philip Nordis Company laid off 200 people last week.

   B: I heard that they _____ without any warning.

6. **A:** Put on your jacket. It's going to be cold today.

   B: I'll carry it and _____ if I need it.

7. **A:** This is Maple Street. Did you write down the exact address?

   B: Yeah. I _____ here in my address book.

8. **A:** How are you getting along with your new boss?

   B: Sarah Latham? I _____ very well.

9. **A:** Would you mind putting away the dishes?

   B: Not at all. I'll _____ as soon as I finish reading the newspaper.

10. **A:** Would you read this report and point out any problems to me?

    B: Sure. How should I _____? Can I write comments right on the page?

IV. Phrasal Verbs: Meaning. *Complete each sentence with the phrasal verb closest in meaning to the word in parentheses. Remember to use the correct form of the verb.*

bring up	look over	set up
tear down	break out	get up
come up with	put away	hand over
hang up	eat out	come in
look out for		bring̶ out

1. Play Around, Inc. is ___bringing out___ a new line of toys for the holidays.
   (presenting)

2. _____ a child is a big responsibility.
   (Raising)

3. Can I _____?
   (enter)

4. Listen to this. I just _____ a way to solve that problem.
   (imagined)

5. Citizens are being encouraged to _____ weapons to the police.
   (submit)

6. A lot of people just _____ when a salesperson calls.
   (end the telephone conversation)

7. _____ potholes. The roads are in very bad shape.
   (Be careful of)

8. After Sandra _____ the contract carefully, she decided not to sign it without some
   (examined)

   important changes.

9. The workers didn't _____ their tools after they finished working.
   (return to the proper place)

10. The city plans to _____ a new program for homeless people.
    (establish)

11. They won't _____ that building. It's a famous landmark.
    (destroy)

12. Let's _____. I'm too tired to cook.
    (eat in a restaurant)

13. After a week in the hospital, Fayeza was able to _____ and walk around a little.
    (rise from bed)

14. Fire _____ in the basement of the building next door.
    (occurred suddenly)

V. Synthesis: Error Correction. *Correct these sentences.*

1. That was a lovely gift you picked out for myself.

   That was a lovely gift you picked out for me.

2. Gary and I were talking to each other on the telephone when he suddenly hung down without saying goodbye.

3. When Craig's college application was turned down, he blamed hisself for not handing it in sooner.

4. The committee chairperson herself called the meeting up and rescheduled it for the following week.

5. Flu broke out in the school, and everyone seemed to be catching it from themselves.

6. The lights were still on in the bedroom, so I shut off them and lay down.

7. The students couldn't figure out the problem theirselves, but they knew they'd be able to work it out with some help from their teacher.

8. I hate eating out by herself.